MURTY CLASSICAL
LIBRARY OF INDIA

*Sheldon Pollock, General Editor*

# YAJNAVALKYA

# A TREATISE ON DHARMA

MCLI 20

YAJNAVALKYA

याज्ञवल्क्य

# A TREATISE ON DHARMA

Edited and translated by

PATRICK OLIVELLE

MURTY CLASSICAL LIBRARY OF INDIA

HARVARD UNIVERSITY PRESS

Cambridge, Massachusetts

London, England

2019

Printed in the United States of America

SERIES DESIGN BY M9DESIGN

*Library of Congress Cataloging-in-Publication Data*

Names: Yājñavalkya, author. | Olivelle, Patrick, editor, translator. |
Container of (expression): Yājñavalkya. Yājñavalkyasmṛti. |
Container of (expression): Yājñavalkya. Yājñavalkyasmṛti. English.
Title: Yajnavalkya : a treatise on dharma /
edited and translated by Patrick Olivelle.
Other titles: Murty classical library of India ; 20.
Description: Cambridge, Massachusetts : Harvard University Press, 2019. |
Series: Murty classical library of India ; 20 |
English and on facing page
Sanskrit ; Devanagari script |
Includes bibliographical references and index.
Identifiers: LCCN 2018015226 | ISBN 9780674277069 (cloth : alk. paper)
Subjects: LCSH: Hindu law—Early works to 1800. |
Inheritance and succession
(Hindu law)—Early works to 1800.
Classification: LCC KNS127.8.A4 E54 2019 | DDC 294.5/94—dc23
LC record available at https://lccn.loc.gov/2018015226

# CONTENTS

# INTRODUCTION

The treatise on dharma edited and translated here, the *Yājñavalkya Dharmaśāstra* (*YDh*), belongs to a rich expert tradition called *dharmaśāstra* spanning two and a half millennia.[1] The term *śāstra* indicates both a scientific discipline and presentations of that science in textual form.[2] The beginnings of *dharmaśāstra* go back possibly to the fourth century B.C.E., although the earliest extant text, that of Apastamba, dates to the late third century B.C.E. The four early texts ascribed to Apastamba, Gautama, Baudhayana, and Vasishtha, were written in the style of aphoristic prose called *sūtra*. The watershed moment in the history of *dharmaśāstra* was the composition of the text ascribed to Manu in the second century C.E. Written in a simple verse called *śloka*, it set the standard for all later compositions of the genre.

Yajnavalkya, to whom this treatise on dharma is ascribed, has a long and illustrious history within the literature of ancient India.[3] He first comes to light in the *Śatapatha Brāhmaṇa* of the *Śukla Yajur Veda*, within which is embedded the most celebrated Upanishad, the *Bṛhadāraṇyaka Upaniṣad*. In both, but especially in the Upanishad, Yajnavalkya occupies a central position. He is the most colorful personality in the early Brahmanical literature: blunt, provocative, and often sarcastic. He is also presented as a philosopher, the seer who received the text of the *Śukla Yajur Veda* directly from the sun, and is thus the founder of the *Śukla Yajur Veda* tradition. He is also associated with asceticism; he left his two wives to begin a life of wandering mendicancy. His literary biography continues in later texts, including the *Mahābhārata* and the Puranas, where he comes to be associated with yoga. It is somewhat surprising that a legal treatise would come to be ascribed to him. The reasons for this ascription are unclear; we can only offer educated guesses.

Yajnavalkya's is the most well known and most commented on legal text of ancient India after Manu's. Its significance for law became more prominent in medieval times partly due to the major twelfth-century commentary on it by Vijnaneshvara called *Mitākṣarā* (*Concise Commentary*). The British colonial administration accepted it as the fundamental text of what they thought to be Hindu law. One modern scholar puts it succinctly: "If it is true that all Hindus bow before the authority of Manu, we must not forget that in reality they are ruled by the Code of Yājñavalkya."[4] As a legal text, Yajnavalkya's work is far superior to Manu's in terms of precision and organizational skill.[5] The only other jurist of the period who surpasses Yajnavalkya in this regard is Narada, but his work is brief and covers only legal procedure.

### *Authorship, Provenance, and Date*

The text presents itself as the oral instruction of Yajnavalkya to a group of sages who ask him to teach them all the dharmas or laws. Thus, the authorship of Yajnavalkya is intrinsic to and guaranteed by the frame narrative of the text. Even though for the sake of convenience I will call the author

Yajnavalkya, from a historical perspective it is impossible for Yajnavalkya, or at least the Yajnavalkya of the Upanishads, to have authored the text, because his earliest appearance predates it by over a millennium. The issue, however, is why the historical author or authors wanted to credit Yajnavalkya with authoring their own work. While the pseudonymous ascription of texts to individuals well known from the distant past or even to divine beings is not uncommon, its function here is more complex and provides insights into the composition of the text.

The ascription to Yajnavalkya in the frame narrative is confirmed by the internal evidence showing that the historical author of the text belonged to tradition of the *Śukla Yajur Veda* reputedly founded by Yajnavalkya. Scholars have noted that most of the mantras in the text are derived from the *Vājasaneyi Saṃhitā* and that it follows the *Pāraskaragṛhyasūtra,* both belonging to the *Śukla Yajur Veda.* Furthermore, the historical author has repeatedly used passages from the *Bṛhadāraṇyaka Upaniṣad* belonging to the *Śukla Yajur Veda* that are spoken by Yajnavalkya, often prefacing these extracts with the first-person interjections of Yajnavalkya: "Anyone who desires to master yoga should know the *Āraṇyaka* that I received from the sun, as well as the yoga treatise that I proclaimed" (3.110); "The primordial god with a thousand bodies that I have declared to you" (3.126). We also see an echo of Yajnavalkya's wife Maitreyi's puzzlement (*BāU* 2.4.13; 4.5.14) in the queries posed by the sages at 3.118: "We are bewildered! How did this world with its gods, demons, and humans come into being? And how did the self come into being in this world? Tell us that."[6]

Yet, choosing Yajnavalkya to be the author of the *Dharmaśāstra* is somewhat unusual, given that he has a well-defined character and biography, including the geographical region where he lived. Why was he chosen? Finding a tentative answer will permit us to see behind the text itself to the intentions of its actual author (or authors). Besides the Vedic tradition to which the historical authors belonged, at least three interrelated factors probably influenced the selection of Yajnavalkya: geography, dynastic legitimation, and the rising importance of yoga. The *Bṛhadāraṇyaka Upaniṣad* clearly places Yajnavalkya in the eastern kingdom of Videha. He was the great philosopher of the east, something of a backwater of the time, and his defeat of conceited theologians from the more famous western region is celebrated in the Upanishad. Furthermore, his constant interlocutor was King Janaka of Videha, who is celebrated in later literature as also a great yogi. These associations with the east, with what has been called Greater Magadha,[7] may have been a significant factor in the choice of Yajnavalkya. The second verse of the text in fact locates him in the famous eastern city of Mithila, the capital of Videha. Its fame is also related to Sita, the wife of Rama, who was the daughter of Janaka. So multiple associations place Yajnavalkya at the heart of the eastern region, not too distant from the Magadha capital of Pataliputra, the modern Patna in Bihar.

The significance of this geographical information relates to the Gupta Empire that arose in this region with its capital precisely in Pataliputra early in the fourth century C.E. While the connection of the Gupta rulers to the composition of Yajnavalkya's treatise cannot be demonstrated, the timing is intriguing. As I will presently show, the treatise was composed in the fourth or fifth century C.E., thus overlapping considerably with the Gupta dynasty. It is most likely that not just its literary setting but also the location of its composition was Magadha. The issue then is: what connection, if any, is there between the Guptas and the composition of this text?

Given the lack of external evidence, framing a reasonable hypothesis is all one can do at present. The Gupta dynasty sought to establish and enhance its authority through a variety of symbolic means, including art, architecture, ritual, and particularly literature.[8] A political drama called *Mudrārākṣasa* (Rakshasa and the Signet Ring) traces the ascent to power of Chandragupta, the founder of the Maurya dynasty, toward the end of the fourth century B.C.E. Many scholars have argued that the play's author, Vishakhadatta, was a contemporary or courtier of Chandragupta II (375–413/15 C.E.), and that the drama itself was a eulogy of the Gupta emperor.[9] Although the historical data are not certain, the identity of the names of the emperors of the dynasties separated by over seven hundred years makes the literary connection through the historical drama suggestive.

Another interesting convergence concerns the hero of the play, the Brahman Chanakya, who singlehandedly defeats the last of the Nanda kings and installs Chandragupta on the throne of Pataliputra. Now, Vishakhadatta identifies Chanakya with Kautilya, author of the famous *Arthaśāstra,* and from this time this ascription of the text to Chanakya will become commonplace, making it a work of the Maurya period. This connection between Chanakya, the *Arthaśāstra,* and Chandragupta Maurya may have been intended to buttress the link between the two "Chandragupta" empires, the Maurya and the Gupta, both with their capitals at Pataliputra. It was during Gupta times that the law book of Manu and Kautilya's work on political science rose to prominence.[10]

All this probably explains the close dependence of Yajnavalkya, as we will see, on both those works. Willis argues that some version of this text must have been known in the courts that issued grants during the Gupta period.[11] I want to tentatively suggest that, like the *Mudrārākṣasa,* the law book of Yajnavalkya was composed during the Gupta period, perhaps under imperial patronage, to support Gupta legitimacy. The reputed author, Yajnavalkya, goes even further back in the Magadha history than Chanakya, to the legendary king Janaka of Videha celebrated both in the Vedas and in the Sanskrit epics. All three texts also support the preeminence of Brahmans within the social structure. It was the Brahman Chanakya who both installed Chandragupta on the throne, thus inaugurating the Maurya Empire, and wrote the textbook that provided kings with the blueprint for governance, diplomacy, and warfare. The Brahman seer, Yajnavalkya, wrote the treatise that proclaimed the dharma to be followed by kings and subjects alike. The ideal king follows the advice of Brahmans.

Whether or not it was written under royal patronage, Yajnavalkya's treatise shows features that correspond to the bureaucratic and legal advances that must have accompanied the formation of a territorially vast empire.

The prominence given to law and legal procedure, occupying the second of its three chapters and accounting for almost one-third of the entire text, is unprecedented. Even more significant is the development of the technical legal vocabulary discussed below, which was only incipient in Manu. The prevalence of legal documents and the weight given to them in court proceedings also point to a period of bureaucratic complexity when literacy, at least among the elite, was on the ascendency. Documents are required for a contract, especially for a loan. When a party is illiterate, he is expected to get a scribe to write on his behalf (2.90). Yajnavalkya is the first to use the technical term *lekhya* for a legal document. The importance of documents is evident in the rise of a professional scribal class called *kāyastha* mentioned for the first time by Yajnavalkya, who makes the somewhat off-the-cuff remark that a king should protect his subjects when they are harassed "especially by scribes" (1.332).

The third element of Yajnavalkya is the prominence given to yoga, the discipline of body and mind leading to ultimate liberation (*mokṣa*). The very first word of the very first verse of the text is *yogīśvara,* the king of yogis, used as an epithet of Yajnavalkya. The first word of Sanskrit texts often signals its centrality. In the very next verse he is called *yogīndra,* the chief of yogis, an epithet repeated at the very end of the text (3.329). This depiction matches the portrait of Yajnavalkya in the *Bṛhadāraṇyaka Upaniṣad,* where he leaves his two wives and departs from home to live as a wandering ascetic. In the definition of dharma (1.8), it is said that among all ritual and meritorious actions the highest dharma is "to perceive the self by means of yoga." One of the longest sections of the text, comprising 15 percent (151 verses), is devoted to the renouncer and meditation, and the terms *yoga* and *yogin* are used there frequently. Yajnavalkya devotes considerable space to describing both the gestation of the human embryo (3.73–83) and human anatomy (3.84–107), both passages dependent on the Ayurvedic text *Caraka Saṃhitā*. These are clearly intended to be subjects of meditation on the transience of human life, on the suffering nature of samsara, the cycle of births and deaths, reminiscent of Buddhist forms of meditation: "a person who in this manner considers this body as impermanent is capable of achieving liberation" (3.107). In a remarkable passage, Yajnavalkya talks about the use of music as an aid in reaching the higher mystical states (3.112–116).[12] These sections show the author's knowledge of medical and musical texts, as well as the innovative use of such technical information for religious purposes.

Although we can reasonably date Yajnavalkya's text to the period of the Guptas, any further narrowing of the date is not possible without additional evidence. The most likely date would be the reign of Chandragupta II, that is 375–415 C.E.

Establishing early fifth century C.E. as the *terminus post quem* is also assisted by the section on the worship of Vinayaka (*YDh* 1.268–290), who is identified with the "lord of Ganas" and "Great Ganapati" (1.268, 290).[13] The historical origins of this elephant-headed god are quite unclear, but he does not make a definite appearance in text or iconography until Gupta times.[14] This timeframe is also consistent with the knowledge of Greek astronomy in the text and the mention of *nāṇaka,* a generic name for a coin.

Its earliest literary use is by Yajnavalkya, and its earliest inscriptional use is a third-century inscription from Mahar.[15]

Nothing is certain or precise in ancient Indian history, especially in literary history. But historical hypothesis and conjecture can be useful tools in helping us understand the larger historical landscape. The confluence of three major literary works—the historical drama *Mudrārākṣasa* set at the beginning of the Maurya Empire; the political science treatise *Arthaśāstra* presented as being authored by Chanakya, the hero of the *Mudrārākṣasa* and the power behind the throne of Chandragupta, the first Maurya emperor; and the *Dharmaśāstra* authored by Yajnavalkya, the royal theologian of King Janaka of Videha—is suggestive of a literary project aimed at buttressing the claim of the Gupta Empire that it was the successor state to the celebrated Maurya Empire.

### *Sources*

Ancient Indian authors, much like their modern counterparts, did not compose texts in a literary and historical vacuum. This was especially true in the composition of texts within what may be called expert traditions, whether medicine, astronomy, or in our case law. The authors consulted, copied verbatim, and condensed or expanded material from older texts, most often without explicit attribution. Yajnavalkya is no different. He used a variety of sources that I will discuss below, but two stand out: Manu's legal treatise and Kautilya's *Arthaśāstra*.

Yajnavalkya's dependence on Manu is well known and

has been discussed repeatedly.[16] A characteristic of Yajnavalkya's writing is his aphoristic brevity that permitted him to shorten his text to just over one thousand verses as opposed to Manu's 2688. Some verses, especially in the first chapter, appear to be condensations of the more prolix style of Manu.[17] Yajnavalkya also follows the broad structure of Manu's work and his sequence of topics with, however, significant modifications, which I will discuss in the next section.

As chapter 1, and to a lesser degree chapter 3, are dependent on Manu, so chapter 2 on legal procedure is based both on Manu and in particular on Kautilya's *Arthaśāstra.* The connection between the latter and Yajnavalkya, although repeatedly noted, has not been subjected to deep analysis. I can deal with that close connection only briefly here. The text of Kautilya's treatise underwent a major redaction sometime after Manu—what I have called the "śāstric redaction"—that brought it closer to the dharmashatric model.[18] It is significant that Yajnavalkya had before him this new version. Thus, for example, *YDh* 2.236 reads: "A man who gets someone to commit forcible seizure should be made to pay double the above fine. When a man gets someone to do it by saying: 'I will compensate you,' he should be made to pay four times that fine." This is clearly a versification of *KAŚ* 3.17.11–12: "A man who gets someone to commit forcible seizure, saying 'I will take responsibility,' should pay double. One who does so, saying 'I will give as much money as will be needed,' should pay a quadruple fine."[19] What is interesting here is that this entire section of the *Arthaśāstra* is a dialogue between Kautilya and other authorities, and I have shown that these dialogues, along with the chapter-ending verses, are the work of the later redactor. The section on investigating a sudden death (2.284–285) is clearly a condensation of the much longer passage in *KAŚ* 4.3.14–22. Not infrequently we are able to improve the received text that misunderstood or misread a *KAŚ* passage, as at *YDh* 2.221. An important such misunderstanding is found at *YDh* 2.235, where the scribes or readers were unable to understand the technical term *anvayavat* of *KAŚ* 3.17.1. The close adherence to the *KAŚ* permits us to make editorial choices between the Vulgate version and the older text commented on by Vishvarupa.[20]

Even though Manu and Kautilya provided the main sources for Yajnavalkya, he used others for smaller sections that are novel and not found in other *dharmaśāstras*. Thus, he appears to have used the *Mānavagṛhyasūtra* for the section on the worship of Vinayaka (1.268–290). The section on embryology and anatomy (3.75–109) are taken from medical texts, principally the *Caraka Saṃhitā*.[21] The brief section on music (3.112–116) must be based on an early treatise on music, while the description of yogic meditation (3.199–204) is probably derived from a treatise on yoga, both unidentified. At 3.110 Yajnavalkya says that he himself authored a yoga treatise (*yogaśāstra*).

### *Structure and Composition*

The structure of the received text, the one commented on by the ninth-century scholar Vishvarupa, needs our attention first. Possible redactions and interpolations that may have altered the structure of the original text will be addressed in the final section of the introduction.

The broadest division of the text is into three chapters (*adhyāya*) of roughly equal length. Most editions and translations contain only this division. Yet, all the commentaries and a substantial number of manuscripts contain a second division into forty-two "topics" (*prakaraṇa*) of varying lengths ranging from three to 151 verses and spread unevenly across the three chapters: thirteen, twenty-four, and five. Whether one or both divisions were original is difficult to say, but the topical division is integral also to Kautilya's *Arthaśāstra,* and it is possible that the author adopted this division from it. There is also a parallel in the text of Vishnu written a couple of centuries after Yajnavalkya's, which is also segmented into *prakaraṇas.*

Beyond these external divisions, Yajnavalkya closely follows the sequence of subjects of his model, the treatise of Manu. This treatise has an intricate internal structure signaled by what I have called "transitional verses."[22] There are, however, notable exceptions where Yajnavalkya deviates from his model. What Manu calls *anāpaddharma,* that is, dharma outside times of adversity, covers eight central chapters (2–9) of his text. That, for the most part, is the subject matter of Yajnavalkya's first chapter on proper conduct (*ācārādhyāya*). Manu, however, concludes this long section with brief statements about the dharma of Vaishyas and Shudras. The implication is that the rules given in chapters 2–6 are specifically intended for Brahmans, while chapters 7–9 deal with the dharma of kings, including legal procedure. With the brief statements on Vaishyas and Shudras

(9.326–335), Manu assumed that, *mutatis mutandis,* the dharma of a Brahman would apply to the other classes as well. This follows the general hermeneutical model adopted by ritual texts, which describe in full only one rite taken as the archetype. In the case of other rites falling under it, only those elements that are different from the archetype are described. For Manu, the Brahman is the archetype with respect to dharma. Yajnavalkya, on the other hand, omits the sections on Vaishyas and Shudras, implying that his discussion takes into account all the twice-born classes. Two other sections that Manu includes in his discussion of the dharma of a Brahman are moved by Yajnavalkya to the third chapter on expiation (*prāyaścittādhyāya*): the period of impurity following a birth or death and the discussion of the two ascetic modes of life, namely, the forest hermit and the wandering ascetic. I will discuss in the next section the possible motivation for this change.

Besides these omissions and changes, there is also a conspicuous novelty: Yajnavalkya introduces two topics between the discussion of proper conduct and that of the duties of a king. The first is the worship of Vinayaka or Ganapati, and the second is the pacification of planets. These are completely novel topics not found in any other *dharmaśāstra.* In a curious way, these two replace the two sections on the forest hermit and wandering mendicant at precisely the same place they are found in Manu, right before the section on the king. Yet, it appears that Yajnavalkya makes an effort at a smooth transition to the section on kings by showing, in the last verse (1.304) of the pacification of planets, that "the upturns and downturns of great kings are dependent on the planets.... Therefore, planets are most worthy of worship."

The organization of topics in the second chapter on legal procedure (*vyavahāra*) differs considerably from both Manu and Kautilya. Yajnavalkya follows Manu in placing "non-payment of debts" as the first subject of litigation (*vyavahārapada*)—which becomes the norm in later *dharmaśāstras*—while he follows Kautilya in placing inheritance and the partition of an estate very early in the enumeration of subjects of litigation.

Chapter 3 contains the fewest number of topics, just five. The two topics on the ascetic and expiation are the longest, containing 151 and 124 verses, or 15 and 12 percent of the entire text, respectively.

A brief introduction consisting of nine verses (1.1–9) presents the narrative framework of the text. Here Yajnavalkya follows the example of Manu, but dramatically condenses his entire first chapter, eliminating the discourse on the creation of the world and the table of contents. The conclusion is even briefer, just seven verses, and brings the narrative to a conclusion with the sages thanking Yajnavalkya.

### *Innovations of Yajnavalkya*

Writing two or three centuries after Manu and, very likely, at the height of Gupta power, Yajnavalkya reflects changes in religion, society, and culture, as well as in jurisprudence and court procedures. Even though Yajnavalkya borrows extensively from Manu and Kautilya, he introduces numerous innovations that are significant in the history of *dharmaśāstra.* Here I have space only to highlight a few noteworthy changes and advances.

Some of the most significant of these appear in the second chapter and are likely responsible for making his text the main object of study and commentary in the medieval period. Yajnavalkya represents an advanced stage of jurisprudence; brevity and precision of language characterize his discussions. If we compare Yajnavalkya's account of the general rules of procedure in a case brought before a court (2.1–38) with the parallel section of Manu (8.1–46), we detect a vast difference both in the precision with which Yajnavalkya presents the issues in contrast to the rambling account of Manu—with numerous digressions or "excursi"—and in the technical vocabulary employed by Yajnavalkya.[23]

Yajnavalkya sees the entire legal process of the court, from the initial filing of the complaint until the court's final verdict, as divided into four steps (2.8): plaint, plea, evidence, and verdict.[24] He presents clear descriptions of these steps, except perhaps the verdict, which is dealt with cursorily and in the context of an appeal from an unjust court proceeding. He delineates for the first time the five forums for adjudicating lawsuits (2.34). The technical legal vocabulary he employs indicates the rapid development of jurisprudence between the second century when Manu wrote his treatise and the Gupta period. I give here a sample of these terms:

*abhiyoga* and *pratyabhiyoga:* suit and counter-suit
*arthin* and *pratyarthin:* plaintiff and defendant
*āvedita:* the initial charges filed with the court, as opposed to *pratijñā*

*bhāvita:* proved, convicted
*divya:* ordeal
*hīna:* defeated in a lawsuit
*kriyā:* evidence
*lekhya:* documentary evidence
*nihnava:* plea of denial
*nirṇaya:* verdict
*pratijñā:* formal written plaint
*prativādin:* defendant
*pūrvavādin, pūrvapakṣa:* plaintiff, the person who has the burden of proof
*pūrvāvedaka:* person filing the charges, plaintiff
*sapaṇa:* a suit that involves a stake or wager
*upagata:* receipt for partial payment of a loan

A significant point both for jurisprudence and for cultural history in general is the emphasis Yajnavalkya places on documents. In Manu we do not even have a technical term for a legal document, and he does not formally recognize documents as evidence in a court of law. Yajnavalkya devotes an entire topic to the subject (2.86–97), showing for the first time in Indian legal history how a legal document is to be executed and what elements, such as the signatures of the executor, witnesses, and scribe, should be present for it to be valid. He is also the first in the legal tradition to use the technical term *lekhya* for a legal document.[25] Professional scribes appear to have been commonplace during his time: he notes the function of scribes and their employment by illiterate people who take out loans (2.90–91). An *obiter dictum* regarding the king's duty to protect his subjects from thieves, rogues, and *especially from scribes* (1.332), using for the first time in the tradition the term *kayastha,* shows the emergence of an established group or caste of the scribal profession.

Another area of jurisprudence relating to evidence is ordeals. Although ordeals are known in early literature and Manu refers in passing to ordeals with the term *śapatha,* which refers more specifically to oaths, Yajnavalkya is the first author to deal with ordeals explicitly, using, again for the first time in the literature, the technical term *divya* and describing in detail the ordeals of the balance, fire, water, poison, and holy water (2.98–117).

Turning to issues beyond jurisprudence, Yajnavalkya is the first to present a canon of *dharmaśāstras.* It contains the names of twenty authors (1.4–5), including some, such as Parashara, Brihaspati, and Katyayana, whose existing works are definitely posterior to Yajnavalkya. This may well be an indication that these two verses, with two widely different versions in my edition and the Vulgate, may have been a later interpolation. They are commented on, however, by the early ninth-century scholar Vishvarupa, and are also cited by the later ninth-century scholar Medhatithi in his commentary on Manu (2.6), who, however, rejects the list as unauthoritative. Given that *dharmaśāstras* were viewed as being based on the Veda and uniformly authoritative, it may well be that Medhatithi considered these verses to be interpolations inserted into Yajnavalkya's original composition.

With reference to social and religious norms, Yajnavalkya departs radically from the tradition in forbidding twice-born men, whether Brahman, Kshatriya, or Vaishya, from marrying Shudra women. Indeed, he acknowledges that other authorities do permit such marriages, an opinion with which he vehemently disagrees: "With respect to what has been stated about twice-born men taking wives from the Shudras—I do not approve of it, because that man is himself born in her" (1.56).[26]

The historical author of our text was writing at a time when the devotional (*bhakti*) traditions of Hinduism were in the ascent. The Guptas themselves were Vaishnavites, although many writers, including the famous Kalidasa whom they supported, were Shaivites. Our author gives a few hints that he also may have been a Shaivite: references to Uma, the wife of Shiva, at 1.75, and to Rudra at 3.116; and the section on the worship of Vinayaka or Great Ganapati at 1.268–290. Yet a strong devotional bias, such as what we see in the *dharmaśāstra* of Vishnu,[27] is absent in it.

Yoga, as I have already noted, is a central concern for Yajnavalkya. The most explicit and elaborate discussion of yoga and meditative practices in general is in the long and detailed section on the wandering mendicant (3.72–204). The meditative practices appear to involve contemplation of the transient nature of human life by examining the process of the development of the fetus and human anatomy. Another discussion centers on music and how singing and playing musical instruments can further an ascetic's path to liberation. All these are unique and unprecedented in *dharmaśāstra* literature.

The question remains why Yajnavalkya shifted the topics of the forest hermit and wandering mendicant, as also the discussion of dharma in times of adversity (*āpaddharma*) and of the period of impurity (*āśauca*), to the chapter on expiation (*prāyaścitta*). At first sight their inclusion is incongruous. But what did *prāyaścitta* mean to Yajnavalkya? The earliest use of the term refers to the rectification of ritual faults of commission or omission, and its use for the expiation of sins is a secondary development.[28] The term also appears to have assumed a broader semantic compass, extending to areas of austerity and self-control that are not directly related to the expiation of sins. Thus a verse cited in medieval sources defines the term thus: "The term *prāya* is said to be austerity and *citta* is said to be resolve. It is said to be *prāyaścitta* because of the conjunction of austerity and resolve."[29] I think Yajnavalkya is giving the term a broad meaning: it includes activities that are "out of the ordinary." So, it would include the expiation of sins but also other extraordinary actions, such as those undertaken in an emergency or when one is in a state of impurity because of a death in the family, as well as extraordinary modes of life, such as those connected with forest hermits and wandering mendicants. We get a hint to this conception when Yajnavalkya (3.50) says that a forest hermit "should spend his time engaged in lunar fasts (*cāndrāyaṇa*), or live his life always engaged in arduous penances (*kṛcchra*)." These are precisely the penances prescribed to expiate sins. But the same acts can be performed not to expiate sins but "for the sake of dharma" (3.327–328), and apparently Yajnavalkya places the activities of an ascetic in this category.

The influence of ascetic practices, especially as it relates to food and sex, in Yajnavalkya's view of the ideal religious life is obvious. At a somewhat abstract level, the acquisition of the liberating knowledge, equated here with the "knowledge of the self" (*ātmadarśana*), through the practice of yoga is said to be the "highest dharma" (*paramo dharmaḥ*, 1.8). Yajnavalkya, however, attempts to co-opt the householder into this vision. A person does not have to formally leave home and family and don special attire in order to be a true ascetic. He observes that "By refraining from meat...while still living at home he becomes a sage," and asserts that a householder actually remains a celibate (*brahmacārin*) by strictly observing the rules with regards to sexual intercourse with his wife. He ends the topic of the householder by exhorting him to end his life by adopting some of the ascetic behaviors with regard to food: "Let him be a man who stores grain sufficient to fill a granary or sufficient to fill a jar, a man who has grain sufficient for three days, or a man who keeps nothing for the next day; or else, he may live by gleaning. Of these, each succeeding one is superior to each preceding." And at the end of his discussion of the wandering ascetic, he returns to the possibility that even a householder may become liberated if he follows certain practices: "Even a householder is liberated when he acquires wealth by lawful means, is firmly established in the knowledge of the truth, loves guests, performs ancestral offerings, and speaks the truth."[30]

### *Yajnavalkya's Dharma*

Given his innovations with respect to the science of dharma, does Yajnavalkya demonstrate similar originality with respect to the conception of dharma? This is a difficult question to answer because he does not provide in one place an explanation of what he means by dharma. Yet, by piecing together comments made within diverse contexts, we can gain some insight into his thinking on the subject.

First, dharma is multiple, as shown in the use of the plural dharmas in the very opening verse (*dharmān;* 1.1). There are multiple epistemic sources of dharma (1.7): Veda, texts of recollection (*smṛti*), conduct of good people, satisfaction of the self, and desire (*kāma*) springing from right intention. The last is innovative and lacking in Manu; it appears to connect the last of the triple set (*trivarga*) or human aims with dharma. The two most significant statements, however, are his claims that giving gifts (*dāna*) constitutes the essence of dharma (1.6) and that the highest dharma is "to perceive the self (*ātmadarśana*) by means of yoga" (1.8). The centrality accorded to gift giving is unprecedented; even though the topic is discussed in earlier texts, it is never provided a separate section (Topic 9: 1.197–214) or this kind of prominence.

The centrality given to yogic practice and the mystical knowledge of the self (*ātman*), as already noted, is a distinctive feature of Yajnavalkya's text. Whatever a person who knows the self says is dharma (1.9), and he is superior even to Brahmans who know the Veda and perform Vedic rites. Yet, elsewhere Yajnavalkya concedes that dharma operates in this world and is unconnected to the liberated state (*mokṣa*). Those people who return to this word after death and are reborn as humans are said to become "promulgators of dharma" (3.187), that is, authors of *dharmaśāstras.* Thus, we detect multiple meanings or nuances in Yajnavalkya's conception of dharma.

The multiplicity of dharma is evident in the very threefold division of his text. The numerous rules that govern the quotidian life of twice-born individuals and the norms that regulate the conduct of the king himself given in chapter 1 are as much dharma as the courtroom procedures presented in chapter 2. Then in chapter 3 Yajnavalkya turns to rules for extraordinary times such as emergencies and impurity, and for extraordinary individuals whether undertaking ascetic practices or attempting to expiate their sins. Not only are all these part of dharma, but at one point he even says explicitly that the king can proclaim dharma (2.190), which must be followed by his subjects.

For Yajnavalkya, then, not all of dharma is *vaidika,* that is, derived from the Veda and its subsidiary texts, such as the *dharmaśāstras.* Some dharmas are worldly (*laukika*) based on local customs or promulgated by the ruler. Indeed, he accepts the power of the world, of "what people say," in determining what sort of dharma a person should follow. One should not perform even an act prescribed by the Veda if it is repulsive to the world (1.155).

### *Textual History*

With regard to the history of Yajnavalkya's text in the centuries following its composition—a text that has a remarkable and traceable literary history—what I wrote about the legal treatise of Manu a decade ago is pertinent:

> After it leaves the hands of the author, every text assumes an independent life. This is especially true in the case of texts published before the advent of printing. These

> pre-modern texts continue their life as they are copied by hand, read, studied, interpreted, and commented on by succeeding generations of scribes, readers, and scholars. It is this after-life of a text that a critical edition uncovers through the collation of manuscripts and presents to the reader in its critical apparatus. This aspect of a critical edition is as important as its better known feature of attempting to reconstruct the text as composed by the author.[31]

On the reasonable assumption that the *YDh* was written in early fifth century C.E., we have a period of about four centuries during which there is no manuscript or mention of it in the historical record. This is the dark period in the textual history of the work. Some scholars have argued that certain sections of the text were interpolated during this period. These include the second chapter on legal procedure, the long discourses on anatomy and music, and ritual passages such as those on the worship of Vinayaka and the planets. The evidence given for these conclusions, however, is not convincing. We must acknowledge the limitations of available evidence; the best we can say is that some changes must have occurred, but it is impossible to identify them with certainty.

The text comes into historical view in the commentary written by Vishvarupa in the first quarter of the ninth century. This commentary is significant for establishing the text as it was available to Vishvarupa, because he often comments on the form and meaning of individual words. He may have had access to one or more earlier commentaries.[32] We also see evidence that the textual tradition already had variants during his time. For example, commenting on 1.2 where we have the reading *dharmān* in the plural, he points to some people who read *dharmam* in the singular.[33] So the upshot is that even in the early ninth century our text was somewhat fluid with numerous variant readings that had crept into it either due to revisions or through scribal errors. A bit of evidence regarding the state of the text in the ninth century comes also from a couple of citations in the voluminous commentary on Manu by Medhatithi, who wrote about fifty years after Vishvarupa. These citations broadly confirm some of Vishvarupa's readings, as well as the fluid state of the text during his time.[34]

Evidence suggests that sometime between the early ninth and early twelfth centuries, a radical redaction amounting to a new edition was carried out by some scholar, an edition that I have called the Vulgate. The evidence for this lies in the two twelfth-century commentaries of Vijnaneshvara and Apararka, as well as in the vast majority of manuscripts written in a wide variety of southern and northern scripts—except those in the Malayalam script. They all reproduce basically a text that is quite distinct from the one commented on by Vishvarupa. We can push back the *terminus ante quem* of this new edition because of a fragment of a thus-far unknown and anonymous commentary preserved in Kathmandu, Nepal.[35] The manuscript is written in a script known as *bhujīmola* and is dated 122, which in all likelihood refers to *Nepāla Saṃvat* and is thus 1002 C.E. The commentary itself must be somewhat earlier than the age of this manuscript, and we could reasonably date it to the tenth century C.E. The text accompanying and presupposed by the commentary is the Vulgate. We also have a few references to Yajnavalkya in Abhinavagupta's *Abhinavabhāratī* that follow the Vulgate readings.[36] Abhinavagupta wrote during the last quarter of the tenth and the first quarter of the eleventh century. So, these provide us a somewhat narrower window of time—one century—when this new edition could have been created: between the middle of the ninth and the middle of the tenth century.

This edition, however, was subjected to further revisions, because there are substantive differences between the texts commented on by Vijnaneshvara and Aparарka. The latter often agrees with the text of Vishvarupa. All medieval citations of Yajnavalkya, as well as the sub-commentaries on Vijnaneshvara, are based on the Vulgate version.

Two pieces of evidence further complicate the picture. The entire text of Yajnavalkya is incorporated into two Puranas: the second chapter in the *Agni Purāṇa* (ch. 253–258), and much of the first and third chapters in the *Garuḍa Purāṇa* (1.93–106). The text given in the *Agni Purāṇa* agrees often with the readings of Vishvarupa but in some places with those of the Vulgate.[37] The issue is more complex in the *Garuḍa,* whose readings follow both the Vulgate and Vishvarupa's. Given the quite deficient editions we have of these texts, it is not possible to eliminate contamination from the Vulgate version, which was the one commonly known by and accessible to their editors. It is, however, likely that these two Puranas incorporated a text that was still in flux. The usual dating of the two works to the tenth century coincides with my broad dating of the Vulgate edition.[38]

Two other commentaries on Yajnavalkya were composed in late medieval times. The first is by Shulapani, whom Kane dates to between 1365 and 1445 C.E.[39] The other is by Mitramishra, who lived in the first half of the seventeenth century C.E. There were also sub-commentaries on Vijnaneshvara's *Mitākṣarā:* the first called *Subodhinī* by Vishveshvara (1360–1390 C.E.), the second called *Pramitākṣarā* by Nandapaṇḍita (1580–1630 C.E.), and finally the *Bālambhaṭṭī* by Bālambhaṭṭa (1730–1820 C.E.). This is the most commentarial attention paid during the medieval times to any ancient *dharmaśāstra.* Yet, the attention was also due, at least in part, to the popularity and growing authority of Vijnaneshvara's own commentary. Its authority spread throughout the Indian subcontinent, perhaps with the exception of Bengal. This authority was given state and court recognition during the British colonial period; Vijnaneshvara's commentary was "Hindu law" for inheritance and family law in all parts of India apart from Bengal, where Jimutavahana's *Dāyabhāga* was considered authoritative.[40]

### *Acknowledgments*

The project to produce a critical edition of Yajnavalkya's treatise started around ten years ago, soon after my critical edition and translation of Manu's *Treatise on Dharma.*[41] This long and complex project could not have succeeded without the generous support of numerous institutions and individuals. Foremost among the individuals is Dr. Saroja Bhate and her group of students who collated many manuscripts. The collators include Prajakta Deodhar, Mukta Keskar, Tanuja Ajotikar, Anuja Ajotikar, Anindya Bandyopadhyay, Phillip Ernest, Justin Fifield, Amy Hyne, Rohan Kulkarni, Radhesh Kulkarni, Sarita Kulkarni, Suman Olivelle, Amogh Prabhudesai, and Saraju Rath. Friends and colleagues who assisted me in procuring copies of manuscripts include Radhavallabh Tripathi, Daniel Majchrowicz, Trupti Kulkarni, Viswanatha Gupta, and P. L. Shaji. The following institutions provided generous access to their manuscript collections: Bhandarkar Oriental Research Institute (Pune), Bharatiya Itihasa Samsodhana Mandala (Pune), Oriental Manuscripts Library (Trivandrum), Government Oriental Library (Mysore), Government Oriental Manuscript Library (Chennai), Adyar Library (Chennai), Akhil Bhartiya Samskrita Parishad (Lucknow), Oriental Institute (Baroda), National Archive (Kathmandu, Nepal), Orissa State Museum, Deccan College (Pune), and Sanskrit College (Kolkata). My thanks also to the many colleagues who assisted me in various ways: Joel Brereton, Donald Davis, Timothy Lubin, Mark McClish, Oliver Freiberger, Martha Selby, Stephanie Jamison, Ashok Aklujkar, Dominik Wujastyk, Madhav Deshpande, George Cardona, Philipp Maas, and Elisa Ganser. Funds from the University of Texas at Austin and, in 2016, from the University of Chicago assisted in the procurement of manuscripts and in their collation. Sheldon Pollock accepted this for publication in the MCLI and provided vital feedback on the introduction. To all of them, a big Thank You.

As always my wife, Suman, has participated in this

project fully not only in collating several manuscripts but also in numerous other ways. To her a special thanks. During the long period of gestation of this project, my daughter Meera got married to Mark and gave us three wonderful grandchildren: Keya, Maya, and Max. To them—*mātāmahaharṣavardhanāḥ*—this book is dedicated.

## NOTES

1. For the history of *dharmaśāstra*, the science of dharma, see Kane 1962–1975; Lingat 1973; Derrett 1973a, 1973b. For a more succinct account, see Olivelle 2010.
2. For a detailed study of the category of *śāstra*, see Pollock 1989.
3. For a detailed study of the character of Yajnavalkya in ancient literature, see Lindquist 2018.
4. J. C. Ghose (*Principles of Hindu Law,* Calcutta, 1906: xi), cited by Lingat 1973: 98.
5. Lingat (1973: 98) is correct in his assessment: "Of all the *smṛtis* which have come down to us that of Yājñavalkya is assuredly the best composed and appears to be the most homogeneous....We are struck, especially if we have just read Manu, by the sober tone, the concise style, and the strictness with which the topics are arranged."
6. See also 1.129. The frequent use of first-person pronouns marks the whole text as the oral instruction of Yajnavalkya in a way that Manu's text is not. See the first person used at 1.5; 2.137; 3.110, 126, 182, 217.
7. See Bronkhorst 2007.
8. For an extended discussion, see Willis 2009. He also gives helpful hints with respect to the *Mudrārākṣasa* (2009: 46–55, 248–250).
9. The date of the *Mudrārākṣasa* is quite uncertain. For a comprehensive evaluation, see Balogh 2015: 226–231. Stietencron (1985–1986: 21) argues: "the concluding verse of Viśākhadatta's drama *Mudrārākṣasa*..., while dealing with events of the time of Candragupta Maurya, refers indirectly also to Candragupta II, who was the poet's contemporary and may have been his patron."

10 For the literary history of the *Arthaśāstra*, see Olivelle 2013. See also Willis 2009: 205.
11 Willis 2009: 206.
12 This section is referred to and cited by Abhinavagupta in his commentary on the treatise on dramaturgy, the *Nāṭyaśāstra* (see below, note 36). At 3.162, Yajnavalkya refers to the makeup that an actor puts on his body to act his part to the way the one self is displayed in various bodies.
13 The earliest and only occurrence of *vināyaka* in the *dharmaśāstras* is in *BDh* 2.9.7, where we also find the epithets *vighna*, *ekadanta*, and *lambodara*. However, given the bad textual tradition of this text and the numerous later additions (Olivelle 2000: 191), this passage in a section on offering water libations (*tarpaṇa*) cannot be a solid basis for dating the emergence of this deity.
14 Courtright (1985: 8) summarizes the previous scholarship: "Gaṇeśa seems to make an abrupt and dramatic appearance into the mythology and iconography of Hinduism in the post-Epic or early Purāṇic period, around the fifth century A.D."
15 Malhar Memorial Stone Inscription of Isinaga. See Majumdar and Bajpai 2015: 56–59.
16 See Kane 1962–1975, I: 430; Jayaswal 1930; Kangle 1964. Stenzler (1849) in his translation provides convenient marginal references to parallel verses in Manu.
17 Thus the content of *MDh* 2.243, 247–248 are given in *YDh* 1.49, and that of *MDh* 3.46–48, 50 in *YDh* 1.48. For further examples, see Kane 1962–1975, I: 430.
18 For an extended treatment of this issue, see Olivelle 2013.
19 The parallel is clearer in the Sanskrit original. Yajnavalkya:
*yaḥ sāhasaṃ kārayati sa dāpyo dviguṇaṃ damam* ।
*yas tv evam uktvāhaṃ datā kārayet sa caturguṇam* ॥
Kautilya: *yaḥ sāhasaṃ pratipattā iti kārayati sa dviguṇaṃ dadyāt* । *yāvad dhiraṇyam upayokṣyate tāvad dāsyāmi iti sa caturguṇaṃ daṇḍaṃ dadyāt* ॥
20 For the editorial principles, see my "Note on the Text."
21 See Yamashita 2001–2002.
22 Olivelle 2005: 7–18.
23 For these digressions, see Olivelle 2005: 168–207. As Lingat (1973: 98) notes, the text of Yajnavalkya is the best composed and the most homogeneous of all the *dharmaśāstras* (see note 5 above).

24 See Olivelle and McClish 2015.

25 Both Manu (8.52–57) and Kautilya (*KAŚ* 3.1.19) use the interesting and obscure term *deśa* to refer to a legal document. On this usage, see Olivelle 2004.

26 That a man takes birth again in his wife and is reborn as the son is already expressed in the *Aitareya Brāhmaṇa* 7.13: "The husband enters the wife. Becoming an embryo, he enters the mother. Becoming in her a new man again, he is born in the tenth month." Manu permits marrying a Shudra woman at 3.13, but he gives another opinion that prohibits it at 3.14–19.

27 See Olivelle 2009.

28 See Kane 1962–1975, IV: 57–59.

29 For a discussion of this verse and its sources, see Kane 1962–1975, IV: 59.

30 See respectively *YDh* 1.180; 1.78; 1.127; 3.206. For the food of an ascetic, see Olivelle 1991.

31 Olivelle 2005: 50.

32 If, that is, my hypothesis regarding the verse he adds after 2.216 is correct: see note 36 to the Sanskrit text of chapter 2.

33 Significantly, the singular form is given in the text as preserved in the *Garuḍa Purāṇa*. Vishvarupa also rejects the authenticity of verse 1.195, which he says some insert at this point (*atraiva pradeśe kecid imaṃ ślokaṃ paṭhanti*), and of verse 2.143 (*atrāpare pūrvaślokavivaraṇasthānīyam imaṃ ślokaṃ paṭhanti*). Vishvarupa gives other variant readings at 1.1c (*varṇānāṃ sāśramāṇām*), 1.51c (*vedavratāni*), and 2.179d (*pratiśrutam*).

34 Medhatithi's citations (sometimes anonymously) are: 1.4 (on *MDh* 2.6); 2.24, 89, 92, 96 (all on *MDh* 8.3), and 2.309 (on *MDh* 8.2).

35 Nepal-German Manuscript Preservation Project, National Archives, Kathmandu, Nepal. Manuscript number 5-696/ dharmaśāstra 65 (Reel No. A51/12). Both the script and the date of this manuscript have been confirmed by Axel Michaels and Rajan Sharma. I thank them for their help.

36 He cites, for example, a portion of *YDh* 3.115, reading *mokṣamārgam* instead of Vishvarupa's *yogamārgam*. See *Nāṭyaśāstra*, IV: 173.

37 For a comparison, see Kane 1962–1975, I: 425.

38 See Rocher 1986: 136–137 for the *Agni*, and Rocher 1986: 177 for the *Garuḍa*, with additional bibliography given there. The estimates of their dates, however, are educated guesses.

39 Kane 1962–1975, I: 839.
40 Rocher 2002b.
41 Olivelle 2005.

# NOTE ON THE TEXT

The text of Yajnavalkya given in this volume is the critical edition I have prepared on the basis of the following witnesses: thirty-three manuscripts in seven scripts, four commentaries, *Agni Purāṇa* and *Garuḍa Purāṇa*, and citations in medieval legal digests. The full critical edition along with the critical apparatus will be published later.[1] Here I want to present briefly some of the highlights of the new edition.

This critical edition could not be prepared according to the classical method of preparing a *stemma codicum*, because almost all the manuscripts presented no real variants. They all belonged to a single family, which I have called the Vulgate. I turned my attention from the vast majority of my manuscripts from all over the subcontinent to the seven from Kerala in the Malayalam script. Some of them had only the text, while others contained also the early ninth-century commentary *Bālakrīḍā* by Vishvarupa. These manuscripts presented a text that was different, often radically different, from the Vulgate. So, now I had two transmission lines, two recensions, the one represented by Vishvarupa and the Malayalam manuscripts, and the other represented by over thirty manuscripts in seven scripts and by the medieval commentaries. But such a *stemma* with two branches is of little use, because there is no criterion within the *stemma* itself for choosing one of the two lines of transmission over the other. To my great good fortune,

I found precisely such criteria external to the *stemma.*

First, there are two Puranas, *Agni* and *Garuḍa,* that reproduce large chunks of the text. Second, and even more importantly, the author followed very closely several sources. I have already referred to these sources in the introduction. For the critical edition, however, two sources of Yajnavalkya are of special importance: Manu and Kauṭilya's *Arthaśāstra,* which were followed closely by him, as demonstrated by Kobayashi.[2] The third and final criterion is the bedrock principle of *lectio difficilor.* Using these external criteria, I found that the Malayalam or what I call the "M" tradition based on the text commented on by Vishvarupa is far superior to the Vulgate and brings us as close to the original as we can without fresh evidence.

That is the text reproduced here. Whenever I depart from Vishvarupa's readings, I explain the reasons. Only the major variants in the two versions that affect the meaning are given in the Notes to the Text; the full critical apparatus is given in my forthcoming critical edition.[3] Endnote numbers are given at the end of verses; sometimes several variant readings of a single verse are given in a single note. The verse numbering of my text, furthermore, differs from those of the three major commentators, Vishvarupa, Vijnaneshvara, and Aparaka. The four numbering systems are given in the Concordance of Verses.

NOTES

1 Olivelle Forthcoming.
2 Kobayashi 2001–2002.
3 Olivelle Forthcoming.

# *A Treatise on Dharma*

# आचाराध्यायः

## ॥ अथोपोद्घातप्रकरणम् ॥

१ योगीश्वरं याज्ञवल्क्यं संपूज्य मुनयोऽब्रुवन् ।
वर्णाश्रमेतरेषां नो ब्रूहि धर्मानशेषतः ॥

२ मिथिलास्थः स योगीन्द्रः सम्यग्ध्यात्वाब्रवीन्मुनीन् ।
यस्मिन्देशे मृगः कृष्णस्तस्मिन्धर्मान्निबोधत ॥

३ पुराणन्यायमीमांसाधर्मशास्त्राङ्गमिश्रिताः ।
वेदाः स्थानानि विद्यानां धर्मस्य तु चतुर्दश ॥

४ वक्तारो धर्मशास्त्राणां मनुर्विष्णुर्यमोऽङ्गिराः ।
वसिष्ठदक्षसंवर्तशातातपपराशराः ॥

५ आपस्तम्बोशनोव्यासाः कात्यायनबृहस्पती ।
गौतमः शङ्खलिखितौ हारीतोऽत्रिरहं तथा[१] ॥

६ देशे काल उपायेन द्रव्यं श्रद्धासमन्वितैः ।
पात्रे प्रदीयते यत्तत्सकलं धर्मलक्षणम् ॥

# 1 Proper Conduct

## TOPIC 1: INTRODUCTION

### *Preamble*

To the king of yogis, Yajnavalkya, the sages paid homage and said: "Tell us in their entirety the dharmas pertaining to social classes, to orders of life, and to the rest."[1] 1

Residing in Mithila, that chief of yogis, after pondering it thoroughly, said to the sages: "Listen to the dharmas found in the region of the blackbuck."[2] 2

### *Sources of Dharma*

The Vedas coupled with Puranas, logic, hermeneutics, legal treatises, and supplements—these are the fourteen sites of the sciences, and of dharma.[3] 3

The promulgators of legal treatises are: Manu, Vishnu, Yama, Angiras, Vasishtha, Daksha, Samvarta, Shatatapa, Parashara, Apastamba, Ushanas, Vyasa, Katyayana, Brihaspati, Gautama, Shankha, Likhita, Harita, Atri, as well as myself.[4] 4–5

When an article is given by individuals imbued with the spirit of generosity, at a proper place and time, to a worthy recipient, and following the proper procedure—that constitutes the complete distinguishing mark of dharma. 6

७ वेदः स्मृतिः सदाचारः स्वस्य च प्रियमात्मनः ।
सम्यक्संकल्पजः कामो धर्ममूलमिदं स्मृतम् ॥

८ इज्याचारदमाहिंसादानस्वाध्यायकर्मणाम् ।
अयं तु परमो धर्मो यद्योगेनात्मदर्शनम् ॥

९ चत्वारो वेदधर्मज्ञाः पर्षत्त्रैविद्यमेव वा ।
सा ब्रूते यं स धर्मः स्यादेको वाध्यात्मवित्तमः ॥

॥ इत्युपोद्घातप्रकरणम् ॥

## ॥ अथ ब्रह्मचारिप्रकरणम् ॥

१० ब्रह्मक्षत्रियविड्शूद्रा वर्णास्त्वाद्यास्त्रयो द्विजाः ।
निषेकाद्याः श्मशानान्तास्तेषां वै मन्त्रतः क्रियाः ॥

११ गर्भाधानमृतौ पुंसः सवनं स्पन्दनात्पुरा ।
षष्ठेऽष्टमे वा सीमन्तो मास्येते जातकर्म च ॥

Veda, text of recollection, practice of good people, what is pleasing to one's self, and desire springing from right intention—that, texts of recollection state, is the root of dharma. 7

Sacrifice, normative practice, self-control, abstaining from injury, gift giving, and Vedic recitation—among these activities, however, this is the highest dharma: to perceive the self by means of yoga. 8

Four persons who know the Vedas and dharma constitute a legal assembly; or just an expert in the triple Veda. What that assembly declares—or even a single individual who knows the inner self completely—is dharma.[5] 9

## TOPIC 2: THE VEDIC STUDENT

### *Early Childhood Rites*

Brahman, Kshatriya, Vaishya, and Shudra are the social classes. The first three, however, are twice-born, and it is only for these males that the rites performed with the use of ritual formulas are intended, rites beginning with the impregnation ceremony and ending with the funeral.[6] 10

The impregnation ceremony is performed during the season; the quickening of the male fetus before it stirs; the parting of the hair in the sixth or the eighth month; the birth rite after he is born;[7] 11

१२ अहन्येकादशे नाम चतुर्थे मासि निष्क्रमः।
षष्ठेऽन्नप्राशनं मासि चूडा कार्या यथाकुलम् ॥

१३ एवमेनः शमं याति बीजगर्भसमुद्भवम्।
तूष्णीमेताः क्रियाः स्त्रीणां विवाहस्तु समन्त्रकः ॥

१४ गर्भाष्टमेऽष्टमे वाब्दे ब्राह्मणस्योपनायनम्।
राज्ञामेकादशे सैके विशामेके यथाकुलम् ॥

१५ उपनीय गुरुः शिष्यं महाव्याहृतिपूर्वकम्।
वेदमध्यापयेत्पश्चाच्छौचाचारांश्च शिक्षयेत् ॥

१६ दिवासंध्यासु कर्णस्थब्रह्मसूत्र उदङ्मुखः।
कुर्यान्मूत्रपुरीषे तु रात्रौ चेद्दक्षिणामुखः ॥

१७ गृहीतशिश्नश्चोत्थाय मृद्भिरभ्युद्धृतैर्जलैः।
गन्धलेपक्षयकरं शौचं कुर्यादतन्द्रितः ॥

the naming ceremony on the eleventh day; going out in the fourth month; and feeding solid food in the sixth month; while the cutting of the hair should be performed according to the custom of each family. 12

In this manner the taint arising from semen and womb is erased. These rites should be performed silently for females; but their marriage rite is performed with ritual formulas. 13

### *Vedic Initiation*

The Vedic initiation of a Brahman is performed in the eighth year from conception or in the eighth year from birth; of royals, in the eleventh; and of Vaishyas, in the twelfth—according to the custom of each family, some say. 14

Having initiated the pupil, the teacher should teach him the Veda preceded by the great calls, and afterwards also train him in purification and proper conduct.[8] 15

### *Duties of a Vedic Student*

During the day and the twilights he should void urine and excrement facing the north and with his sacred cord wrapped around his ear, and if it is during the night, facing the south. 16

Getting up holding his penis, he should tirelessly perform the purification that eliminates the smell and the stain using earth and water drawn out. 17

१८ अन्तर्जानु शुचौ देश उपविष्ट उदङ्मुखः।
प्राग्वा ब्राह्मेण तीर्थेन द्विजो नित्यमुपस्पृशेत्॥

१९ कनिष्ठादेशिन्यङ्गुष्ठमूलान्यग्रं करस्य च।
प्रजापतिपितृब्रह्मदैवतीर्थान्यनुक्रमात्॥

२० त्रिः प्राश्यापो द्विरुन्मृज्यात् खानि चोर्ध्वमुपस्पृशेत्।
अद्भिस्तु प्रकृतिस्थाभिर्हीनाभिः फेनबुद्बुदैः॥

२१ हृत्कण्ठतालुगाभिस्तु यथासंख्यं द्विजातयः।
शुध्येरन्स्त्री च शूद्रश्च सकृत्स्पृष्टाभिरन्ततः॥

२२ स्नानमब्दैवतैर्मन्त्रैर्मार्जनं प्राणसंयमः।
सूर्यस्य चाप्युपस्थानं गायत्र्याः प्रत्यहं जपः॥

२३ गायत्रीं शिरसा सार्धं जपेद्व्याहृतिपूर्विकाम्।
प्रतिप्रणवसंयुक्तां त्रिरयं प्राणसंयमः॥

२४ प्राणानायम्य संशुद्धः तृचेनाब्दैवतेन तु।
जपन्नासीत सावित्रीं प्रत्यगातारकोदयात्॥

Seated in a clean spot, facing the north or the east, and with his hand between his knees, a twice-born man should sip water every day with the part of the hand sacred to Brahma.[9] 18

The bases of the little finger, ring finger, and the thumb, and the tip of the hand are the parts of the hand sacred to Prajapati, forefathers, Brahma, and gods, respectively. 19

After sipping water three times, he should wipe his mouth twice and rub water on the upper orifices, using water in its natural state, however, free of froth or bubbles.[10] 20

Persons with two births become purified by water reaching the heart, throat, and palate, respectively, while a woman or Shudra is purified by water touching the ends of the lips just once.[11] 21

He should bathe, rub water on his body while reciting the formulas addressed to water, control his breath, worship the sun, and perform daily the soft recitation of the *gāyatrī* verse.[12] 22

He should recite the *gāyatrī* verse along with the *śiras* formula, preceded by the calls, to each of which is added the syllable OṂ; when repeated three times this constitutes a control of breath.[13] 23

After controlling his breath and purifying himself while reciting the three verses addressed to water,[14] he should remain seated facing the west and reciting the *sāvitrī* verse until the stars appear. 24

२५ संध्यां प्राङ्गातरेवं हि तिष्ठेदासूर्यदर्शनात् ।
अग्निकार्यं ततः कुर्यात्संध्ययोरुभयोरपि ॥

२६ ततोऽभिवादयेद्वृद्धानसावहमिति ब्रुवन् ।
गुरुं चैवाप्युपासीत स्वाध्यायार्थं समाहितः ॥

२७ आहूतश्चाप्यधीयीत लब्धं चास्मै निवेदयेत् ।
हितं चास्याचरेन्नित्यं मनोवाक्कायकर्मभिः ॥

२८ कृतज्ञोऽद्रोही मेधावी शुचिः कुल्योऽनसूयकाः ।
अध्याप्याः साधुशक्ताप्तस्वार्थदा धर्मतस्त्विमे[२] ॥

२९ दण्डाजिनोपवीतानि मेखलां चैव धारयेत् ।
ब्राह्मणेषु चरेद्भैक्षमनिन्द्येष्वात्मवृत्तये ॥

३० आदिमध्यावसानेषु भवच्छब्दोपलक्षिता ।
ब्राह्मणक्षत्रियविशां भैक्षचर्या यथाक्रमम् ॥

In the morning he should remain standing in the same manner facing the east until the sun comes into view. After that, at both twilights, he should perform the fire ritual. 25

Then, he should pay homage to elderly persons, saying: "I am so-and-so." With a collected mind, moreover, he should pay obeisance to his teacher in order to carry out the Vedic recitation. 26

And, when called upon, he should recite the Veda. He should present to the teacher whatever he has received and always do what is beneficial to him through mental, verbal, and physical activities. 27

A person who is grateful, not inimical, intelligent, pure, or from a good family; persons who are free from envy; or persons who are virtuous, competent, close to him, or part of his family, or who give him money—these are fit to be taught the Veda in accordance with dharma.[15] 28

### *Begging and Food*

He should carry a staff and wear an antelope skin, a sacrificial cord, and a girdle. To maintain himself, he should beg for almsfood among irreproachable Brahmans. 29

Begging for almsfood is done by Brahmans, Kshatriyas, and Vaishyas by placing the word "Lady" at the beginning, middle, and end, respectively.[16] 30

३१ ब्रह्मचर्ये स्थितो नैकमन्नमद्यादनापदि ।
ब्राह्मणः काममश्नीयाच्छ्राद्धे व्रतमपीडयन् ॥

३२ मधुमांसाञ्जनोच्छिष्टशुक्तस्त्रीप्राणिहिंसनम् ।
भास्करालोकनाश्लीलपरिवादांश्च वर्जयेत् ॥

३३ स गुरुर्यः क्रियाः कृत्वा वेदमस्मै प्रयच्छति ।
उपनीय ददद्वेदमाचार्यः स उदाहृतः ॥

३४ एकदेशमुपाध्याय ऋत्विग्यज्ञकृदुच्यते ।
एते मान्या यथापूर्वमेभ्यो माता गरीयसी ॥

३५ कृताग्निकार्यो भुञ्जीत वाग्यतो गुर्वनुज्ञया ।
अपोशानक्रियापूर्वं सत्कृत्यान्नमकुत्सयन् ॥

३६ प्रतिवेदं ब्रह्मचर्यं द्वादशाब्दानि पञ्च वा ।
ग्रहणान्तिकमित्येके केशान्तश्चैव षोडशे ॥

While he remains a Vedic student, he should not eat the food given by a single individual outside a time of adversity. A Brahman may freely eat at an ancestral offering without violating his vow. 31

He should shun honey, meat, unguents, leftover food, food that has turned sour, women, and injuring living beings, as well as looking at the sun, vulgar language, and slander. 32

*The Teacher*

"Teacher" is the man who, after he has performed the rites, transmits to him the Veda, while the man who performs his Vedic initiation and imparts the Veda is called "Instructor." 33

A man who imparts one section of the Veda is called "Tutor," while a man who performs one's sacrifices is called "Officiating Priest." Respect should be paid to them in that order. The mother is more venerable than all these. 34

Having performed the fire ritual, obtained his teacher's permission, and performed the rite of sipping water, he should eat silently after revering the food and without showing disdain.[17] 35

*Period of Studentship*

For each Veda the period of studentship lasts twelve years or five; according to some, until he has grasped it. The shaving ceremony is done in the sixteenth year. 36

३७ आ षोडशाद्द्वाविंशाच्च चतुर्विंशाच्च वत्सरात्।
ब्रह्मक्षत्रविशां काल औपनायनिकः परः॥

३८ अत ऊर्ध्वं पतन्त्येते सर्वधर्मबहिष्कृताः।
सावित्रीपतिता व्रात्या व्रात्यस्तोमादृते क्रतोः॥

३९ मातुरग्रेऽधिजायन्ते द्वितीयं मौञ्जिबन्धने।
ब्राह्मणक्षत्रियविशस्तस्मादेते द्विजातयः॥

४० यज्ञानां तपसां चैव शुभानां चैव कर्मणाम्।
वेद एव द्विजातीनां निःश्रेयसकरः परः॥

४१ मधुना पयसा चैव स देवांस्तर्पयेद्द्विजः।
पितॄन्मधुघृताभ्यां च ऋचोऽधीते हि योऽन्वहम्॥

४२ यजूंषि शक्तितोऽधीते योऽन्वहं स घृतामृतैः।
प्रीणाति देवानाज्येन मधुना च पितॄंस्तथा॥

४३ स तु सोमघृतैर्देवांस्तर्पयेद्योऽन्वहं पठेत्।
सामानि तृप्तिं कुर्याच्च पितॄणां मधुसर्पिषा॥

The sixteenth, the twenty-second, and the twenty-fourth year are the upper time limits for the Initiation of a Brahman, Kshatriya, and Vaishya, respectively. 37

After that time they become fallen and are excluded from all dharmas; they become *vrātyas,* fallen from *sāvitrī,* unless they perform the rite of *vrātyastoma.*[18] 38

Brahmans, Kshatriyas, and Vaishyas are born initially from the mother, and a second time at the tying of the *muñja* grass girdle; therefore they are persons with two births.[19] 39

### *Vedic Study*

Among sacrifices, ascetic toils, and auspicious rites, the Veda alone is the highest means of securing supreme bliss for men with two births.[20] 40

A twice-born man who recites the *ṛc* verses every day satisfies thereby the gods with honey and milk, and the ancestors with honey and ghee. 41

Someone who recites the *yajus* formulas every day to the best of his ability gratifies thereby the gods with ghee and nectar, and the ancestors with clarified butter and honey. 42

Someone who recites the *sāman* chants every day satisfies thereby the gods with *soma* and ghee, and brings satisfaction to the ancestors with honey and clarified butter. 43

४४ मेदसा तर्पयेद्देवानथर्वाङ्गिरसः पठन् ।
पितृंश्च मधुसर्पिर्भ्यामन्वहं शक्तितो द्विजः ॥

४५ वाकोवाक्यं पुराणं च नाराशंस्योऽथ गाथिकाः ।
इतिहासांस्तथा विद्या योऽधीते शक्तितोऽन्वहम् ॥

४६ मांसक्षीरौदनमधुतर्पणं स दिवौकसाम् ।
करोति तृप्तिं च तथा पितॄणां मधुसर्पिषा ॥

४७ ते तृप्तास्तर्पयन्त्येनं सर्वकामफलैः शुभैः ।
यं यं क्रतुमधीते च तस्य तस्याप्नुयात्फलम् ॥

४८ त्रिर्वित्तपूर्णपृथिवीदानस्य फलमश्नुते ।
तपसश्च परस्येह नित्यस्वाध्यायवान्द्विजः ॥

४९ नैष्ठिको ब्रह्मचारी तु वसेदाचार्यसंनिधौ ।
तदभावेऽस्य तनये पत्न्यां वैश्वानरेऽपि वा ॥

५० अनेन विधिना देहं साधयन्विजितेन्द्रियः ।
ब्रह्मलोकमवाप्नोति न चेहाजायते पुनः ॥

॥ इति ब्रह्मचारिप्रकरणम् ॥

A twice-born man who recites the *atharva-aṅgiras* verses every day to the best of his ability satisfies thereby the gods with marrow, and the ancestors with honey and clarified butter. 44

Someone who recites the dialogues, Purana, eulogies, epic songs, epic tales, and sciences every day to the best of his ability satisfies thereby the heavenly denizens with meat, milk, rice, and honey, and also brings satisfaction to the ancestors with honey and clarified butter.[21] 45–46

When they are satisfied, they will satisfy him with the marvelous fruits of all his desires. Further, whatever ritual he recites, he will obtain its fruit.[22] 47

A twice-born man who always performs here his daily Vedic recitation obtains the fruit of giving three times as a gift the earth filled with wealth, as well as the fruit of the highest ascetic toil. 48

### *Perpetual Vedic Student*

A perpetual Vedic student, however, should live near his teacher; in his absence, near his son, wife, or sacred fire. 49

By subduing his body in this manner, with his senses under control, he will attain the world of Brahma and will not be born again in this world.[23] 50

## ॥ अथ विवाहप्रकरणम् ॥

५१ गुरवे तु वरं दत्त्वा स्नायीत तदनुज्ञया ।
वेदं व्रतानि वा पारं नीत्वाप्युभयमेव वा ॥

५२ अविप्लुतब्रह्मचर्यो लक्षण्यां स्त्रियमुद्वहेत् ।
अनन्यपूर्विकां कान्तामसपिण्डां यवीयसीम् ॥

५३ अरोगिणीं भ्रातृमतीमसमानर्षिगोत्रजाम् ।
पञ्चमीं सप्तमीं चैव मातृतः पितृतस्तथा ॥

५४ दशपूरुषविख्याताच्छ्रोत्रियाणां महाकुलात् ।
स्फीतादपि न संचारिरोगदोषसमन्वितात् ॥

५५ एतैरेव गुणैर्युक्तः सवर्णः श्रोत्रियो वरः ।
यत्नात्परीक्षितः पुंस्त्वे युवा धीमाञ्जनप्रियः ॥

५६ यदुच्यते द्विजातीनां शूद्राद्दारोपसंग्रहः ।
न तन्मम मतं यस्मात्तत्रायं जायते स्वयम् ॥

५७ तिस्रो वर्णानुपूर्व्येण द्वे तथैका यथाक्रमम् ।
ब्राह्मणक्षत्रियविशां भार्या स्वा शूद्रजन्मनः ॥

## TOPIC 3: MARRIAGE

Having given a gift to his teacher, however, and with his permission, he should bathe after he has completely finished either the Veda or the observances, or both.[24] 51

While continuing to maintain his vow of chastity, he should marry a woman who possesses the proper characteristics—a woman who has not been with another man; is affable; does not belong to his ancestry;[25] is younger; 52

is free from disease; has a brother; is not born in a family having the same ancestral seer or belonging to the same lineage as his own; is fifth and seventh removed from his mother and father, respectively;[26] 53

and comes from an eminent family of Vedic scholars, a family renowned over ten generations, but not from one afflicted with a communicable disease even if it is prosperous. 54

The groom should possess these same qualities, and he should be of the same social class, a Vedic scholar, carefully tested with respect to his virility, young, intelligent, and well liked by the people. 55

With respect to what has been stated about twice-born men taking wives from the Shudras—I do not approve of it, because that man is himself born in her.[27] 56

A Brahman, Kshatriya, and Vaishya, in due order, may take three, two, and one wife in the direct order of class; a man of Shudra birth takes a wife of his own class.[28] 57

५८ ब्राह्मो विवाह आहूय दीयते शक्त्यलंकृता ।
तज्जः पुनात्युभयतः पुरुषानेकविंशतिम् ॥

५९ यज्ञस्थ ऋत्विजे दैव आदायार्षस्तु गोद्वयम् ।
चतुर्दश प्रथमजः पुनात्युत्तरजश्च षट् ॥

६० सह धर्मश्चर्यतामित्युक्त्वा या दीयतेऽर्थिने ।
स कायः पावयत्याद्यः षड्वंश्यान्सहात्मना ॥

६१ आसुरो द्रविणादानाद्गान्धर्वः समयान्मिथः ।
राक्षसो युद्धहरणात्पैशाचः कन्यकाछलात् ॥

६२ पाणिर्ग्राह्यः सवर्णासु गृह्णीत क्षत्रिया शरम् ।
वैश्या प्रतोदमादद्याद्वेदने त्वग्रजन्मनः ॥

६३ पिता मातामहो भ्राता स्वकुल्यो जननी तथा ।
कन्याप्रदः पूर्वनाशे प्रकृतिस्थः परः परः[३] ॥

When the bride, adorned according to ability, is given to a man who has been invited, it is the Brahma marriage. A son born from it purifies twenty-one generations on both sides.[29] 58

When she is given to the officiating priest engaged in performing a sacrifice, it is the divine marriage, while it is the seers' marriage when a pair of cows is received. A son born from the former purifies fourteen generations, while a son born from the latter purifies six. 59

"May the two of you carry out the dharma together": when she is given to a suitor after saying this, it is the marriage connected to Prajapati, the primary one that purifies six plus six generations along with himself.[30] 60

It is a demonic marriage when things of value are accepted; when the two get together by mutual consent, it is connected to the Gandharvas; fiendish, when she is abducted by force; and ghoulish, when a virgin girl is taken through deceit. 61

In the case of women of equal social class, her hand should be grasped. A Kshatriya woman, however, should grasp an arrow, and a Vaishya woman should take a goad when she marries a man of the highest birth. 62

Father, mother's father, brother from her own family, and mother may give a virgin girl in marriage—each succeeding one in the absence of each preceding, provided the person is in sound shape.[31] 63

६४ अप्रयच्छन्समाप्नोति भ्रूणहत्यामृतावृतौ ।
गम्यं त्वभावे दातॄणां कन्या कुर्यात्स्वयंवरम् ॥

६५ सकृत्प्रदीयते कन्या हरंस्तां चोरदण्डभाक् ।
दत्तामपि हरेत्पूर्वं श्रेयांश्चेद्वर आव्रजेत् ॥

६६ अनाख्याय ददद्दोषं दण्ड्य उत्तमसाहसम् ।
अदुष्टां यस्त्यजेत्कन्यां दूषयंस्तु मृषा शतम् ॥

६७ अक्षता वा क्षता वापि पुनर्भूः संस्कृता पुनः ।
स्वैरिणी या पतिं हित्वा सवर्णं कामतः श्रयेत् ॥

६८ अपुत्रां गुर्वनुज्ञानाद्देवरः पुत्रकाम्यया ।
सपिण्डो वा सगोत्रो वा घृताभ्यक्त ऋतावियात् ॥

६९ आ गर्भसंभवाद्गच्छेत्पतितस्त्वन्यथा भवेत् ।
अनेन विधिना जातः क्षेत्रिणः स भवेत्सुतः ॥

A person who does not give her away incurs the sin of killing a fetus at every menstrual period of hers. In the absence of persons who may give her away, however, a virgin girl may select on her own a groom with whom marriage is permissible. 64

A virgin girl is given in marriage just once. When someone takes her back, he is subject to the same punishment as a thief. Even though she has been given previously, he should take her back if a superior groom comes along. 65

Someone who gives her without revealing a blemish of hers should be punished with the highest seizure fine, as also a man who abandons a virgin girl who is unblemished. Someone who falsely accuses her of a defect, however, should be fined one hundred.[32] 66

A woman who marries again, whether she has lost her virginity or is still a virgin, is a "remarried woman," while a woman who abandons her husband and lustfully resorts to a man of her own class is a "wanton woman." 67

When authorized by the elders, her brother-in-law—or else a man of the same ancestry or of the same lineage—his body smeared with ghee, should approach a sonless woman once during her season with the desire for a son.[33] 68

He should go to her until she conceives; otherwise he becomes a fallen man. A son born according to this procedure belongs to the owner of the field.[34] 69

७० हृताधिकारां मलिनां पिण्डमात्रोपजीविनीम् ।
परिभूतामधःशय्यां वासयेद्व्यभिचारिणीम् ॥

७१ सोमः शौचं ददौ स्त्रीणां गन्धर्वश्च शुभां गिरम् ।
पावकः सर्वभक्षत्वं मेध्या वै योषितो मताः[४] ॥

७२ व्यभिचार ऋतौ शुद्धिर्गर्भे त्यागो विधीयते ।
गर्भभर्तृवधे चासां तथा महति पातके ॥

७३ सुरापी व्याधिता धूर्ती वन्ध्यार्थघ्न्यप्रियंवदा ।
स्त्रीप्रसूश्चाधिवेत्तव्या पुरुषद्वेषिणी तथा ॥

७४ अधिविन्ना तु भर्तव्या महदेनोऽन्यथा भवेत् ।
यत्रानुकूल्यं दम्पत्योस्त्रिवर्गस्तत्र वर्धते ॥

७५ मृते जीवति वा पत्यौ या नान्यमुपगच्छति ।
सेह कीर्तिमवाप्नोति मोदते चोमया सह[५] ॥

७६ स्त्रीभिर्भर्तृवचः कार्यमेष धर्मः परः स्त्रियाः ।
आ शुद्धेः संप्रतीक्ष्योऽपि महापातकदूषितः ॥

A licentious woman should be compelled to dwell deprived of any rights, wearing dirty clothes, living on just morsels of food, scorned, and sleeping on the ground. 70

The moon bestowed on women purity; Gandharva, a sweet voice; fire, the capacity to eat anything—womenfolk, indeed, are considered ritually pure.[35] 71

When chastity is violated, they are purified by their monthly period, whereas when they become pregnant, as also when they kill their fetus or husband and, likewise, when they have committed a grievous sin causing loss of caste, the rule is that they should be abandoned.[36] 72

A woman who drinks liquor; is ailing, deceitful, barren, profligate, or foulmouthed; or gives birth only to girls should be superseded—likewise, a woman who hates her husband. 73

A superseded woman, however, must be maintained; otherwise, he incurs a great sin. When there is harmony between husband and wife, the triple set prospers.[37] 74

When a woman does not go to another man, irrespective of whether her husband is dead or alive, she attains fame in this world and will rejoice in the company of Uma.[38] 75

Women should do what their husbands say: that is the highest dharma for a woman. When he is tainted with a grievous sin causing loss of caste,[39] furthermore, she should wait for him until he is purified. 76

७७ लोकानन्त्यदिवप्राप्तिः पुत्रपौत्रप्रपौत्रिका।
यस्मात्तस्मात्स्त्रियः सेव्याः भर्तव्याश्च सुरक्षिताः॥

७८ षोडशर्तुर्निशाः स्त्रीणां तस्मिन्युग्मासु संविशेत्।
ब्रह्मचार्येव पर्वाण्याद्याश्चतस्रश्च वर्जयेत्॥

७९ एवं गच्छन् स्त्रियं क्षामां मघामूलं च वर्जयेत्।
सुस्थ इन्दौ सकृत्पुत्रं लक्षण्यं जनयेत्पुमान्॥

८० याथाकामी भवेद्वापि स्त्रीणां वरमनुस्मरन्।
स्वदारनिरतश्चैव स्त्रियो रक्ष्या यतः स्मृताः॥

८१ भर्तृभ्रातृपितृज्ञातिश्वश्रूश्वशुरदेवरैः।
बन्धुभिश्च स्त्रियः पूज्या भूषणाच्छादनाशनैः॥

८२ संयतोपस्करा दक्षा हृष्टा व्ययपराङ्मुखी।
कुर्याच्छ्वशुरयोः पादवन्दनं भर्तृतत्परा॥

८३ क्रीडाशरीरसंस्कारसमाजोत्सवदर्शनम्।
हासं परगृहं यानं त्यजेत्प्रोषितभर्तृका[६]॥

Attainment of the world, eternity, and heaven depend on a son, son's son, and son's grandson, respectively. Therefore, men should have sex with their wives and keep them well-guarded.[40] 77

A woman's season consists of sixteen nights. During that period he should lie with her on even nights; thus he remains a true celibate. And he should avoid the days of the moon's change, as well as the first four days.[41] 78

Approaching his wife in this manner, he should avoid her when she is sick, as also in the constellations of *maghā* and *mūla*. When the moon is well located, the man should beget once a son possessing the proper characteristics.[42] 79

Or else, he may follow his desire, remembering the wish granted to women, and remain faithful to his wife, because texts of recollection state that women should be guarded.[43] 80

Women, moreover, should be honored with adornments, clothes, and food by their husbands, brothers, fathers, paternal relatives, mothers-in-law, fathers-in law, and brothers-in-law, as also by their maternal relatives. 81

Keeping the household implements in order, being skilled, cheerful, and averse to spending, she should worship the feet of her parents-in-law, remaining devoted to her husband. 82

Participating in games, adorning the body, attending fairs and festivals, laughing, visiting other people's houses, and travel—these should be shunned by a woman whose husband has gone abroad.[44] 83

८४ रक्षेत्कन्यां पिता विन्नां पतिः पुत्रस्तु वार्धके ।
अभावे ज्ञातयस्त्वेषां स्वातन्त्र्यं न क्वचित्स्त्रियाः ॥

८५ पितृमातृसुतभ्रातृश्वश्रूश्वशुरमातुलैः ।
हीना न स्याद्विना भर्त्रा गर्हणीयान्यथा भवेत् ॥

८६ सत्यामन्यां सवर्णायां धर्मकार्यं न कारयेत् ।
सवर्णासु विधौ धर्म्ये ज्येष्ठया न विनेतरां ॥

८७ दाहयित्वाग्निहोत्रेण स्त्रियं वृत्तवतीं पतिः ।
आहरेद्विधिवद्दारानग्नींश्चैवाविलम्बितः ॥

८८ पतिप्रियहिते युक्ता स्वाचारा संयतेन्द्रिया ।
सेह कीर्तिमवाप्नोति प्रेत्य चानुत्तमां गतिम् ॥

॥ इति विवाहप्रकरणम् ॥

The father should guard her when she is a girl; the husband, when she is married; the son, when she is old; and, in their absence, the paternal relatives—a woman should never live independently. 84

When she is without her husband, she should never live separate from her father, mother, son, brother, mother-in-law, father-in-law, or maternal uncle; otherwise, she will be subject to reproach. 85

When a wife of equal class is available, he should not employ another wife in the performance of ritual duties, and where there are several wives of equal class, he should not employ in a religious rite anyone other than the most senior wife. 86

After cremating a wife of good conduct with his sacred fire, the husband should take a wife and sacred fires according to rule without delay. 87

When she is intent on what is beneficial to her husband, holds to virtuous conduct, and keeps her senses under control, she attains fame in his world and the highest state after death. 88

## ॥ अथ वर्णजातिविवेकप्रकरणम् ॥

८९ सवर्णेभ्यः सवर्णासु जायन्ते हि सजातयः ।
अनिन्द्येषु विवाहेषु पुत्राः संतानवर्धनाः ॥

९० विप्रान्मूर्धावसिक्तं स्त्री राज्ञोऽम्बष्ठं विशोऽङ्गना ।
शूद्राङ्गना निषादाख्यं सूते पारशवं तथा ॥

९१ माहिष्योग्रौ प्रजायेते विट्छूद्राङ्गनयोर्नृपात् ।
शूद्रायां करणो वैश्याद्विन्नास्वेष विधिः स्मृतः ॥

९२ ब्राह्मण्यां क्षत्रियात्सूतो वैश्याद्वैदेहकस्तथा ।
शूद्राज्जातश्च चण्डालः सर्वधर्मविगर्हितः[७] ॥

९३ क्षत्रिया मागधं वैश्याच्छूद्रात्क्षत्तारमेव च ।
शूद्रादायोगवं वैश्या जनयामास वै सुतम् ॥

९४ माहिष्येण करण्यां तु रथकारः प्रजायते ।
असत्सन्तस्तु विज्ञेयाः प्रतिलोमानुलोमतः ॥

## TOPIC 4: EXAMINATION OF CLASS AND CASTE

From men of the same social class through women of the same social class within unimpeachable marriages are, indeed, born sons of the same caste who increase the family line. 89

From a Brahman man a Kshatriya woman begets a Murdhavasikta; a Vaishya woman, an Ambashtha; a Shudra woman, one called a Nishada, as also a Parashava. 90

From a Kshatriya man through Vaishya and Shudra women are born a Mahishya and an Ugra, respectively; from a Vaishya man through a Shudra woman, a Karana—this is said to be the rule with respect to married women. 91

From a Kshatriya man through a Brahman woman is born a Suta; from a Vaishya man, a Vaidehaka; and from a Shudra man, a Chandala, who is banned from all dharmas.[45] 92

From a Vaishya man a Kshatriya woman gives birth to a Magadha; from a Shudra man, a Kshattri. From a Shudra man a Vaishya woman gives birth to an Ayogava son. 93

From a Mahisha man through a Karani woman, however, is born a Rathakara. They should be recognized as bad or good, however, depending on whether they are from unions in the inverse or the direct order of social class. 94

९५ जात्युत्कर्षो युगे ज्ञेयः पञ्चमे सप्तमेऽपि वा।
व्यत्यये कर्मणां साम्यं पूर्ववच्चाधरोत्तरम्॥

॥ इति वर्णजातिविवेकप्रकरणम्॥

## ॥ अथ गृहस्थधर्मप्रकरणम्॥

९६ कर्म स्मार्तं विवाहाग्नौ कुर्वीत प्रत्यहं गृही।
दायकालाहृते वापि श्रौतं वैतानिकाग्निषु॥

९७ शरीरचिन्तां निर्वर्त्य कृतशौचविधिर्द्विजः।
प्रातःसंध्यामुपासीत दन्तधावनपूर्विकाम्॥

९८ हुत्वाग्नीन्सूर्यदेवत्याञ्जपेन्मन्त्रान्समाहितः।
वेदार्थानधिगच्छेत शास्त्राणि विविधानि च॥

९९ उपेयादीश्वरं चैव योगक्षेमार्थसिद्धये।
स्नात्वा देवान्पितॄंश्चैव तर्पयेदर्चयेत्तथा॥

१०० वेदाथर्वपुराणानि सेतिहासानि शक्तितः।
जपयज्ञार्थसिद्ध्यर्थं विद्यां चाध्यात्मिकीं जपेत्॥

One should recognize that advance in caste takes place in the fifth or seventh generation. When the occupational activities are inverted, one attains the same level; and one attains a lower or higher level in the same way as before.[46] 95

## TOPIC 5: DHARMA OF HOUSEHOLDERS

A householder should perform the rites prescribed in the texts of recollection every day in the fire kindled at his marriage or brought at the time of partition, and the Vedic rites in the three sacred fires.[47] 96

After taking care of his bodily needs and performing the rites of purification, a twice-born man should first clean his teeth and then perform the morning twilight worship. 97

After making the offering in the fires, he should recite softly the ritual formulas addressed to the sun with a collected mind. He should study the meanings of the Veda, as well as diverse scientific treatises.[48] 98

He may, furthermore, approach the lord for securing resources and protection. After bathing, he should satiate and worship gods and forefathers. 99

For the success of his sacrifice of soft recitation, he should softly recite to the best of his ability the Vedas, *atharvans,* and Puranas, along with *itihāsas,* as well as the knowledge pertaining to the highest self.[49] 100

१०१ बलिकर्मस्वधाहोमस्वाध्यायातिथिसत्क्रियाः।
भूतपित्रमरब्रह्ममनुष्याणां महामखाः॥

१०२ देवेभ्यश्च हुतादन्नाच्छेषाद्भूतबलिं हरेत्।
अन्नं भूमौ श्वचण्डालवयोभ्यश्चैव निक्षिपेत्॥

१०३ अन्नं पितृमनुष्येभ्यो देयमप्यन्वहं जलम्।
स्वाध्यायं चान्वहं कुर्यान्न पचेदन्नमात्मनः॥

१०४ बालस्ववासिनीवृद्धगर्भिण्यातुरकन्यकाः।
संभोज्यातिथिभृत्यांश्च दम्पत्योः शेषभोजनम्॥

१०५ अपोशानेनोपरिष्टादधस्तादश्नता तथा।
अनग्नममृतं चैव कार्यमन्नं द्विजन्मना॥

१०६ अतिथित्वेऽपि वर्णेभ्यो देयं शक्त्यानुपूर्वशः।
अप्रणोद्योऽतिथिः सायमपि वाग्भूतृणोदकैः॥

१०७ सत्कृत्य भिक्षवे भिक्षा दातव्या सुव्रताय च।
भोजयेच्चागतान्काले सखिसंबन्धिबान्धवान्॥

He should perform the five great sacrifices to beings, forefathers, gods, Veda, and human beings, sacrifices consisting of the Bali rite, ancestral offering, divine offering, Vedic recitation, and rite of hospitality. 101

From what remains of the food offered to the gods, he should make a Bali offering to beings. He should throw on the ground food for dogs, Chandalas, and crows. 102

Food should be given to forefathers and humans, as also water every day, and every day he should perform the Vedic recitation. Let him not cook food just for himself. 103

After feeding the children, newly married women, the elderly, pregnant women, the sick, and young women, as also guests and dependents, the husband and wife should eat what is left over. 104

As he eats, the twice-born man should make the food non-naked and immortal from above and below through the rite of sipping water.[50] 105

Even in the case of feeding guests, food should be given according to his ability to people belonging to the social classes. A guest should not be turned away in the evening, receiving him at least with a pleasant word, a place on the floor, some straw, and water. 106

After paying homage, moreover, he should present almsfood to a mendicant and to one faithful to his vows. He should also feed friends and affinal and maternal relatives who come at the proper time.[51] 107

१०८ महोक्षं वा महाजं वा श्रोत्रियायोपकल्पयेत् ।
सत्क्रिया सेवनं स्वादु भोजनं सूनृतं वचः[८] ॥

१०९ प्रतिसंवत्सरं त्वर्घ्याः स्नातकाचार्यपार्थिवाः ।
प्रियो विवाह्यश्च तथा यज्ञं प्रत्यृत्विजः पुनः ॥

११० अध्वनीनोऽतिथिर्ज्ञेयः श्रोत्रियो वेदपारगः ।
मान्यावेतौ गृहस्थस्य ब्रह्मलोकमभीप्सतः ॥

१११ परपाकरुचिर्न स्यादनिन्द्यामन्त्रणादृते ।
वाक्पाणिपादचापल्यं वर्जयेच्चातिभोजनम् ॥

११२ अतिथिं श्रोत्रियं तृप्तमासीमान्तादनुव्रजेत् ।
अहःशेषं समासीत शिष्टैरिष्टैश्च बन्धुभिः ॥

११३ उपास्य पश्चिमां संध्यां हुत्वाग्नींस्तानुपास्य च ।
भृत्यैः परिवृतो भुक्त्वा नातितृप्याथ संविशेत् ॥

११४ धर्ममर्थं च कामं च यथाशक्ति न हापयेत् ।
ब्राह्मे मुहूर्त उत्थाय चिन्तयेदात्मनो हितम्[९] ॥

११५ विद्याकर्मवयोबन्धुवित्तैर्मान्या यथाक्रमम् ।
एतैः प्रभूतैः शूद्रोऽपि वार्धक्ये मानमर्हति ॥

To a Vedic scholar, he should prepare a large ox or a large goat, offering him homage, attendance, tasty food, and kind words.[52] 108

A bath-graduate, teacher, king, friend, and son-in-law, however, should be honored with the honey-mixture once a year, and officiating priests at every sacrifice.[53] 109

A traveler should be considered a guest, while a Vedic scholar is someone who has mastered the Veda. These two are to be honored by a householder who desires the world of Brahma. 110

He should not take delight in food cooked by others, except when he is invited by a blameless person. He should avoid being frivolous with his speech, hands, and feet, as also eating too much. 111

When a guest or Vedic scholar has been sated, he should follow him until the boundary. He should spend the rest of the day seated with cultured people and cherished relatives.[54] 112

After he has performed the evening twilight worship, made offerings in the sacred fires and worshiped them, and taken his meal surrounded by his dependents without overeating, he should then go to bed. 113

He should not neglect dharma, success, and pleasure as far as he is able. Rising at the time sacred to Brahma, he should reflect on what is beneficial to himself.[55] 114

People are to be honored according to their learning, occupation, age, relatives, and wealth, in that order. Even a Shudra possessing these qualities in abundance deserves honor in his old age. 115

११६ वृद्धभारिनृपस्नातस्त्रीरोगिवरचक्रिणाम् ।
पन्था देयो नृपस्तेषां मान्यः स्नातश्च भूपतेः ॥

११७ इज्याध्ययनदानानि वैश्यस्य क्षत्रियस्य च ।
प्रतिग्रहोऽधिको विप्रे याजनाध्यापने तथा ॥

११८ प्रधानं क्षत्रिये कर्म प्रजानां परिपालनम् ।
कुसीदकृषिवाणिज्यं पाशुपाल्यं विशः स्मृतम् ॥

११९ शूद्रस्य द्विजशुश्रूषा तयाजीवन्वणिग्भवेत् ।
शिल्पैर्वा विविधैर्जीवेद्द्विजातिहितमाचरेत् ॥

१२० भार्यारतिः शुचिर्भृत्यभर्ता श्राद्धक्रियारतः ।
नमस्कारेण मन्त्रेण पञ्च यज्ञान्न हापयेत् ॥

१२१ अहिंसा सत्यमस्तेयं शौचमिन्द्रियसंयमः ।
दमः क्षमार्जवं दानं सर्वेषां धर्मसाधनम् ॥

१२२ वयोबुद्ध्यर्थवाग्वेषश्रुताभिजनकर्मणाम् ।
आचरेत्सदृशीं वृत्तिमजिह्मामशठां तथा ॥

An elderly person, someone carrying a load, king, bath-graduate, woman, sick person, bridegroom, and a person in a carriage—people should give way to them. The king is to be honored by them, while a bath-graduate is to be honored by the king. 116

Offering sacrifices, studying the Veda, and giving gifts pertain to the Vaishya and the Kshatriya; to Brahmans, in addition, accepting gifts, as well as officiating at sacrifices and teaching. 117

The principle activity of a Kshatriya is the protection of the subjects; that of a Vaishya is money lending, agriculture, trade, and cattle herding; and that of a Shudra is the service of twice-born people. If he is unable to make a living from it, he may become a trader or make a living through various artisan activities. He should engage in what is beneficial to people with two births. 118–119

Taking delight in his wife, keeping himself pure, taking care of his dependents, and taking delight in ancestral offerings, he should not neglect the five sacrifices using the mantra "Homage."[56] 120

Abstention from injuring, truthfulness, refraining from theft, purification, restraining the organs, self-control, forbearance, honesty, and giving gifts—these are the means of fulfilling dharma for everybody. 121

One should follow a conduct that corresponds to one's age, intelligence, wealth, speech, dress, learning, birth, and occupation, a conduct that is not dishonest or crooked. 122

१२३ त्रैवार्षिकाधिकान्नो यः स सोमं हि पिबेद्विजः।
प्राक्सौमिकाः क्रियाः कुर्याद्यस्यान्नं वार्षिकं भवेत्॥

१२४ प्रतिसंवत्सरं सोमः पशुः प्रत्ययनं तथा।
कर्तव्याग्रयणेष्टिश्च चातुर्मास्यानि चैव हि॥

१२५ एषामसंभवे कुर्यादिष्टिं वैश्वानरीं द्विजः।
हीनकल्पं न कुर्वीत सति द्रव्ये फलप्रदम्॥

१२६ चण्डालो जायते यज्ञकरणाच्छूद्रभिक्षिता।
यज्ञार्थं लब्धमदद्भासः काकोऽपि जायते[१०]॥

१२७ कुसूलकुम्भीधान्यो वा त्र्यैहिकोऽश्वस्तनोऽपिवा।
जीवेद्वापि शिलोञ्छेन श्रेयानेषां परः परः॥

॥ इति गृहस्थधर्मप्रकरणम्॥

A twice-born person who has sufficient food to last three years may, indeed, drink the *soma*, while someone who has sufficient food to last one year may perform the rites preliminary to a *soma* sacrifice. 123

One should perform the *soma* sacrifice every year and the animal sacrifice every half-year, as well as the offering of the first fruits and the sacrifices connected to the seasons of the year. 124

When it is impossible to undertake them, a twice-born man should perform the *vaiśvānara* oblation. He should not carry out an inferior ritual procedure in the case of a rite that provides a reward only when the ritual material is present.[57] 125

A man who begs from a Shudra in order to perform a sacrifice is born as a Chandala, whereas a man who does not give what has been obtained for the sake of a sacrifice is born as a vulture or even a crow.[58] 126

Let him be a man who stores grain sufficient to fill a granary or sufficient to fill a jar, a man who has grain sufficient for three days, or a man who keeps nothing for the next day; or else, he may live by gleaning. Of these, each succeeding one is superior to each preceding. 127

## ॥ अथ स्नातकधर्मप्रकरणम् ॥

१२८ न स्वाध्यायविरोध्यर्थमीहेत न यतस्ततः ।
न विरुद्धप्रसङ्गेन संतोषी च भवेत्सदा ॥

१२९ राजान्तेवासियाज्येभ्यः सीदन्निच्छेद्धनं क्षुधा ।
दम्भिहैतुकपाषण्डिबकवृत्तींश्च नार्चयेत्[११] ॥

१३० शुक्लाम्बरधरो नीचकेशश्मश्रुनखः शुचिः ।
न भार्यादर्शनेऽश्नीयान्नैकवासा न संस्थितः ॥

१३१ न संशयं प्रपद्येत नाकस्मादप्रियं वदेत् ।
नाहितं नानृतं चैव न स्तेनः स्यान्न वार्धुषी ॥

१३२ दाक्षायणी ब्रह्मसूत्री यष्टिमान्सकमण्डलुः ।
कुर्यात्प्रदक्षिणं देवमृद्गोविप्रवनस्पतीन् ॥

१३३ न मेहेत नदीछायावर्त्मगोष्ठाम्बुभस्मसु ।
न प्रत्यग्न्यर्कगोसोमसंध्याम्बुस्त्रीद्विजन्मनाम् ॥

१३४ नेक्षेतार्कं न नग्नां स्त्रीं न च संस्पृष्टमैथुनाम् ।
न च मूत्रं पुरीषं वा नाशुची राहुतारकाः ॥

## TOPIC 6: DHARMA OF BATH-GRADUATES

He should not desire wealth that interferes with his Vedic recitation, or from just anyone, or through forbidden activities or excessive attachment. And he should always be content. 128

When he is tormented by hunger, he may request money from the king, resident pupil, or a client at whose sacrifice he officiates. He should not honor hypocrites, sophists, ascetics of heretical sects, and those who follow the way of herons.[59] 129

He should wear white clothes, keep his hair, beard, and nails trimmed, and remain pure. He should not eat within sight of his wife, wearing a single garment, or while standing. 130

He should not undertake anything dangerous, say anything unpleasant without reason, do anything harmful, or speak an untruth. He should not be a thief or a usurer. 131

He should display gold, wear the sacred cord, bear a staff, and carry a water pot. He should circumambulate clockwise a divine image, earth, a cow, a Brahman, and a prominent tree.[60] 132

He should not urinate into a river, on his shadow, on a road, in a cattle shed, into water, on ashes, or toward a fire, sun, a cow, moon, twilight, water, a woman, or a twice-born man. 133

He should not look at the sun, a woman who is naked or engaged in sex, urine, or excrement, or look at an eclipse or stars while he is impure. 134

१३५ अयं मे वज्र इत्येनं सर्वं मन्त्रमुदीरयेत् ।
वर्षत्यप्रावृतो गच्छेत्स्वपेत्प्रत्यक्शिरा न च ॥

१३६ ष्ठीवनासृक्शकृन्मूत्रविषान्यप्सु न संक्षिपेत् ।
पादौ प्रतापयेन्नाग्नौ न चैनमतिलङ्घयेत्[१२] ॥

१३७ जलं पिबेन्नाञ्जलिना न शयानं प्रबोधयेत् ।
नाक्षैः क्रीडेन्न धर्मघ्नैर्व्याधितैर्वा न संवसेत् ॥

१३८ विरुद्धं वर्जयेत्कर्म प्रेतधूमं नदीतरम् ।
केशभस्मतुषाङ्गारकपालेषु च संस्थितिम् ॥

१३९ नाचक्षीत धयन्तीं गां नाद्वारेणाविशेत्क्वचित् ।
न राज्ञः प्रतिगृह्णीयाल्लुब्धस्योच्छास्त्रवर्तिनः ॥

१४० प्रतिग्रहे सूनिचक्रिध्वजिवेश्यानराधिपाः ।
दुष्टा दशगुणं पूर्वात्पूर्वादेते यथोत्तरम् ॥

१४१ अध्यायानामुपाकर्म श्रावण्यां श्रवणेन तु ।
हस्ते वौषधिभावे वा पञ्चम्यां श्रावणस्य वा ॥

१४२ पौषमासस्य रोहिण्यामष्टकायामथापि वा ।
जलान्ते छन्दसां कुर्यादुत्सर्गं विधिवद्द्विजः[१३] ॥

He should recite the entire mantra: "May this, my bolt, drive away evil."[61] He should not go in the rain without a cover or sleep with his head toward the west. 135

He should not throw spittle, blood, feces, urine, or poison into water. He should neither warm his feet over a fire nor step over it.[62] 136

He should not drink water from his cupped hands, awaken a sleeping person, play with dice, or live with those who destroy dharma or with sick people. 137

He should avoid incompatible activities, the smoke from a funeral pyre, crossing rivers, and stepping on hair, ashes, chaff, coals, or shards. 138

He should not report a cow that is suckling her calf, enter anywhere by a passage other than a door, or accept anything from a king who is greedy and deviates from the provisions of authoritative texts. 139

Butcher, oil-presser, tavern keeper, prostitute, and king—with regard to accepting gifts, each succeeding one of these is ten times worse than each preceding. 140

The commencement of the annual course of study takes place on the full moon day of the month *śrāvaṇa,* under the constellation *śravaṇa,* in the constellation *hasta,* when plants sprout, or on the fifth day of the month *śrāvaṇa.*[63] 141

At the water's edge, in the month Pausha, under the asterism *rohiṇī,* or on the eighth day, a twice-born man should perform the rite of terminating the Vedic study according to rule.[64] 142

१४३ त्र्यहं प्रेतेष्वनध्यायः शिष्यर्त्विग्गुरुबन्धुषु ।
उपाकर्मणि चोत्सर्गे स्वशाखे श्रोत्रिये तथा ॥

१४४ संध्यागर्जितनिर्घातभूकम्पोल्कानिपातने ।
समाप्य वेदं द्युनिशमारण्यकमधीत्य च ॥

१४५ पञ्चदश्यां चतुर्दश्यामष्टम्यां राहुसूतके ।
ऋतुसंधिषु भुक्त्वा वा श्राद्धिकं प्रतिगृह्य वा ॥

१४६ पशुमण्डूकनकुलश्वाहिमार्जारसूकरैः ।
कृतेऽन्तरे त्वहोरात्रं शक्रपाते तथोच्छ्रये[१४] ॥

१४७ श्वक्रोष्टुगर्दभोलूकसामबाणार्तनिःस्वने ।
अमेध्यशवशूद्रान्त्यश्मशानपतितान्तिके ॥

१४८ देशेऽशुचावात्मनि च विद्युत्स्तनितसंप्लवे ।
भुक्त्वार्द्रपाणिरम्भोऽन्तरर्धरात्रेऽतिमारुते ॥

१४९ पांसुवर्षे दिशां दाहे संध्यानीहारभीतिषु ।
धावतः पूतिगन्धे च शिष्टे च गृहमागते ॥

The suspension of Vedic recitation lasts for three days at the death of a pupil, officiating priest, elder, or a maternal relative; at the commencement and termination of the annual course of study; and at the death of a Vedic scholar belonging to his own Vedic branch. 143

When there is thunder at twilight, a thunderstorm, an earthquake, or a lightning strike, and after completing the recitation of one Veda, the suspension lasts for a day and night; as also after reciting an Aranyaka; on the fifteenth, fourteenth, and eighth day of a fortnight; at an eclipse; at the junctures between seasons; and after eating or accepting food at an ancestral offering. 144–145

When a farm animal, frog, mongoose, dog, snake, cat, or pig comes in between, however, the suspension lasts for a day and night, as also at the lowering and raising of Indra's flag.[65] 146

At the sound of a dog, jackal, donkey, owl, *sāman* chant, arrow, or someone in distress; in the vicinity of filth, a corpse, a Shudra, a person of the lowest caste, a cemetery, and a person fallen from his caste; 147

in an impure place; when one is impure; when there is a lot of lightning and thunder; while one's hands are wet after eating; while standing in water; in the middle of the night; when there is a strong wind; 148

during a dust storm; when the horizons are ablaze; during twilight, fog, and danger; while running; when there is a foul smell; when a person belonging to the cultured elite has come to his house; 149

१५० खरोष्ट्रयानहस्त्यश्वनौवृक्षेरिणरोहणे।
सप्तत्रिंशदनध्यायानेतांस्तात्कालिकान्विदुः॥

१५१ देवर्त्विक्स्नातकाचार्यराज्ञां छायां परस्य च।
नाक्रामेद्रक्तविण्मूत्रष्ठीवनोद्वर्तनानि च[१५]॥

१५२ विप्राहिक्षत्रियात्मानो नावज्ञेयाः कदाचन।
आ मृत्योः श्रियमाकाङ्क्षन्न कंचिन्मर्मणि स्पृशेत्॥

१५३ दूरादुच्छिष्टविण्मूत्रपादाम्भांसि समुत्सृजेत्।
श्रुतिस्मृत्युदितं सम्यङ्नित्यमाचारमाचरेत्॥

१५४ गोब्राह्मणानलान्नानि नोच्छिष्टो न पदा स्पृशेत्।
न निन्दाताडने कुर्यात्सुतं शिष्यं च ताडयेत्॥

१५५ कर्मणा मनसा वाचा यत्नाद्धर्मं समाचरेत्।
अस्वर्ग्यं लोकविद्विष्टं धर्ममप्याचरेन्न तु[१६]॥

when he has climbed on a donkey, camel, vehicle, elephant, horse, boat, tree, or arid land—they state that these are the thirty-seven occasions when Vedic recitation is suspended for the duration of the event. 150

He should not tread on the shadow of a divine image, officiating priest, bath-graduate, teacher, or king, or of another person, as also on blood, feces, urine, spittle, or bath-powder.[66] 151

He should not treat with contempt a Brahman, a snake, a Kshatriya, and his own self. He should pursue prosperity until death and not cut someone to the quick. 152

He should dispose of leftovers, feces, urine, and water from washing the feet far away. He should always carefully follow the normative practices enjoined by Vedic scriptures and texts of recollection. 153

He should not touch a cow, a Brahman, fire, or food while he is sullied with remnants or with his foot. He should not berate or strike anyone; he may strike a son or pupil.[67] 154

He should follow dharma assiduously with his acts, mind, and speech. He should not perform even an act prescribed by dharma when it does not lead to a good outcome or is repulsive to the people.[68] 155

१५६ मातृपितृतिथिभ्रातृज्ञातिसंबन्धिमातुलैः ।
वृद्धबालातुराचार्यवैद्यसंश्रितबान्धवैः[१७] ॥

१५७ ऋत्विक्पुरोहितामात्यभार्यादाससनाभिभिः ।
विवादं वर्जयित्वा तु सर्वाँल्लोकाञ्जयेद्गृही[१८] ॥

१५८ पञ्च पिण्डाननुद्धृत्य न स्नायात्परवारिषु ।
स्नायान्नदीदेवखातह्रदेषु च सरस्सु च ॥

१५९ परशय्यासनोद्यानगृहयानानि वर्जयेत् ।
अदत्तान्यग्निहीनस्य न चाश्नीयादनापदि ॥

१६० कदर्यबद्धचोराणां क्लीबरङ्गावतारिणाम् ।
वेनाभिशस्तवार्धुषिगणिकागणदीक्षिणाम् ॥

१६१ चिकित्सकातुरक्रुद्धपुंश्चलीमत्तविद्विषाम् ।
क्रूरोग्रपतितव्रात्यदाम्भिकोच्छिष्टभोजिनाम् ॥

१६२ अवीरस्त्रीस्वर्णकारस्त्रीजितग्रामयाजिनाम् ।
शस्त्रविक्रयिकर्मारतुन्नवायश्ववृत्तिनाम् ॥

Mother, father, guest, brother, paternal relative, affinal relative, and maternal uncle; old person, child, sick person, teacher, doctor, dependent, and maternal relative; officiating priest, domestic priest, member of the household, wife, slave, and uterine sibling—by avoiding disputes with these a householder will win all the worlds.[69] 156–157

Without taking out five lumps of mud, he should not bathe in a body of water belonging to someone else. Let him bathe in rivers, natural pools, ponds, and lakes. 158

He should avoid beds, seats, gardens, houses, and vehicles belonging to others so long as they have not been given to him. Except in a time of adversity, he should not eat the food of a man who does not maintain a sacred fire. 159

Misers, prisoners, thieves, impotent men, theatrical performers, musicians, heinous sinners, usurers, prostitutes, associations, persons consecrated for sacrifices, 160

physicians, sick people, wrathful people, promiscuous women, drunkards, enemies, cruel people, fierce people, those fallen from their caste, *vrātyas,*[70] hypocrites, people who eat leftovers, 161

women without husbands, goldsmiths, men bossed by their wives, those who officiate at sacrifices sponsored by villages, arms merchants, blacksmiths, tailors, those who earn a living with dogs,[71] 162

१६३ नृशंसराजरजककृतघ्नवधजीविनाम् ।
चेलधावसुधाजीवसहोपपतिवेश्मनाम्[१९] ॥
१६४ एषामन्नं न भोक्तव्यं सोमविक्रयिणस्तथा ।
पिशुनानृतिनोश्चैव तथा चाक्रिकबन्दिनाम् ॥

॥ इति स्नातकधर्मप्रकरणम् ॥

## ॥ अथ भक्ष्याभक्ष्यप्रकरणम् ॥

१६५ अनर्चितं वृथामांसं केशकीटसमन्वितम् ।
शुक्तं पर्युषितोच्छिष्टं श्वस्पृष्टं पतितेक्षितम् ॥
१६६ उदक्यास्पृष्टसंघुष्टं पर्याचान्तं च वर्जयेत् ।
गोघ्रातं शकुनोच्छिष्टं पादस्पृष्टं च कामतः[२०] ॥
१६७ शूद्रेषु दासगोपालकुलमित्रार्धसीरिणः ।
भोज्यान्ना नापितश्चैव यश्चात्मानं निवेदयेत् ॥

heartless men, kings, dyers, ungrateful people, those who make a living by slaughter, washermen, those who make a living by whitewashing, those who keep their wives' lovers in their houses[72]— 163

the food of these people should not be eaten, as also the food of those who sell *soma,* of slanderers and liars, and of oil pressers and bards. 164

## TOPIC 7: PERMITTED AND FORBIDDEN FOOD

Food given without respect, meat procured capriciously, food contaminated with hair or insects, food that has turned sour or stale, leftovers, food touched by a dog or looked at by someone fallen from caste, 165

food touched by a menstruating woman or given after a public announcement, and food given at a meal where someone sips water during the meal—these he should avoid, as also food smelled by a cow, what is left over by a bird, and food touched deliberately with the foot.[73] 166

Slave, cowherd, family friend, and sharecropper—among Shudras these are the ones whose food is fit to be eaten, as also the barber and someone who has presented himself.[74] 167

१६८ अन्नं पर्युषितं भोज्यं स्नेहाक्तं चिरसंस्थितम् ।
अस्नेहा अपि गोधूमयवगोरसविक्रियाः ॥

१६९ संधिन्यनिर्दशावत्सगोपयः परिवर्जयेत् ।
औष्ट्रमैकशफं स्त्रैणमारण्यकमथाविकम् ॥

१७० देवतार्थं हविः शिग्रुं लोहितान्व्रश्चनानि च ।
अनुपाकृतमांसानि विड्जानि कवकानि च[21] ॥

१७१ क्रव्यादपक्षिदात्यूहशुकप्रतुदटिट्टिभान् ।
सारसैकशफान्हंसान्सर्वांश्च ग्रामवासिनः ॥

१७२ कोयष्टिप्लवचक्राह्वबलाकाबकविष्किरान् ।
वृथाकृसरसंयावपायसापूपशष्कुलीः ॥

१७३ कलविङ्कं सकाकोलं कुररं रज्जुदालकम् ।
जालपादान्खञ्जरीटानज्ञातांश्च मृगद्विजान् ॥

१७४ चाषांश्च रक्तपादांश्च सौनं वल्लूरमेव च ।
मत्स्यांश्चाकामतो जग्ध्वा सोपवासस्त्र्यहं भवेत्[22] ॥

Food that has gone stale or has been left for a long time is fit to be eaten when daubed with oil, as also preparations of wheat, barley, and cow's milk even when they are not daubed with oil. 168

He should avoid the milk of a cow in heat or within ten days of giving birth, or that has lost its calf, as also the milk of camels, single-hoofed animals, women, wild animals, and sheep. 169

An offering meant for a deity; *śigru* horseradish; red sap of trees; growths on tree stumps; meat of an unconsecrated animal; what grows in excrement; mushrooms;[75] 170

carnivorous birds; *dātyūha* waterfowl; parrots; birds that feed by pecking; *ṭiṭṭibha* plovers; *sārasa* cranes; single-hoofed animals; *haṃsa* geese; all animals living in villages;[76] 171

*koyaṣṭhi* cranes; *plava* herons; *cakra* sheldrakes; *balāka* egret; *baka* heron; birds that feed by scratching with their feet; *kṛsara* porridge, *saṃyāva* cake, milkrice, *apūpa* cake, or *śaṣkulī* cake prepared for no good reason;[77] 172

*kalaviṅka* sparrows; *kākola* ravens; *kurara* osprey; *rajjudālaka* fowl; web-footed birds; *khañjarīta* wagtails; unknown animals and birds;[78] 173

*cāṣa* jays; birds with red feet; meat from a slaughterhouse; dried meat; and fish—should someone eat any of these unintentionally, he should remain fasting for three days.[79] 174

१७५ पलाण्डुं विड्वराहं च छत्राकं ग्रामकुक्कुटम् ।
लशुनं गृञ्जनं चैव जग्ध्वा चान्द्रायणं चरेत् ॥

१७६ भक्ष्याः पञ्चनखाः सेधागोधाकच्छपशल्यकाः ।
शशश्च मत्स्येष्वपि हि सिंहतुण्डकरोहिताः ॥

१७७ तथा पाठीनराजीवौ सशल्काश्च द्विजातिभिः ।
अतः शृणुध्वं मांसस्य विधिं भक्षणवर्जने ॥

१७८ प्राणात्यये तथा श्राद्धे प्रोक्षितं द्विजकाम्यया ।
देवान्पितॄंस्तथाभ्यर्च्य खादन्मांसं न दोषभाक् ॥

१७९ वसेत्स नरके घोरे दिनानि पशुरोमभिः ।
संमितानि दुराचारो यो हन्त्यविधिना पशून् ॥

१८० सर्वान्कामानवाप्नोति हयमेधफलं तथा ।
गृहेऽपि निवसन्विप्रो मुनिर्मांसस्य वर्जनात् ॥

॥ इति भक्ष्याभक्ष्यप्रकरणम् ॥

Should someone eat onions, village pigs, mushrooms, village fowl, garlic, or leeks, he should perform the lunar fast.[80] 175

From among the five-nailed animals, people with two births may eat the following: porcupine, monitor lizard, tortoise, hedgehog, and rabbit; and among fish also, the *siṃhatuṇḍa, rohita, pāṭhīna, rājīva,* and *saśalka.*[81] 176–177

Next, listen to the rule on eating and on avoiding meat.

Should he eat meat when his life is at risk, at an ancestral offering, when it has been sacrificially consecrated, at the behest of twice-born persons, and after worshiping gods and forefathers, he incurs no guilt. 178

A man of evil conduct who kills farm animals without following the rule will live in a dreadful hell for as many days as there are hairs on the body of those animals. 179

By refraining from meat, a Brahman obtains all his wishes, as well as the fruit of a horse sacrifice, and while still living at home he becomes a sage. 180

## ॥ अथ द्रव्यशुद्धिप्रकरणम् ॥

१८१ सौवर्णराजताब्जानामूर्ध्वपात्रग्रहाश्मनाम् ।
शाकरज्जुमूलफलवासोविदलचर्मणाम् ॥

१८२ पात्राणां चमसानां च वारिणा शुद्धिरिष्यते ।
चरुस्रुक्स्रुवसस्नेहपात्राण्युष्णेन वारिणा ॥

१८३ स्फ्यशूर्पाजिनधान्यानां मुसलोलूखलानसाम् ।
प्रोक्षणं संहतानां च बहूनां चैव वाससाम्[२३] ॥

१८४ तक्षणं दारुशृङ्गास्थ्नां गोवालैः फलसंभुवाम् ।
मार्जनं यज्ञपात्राणां पाणिना यज्ञकर्मणि ॥

१८५ सोषैरुदकगोमूत्रैः शुध्यत्याविकसौत्रिकम् ।
सश्रीफलैरंशुपट्टं सारिष्टैः कुतपं तथा[२४] ॥

१८६ सगौरसर्षपैः क्षौमं पुनःपाकान्महीमयम् ।
कारुहस्तः शुचिः पण्यं भैक्षं योषिन्मुखं तथा ॥

१८७ भूशुद्धिर्मार्जनाद्दाहात्कालाद्गोक्रमणात् तथा ।
सेकादुल्लेखनाल्लेपाद्गृहं मार्जनलेपनात् ॥

## TOPIC 8: PURIFICATION OF ARTICLES

Gold, silver, and aquatic articles; sacrificial utensils and ladles; stone articles; articles made of vegetable material, rope, roots, fruits, cloth, cane, and skin; sacrificial vessels; and *camasa* cups are required to be cleaned with water. Hot water is used to clean *caru* pots, *sruc* spoons, *sruva* spoons, and oily vessels;[82] 181-182

as also to clean *sphya* swords, *śūrpa* winnows, antelope skins, grain, pestles, mortars, and carts. Solid articles and large quantities of clothes are cleaned by sprinkling them with water.[83] 183

Articles made of wood, horn, and bone are cleaned by planing; articles made of fruit, by rubbing with cow's hair; and sacrificial vessels during a sacrificial rite, by rubbing with the hand. 184

Water and cow's urine are used mixed with saline earth to clean cloth of sheep wool and woven textiles; mixed with bel fruit to clean fine fabric; mixed with *ariṣṭa* fruit to clean goat's wool blankets; and mixed with yellow mustard to clean linen. Earthenware is cleaned by firing it again. The hand of an artisan is pure, as also merchandise for sale, almsfood, and the mouth of a woman.[84] 185-186

The cleansing of land is done by scrubbing and burning, through the lapse of time, by cows walking over it, by sprinkling water on it, or by scraping or smearing it. A house is cleansed by scrubbing and smearing it.[85] 187

१८८ गोघ्रातेऽन्ने तथा केशमक्षिकाकीटदूषिते ।
सलिलं भस्म मृद्वापि प्रक्षेप्तव्यं विशुद्धये ॥

१८९ त्रपुसीसकताम्राणां क्षाराम्लोदकवारिभिः ।
भस्मना कांस्यलोहानां शुद्धिः प्लावो द्रवस्य तु ॥

१९० अमेध्याक्तस्य मृत्तोयैः शुद्धिर्गन्धापकर्षणम् ।
वाक्शस्तमम्बुनिर्णिक्तमज्ञातं च सदा शुचि ॥

१९१ शुचि गोतृप्तिकृत्तोयं प्रकृतिस्थं महीगतम् ।
तथा मांसं श्वचण्डालक्रव्यादादिनिपातितम् ॥

१९२ रश्मिरग्नी रजश्छाया गौरश्वो वसुधानिलः ।
विप्रुषो मक्षिकाः स्पर्शे वत्सः प्रस्नावणे शुचिः ॥

१९३ अजाश्वं मुखतो मेध्यं न गौर्न नृखजा मलाः ।
पन्थानश्च विशुध्यन्ति सोमसूर्यांशुमारुतैः[२५] ॥

१९४ मुखजा विप्रुषो मेध्याः पराचमनबिन्दवः ।
श्मश्रु चास्यगतं दन्तसक्तं त्यक्त्वा ततः शुचिः ॥

१९५ रथ्याकर्दमतोयानि स्पृष्टान्यन्त्यश्ववायसैः ।
मारुतेनैव शुध्यन्ति पक्वेष्टकचितानि च ॥

To clean food when it is smelled by a cow or spoiled by hair, flies, or worms, one should sprinkle water, ash, or earth over it. 188

Tin, lead, and copper are cleaned with alkali, acid, and water; and brass and iron with ash. Liquids are cleansed by straining. 189

Anything smeared with a foul substance is purified by applying earth and water until the smell is removed. What is verbally declared as suitable, what is sprinkled with water, and what is not known to be impure—these are always pure. 190

Water on the ground sufficient to slake the thirst of a cow and in its natural state is pure, likewise meat of an animal killed by a dog, Chandala, carnivorous animal, and the like. 191

Rays of the sun, fire, dust, shadows, cows, horses, earth, wind, droplets of water, and flies are pure when touched, as also a calf when it makes the milk to flow. 192

Goats and horses are pure at the mouth, but not cows and not impurities issuing from the bodily orifices of men. Roads are purified by the rays of the moon and sun and by the wind.[86] 193

Drool splattering from the mouth is ritually pure, as also drops of water from someone else's sipping and hair from the beard getting into the mouth. When anything is stuck between the teeth, one becomes pure after getting rid of it. 194

Mud or water on a road coming into contact with a lowest-born person, a dog, or a crow is purified simply by the wind, as also anything built with burnt bricks. 195

१९६ स्नात्वा पीत्वा क्षुते सुप्ते भुक्त्वा रथ्याप्रसर्पणे ।
आचान्तः पुनराचामेद्वासो विपरिधाय च ॥

॥ इति द्रव्यशुद्धिप्रकरणम् ॥

## ॥ अथ दानप्रकरणम् ॥

१९७ तपस्तप्त्वासृजद्ब्रह्मा ब्राह्मणान्वेदगुप्तये ।
तृप्त्यर्थं पितृदेवानां धर्मसंरक्षणाय च ॥

१९८ सर्वस्य प्रभवो विप्राः श्रुताध्ययनशीलिनः ।
तेभ्यः क्रियापराः श्रेष्ठास्तेभ्यो ह्यध्यात्मचिन्तकाः[२६] ॥

१९९ न विद्यया केवलया तपसा वापि पात्रता ।
यत्र वृत्तमिमे चोभे तद्धि पात्रं प्रकीर्तितम् ॥

२०० गोभूतिलहिरण्यादि पात्रे दातव्यमर्चितम् ।
नापात्रे विदुषा किंचिदात्मनः श्रेय इच्छता ॥

२०१ विद्यातपोभ्यां हीनेन न तु ग्राह्यः प्रतिग्रहः ।
गृह्णन्प्रदातारमधो नयत्यात्मानमेव च ॥

After bathing, drinking, sneezing, sleeping, eating, and walking on a street, having sipped water he should sip water once again; as also after wearing his clothes. 196

## TOPIC 9: GIFT GIVING

Brahma, after performing ascetic toil, created Brahmans to protect the Veda, to bring satisfaction to ancestors and gods, and to safeguard dharma. 197

Brahmans devoted to learning and Vedic recitation are the lords of all. Superior to them are those who are intent on performing rites, and superior even to the latter are those who contemplate the highest self.[87] 198

A person is a worthy recipient not simply by reason of knowledge or even ascetic toil. When a person possesses proper conduct as well as those two, he is said to be a truly worthy recipient. 199

Cows, land, sesame seeds, gold, and the like should be given with due respect to a worthy recipient. A learned man who desires his own welfare should never give anything to an unworthy recipient. 200

A person who does not possess knowledge and ascetic toil, however, should not accept a donation. Should he accept, he leads both the giver and himself to the netherworld. 201

२०२ दातव्यं प्रत्यहं पात्रे निमित्तेषु विशेषतः।
याचितेनापि दातव्यं श्रद्धापूतं तु शक्तितः॥

२०३ स्वर्णशृङ्गी शफै रौप्यैः सुशीला वस्त्रसंयुता।
सकांस्यदोहा दातव्या क्षीरिणी गौः सदक्षिणा॥

२०४ दातास्याः स्वर्गमाप्नोति वत्सरान्रोमसंमितान्।
कपिला चेत्तारयति भूयश्चासप्तमं कुलम्॥

२०५ सवत्सारोमतुल्यानि युगान्युभयतोमुखीम्।
दाता स्वर्गमवाप्नोति पूर्वेण विधिना ददत्[२७]॥

२०६ यथाकथंचिद्दत्त्वा गां धेनुं वाधेनुमेव वा।
अरोगामपरिक्लिष्टां दाता स्वर्गमाप्नुयात्॥

२०७ श्रान्तसंवाहनं रोगिपरिचर्या सुरार्चनम्।
पादशौचं द्विजोच्छिष्टमार्जनं गोप्रदानवत्॥

२०८ भूमिपश्वन्नवस्त्राम्भस्तिलसर्पिःप्रतिश्रयम्।
नैवेशिकं स्वर्णधुर्यं दत्त्वा स्वर्गे महीयते[२८]॥

२०९ गृहधान्याभयोपानच्छत्रमाल्यानुलेपनम्।
यानं वृक्षजलं शय्यां दत्त्वात्यन्तं सुखी भवेत्[२९]॥

A donation should be given to a worthy recipient every day, but especially on special occasions. Also when someone requests him, he should give according to his ability a donation purified by a spirit of generosity. 202

One should give a cow having an amiable disposition and yielding milk, her horns adorned with gold and her hoofs with silver and provided with a cloth, along with a brass milking pail and a sacrificial fee. 203

A person who gives her attains heaven for as many years as there are hairs on her body; and further, if she is tawny, he rescues his lineage up to the seventh generation.[88] 204

A person who gives a cow facing both ways will attain heaven for as many years as there are hairs in her and her calf's body, when he gives her according to the above procedure.[89] 205

By giving in any manner whatsoever a cow that is free from disease and infirmity, whether it is giving milk or not, the giver attains heaven. 206

Rubbing the body of a fatigued person, ministering to the sick, worshiping the gods, washing the feet, and cleaning the leftovers of a twice-born person is similar to donating a cow. 207

By giving land, a farm animal, food, clothes, water, sesame seeds, ghee, shelter, a bridal gift, gold, or a beast of burden, a person is exalted in heaven.[90] 208

By giving a house, grain, safety, shoes, umbrella, garland, unguent, vehicle, water for trees, or bed, a person becomes endlessly happy.[91] 209

२१० सर्वधर्ममयं ब्रह्म प्रदानेभ्योऽधिकं ततः।
प्रददत्तत्समाप्नोति ब्रह्मलोकमविच्युतः॥

२११ प्रतिग्रहसमर्थोऽपि नादत्ते यः प्रतिग्रहम्।
ये लोका दानशीलानां स तानाप्नोति पुष्कलान्॥

२१२ कुशाः शाकं पयो मत्स्या गन्धाः पुष्पं दधि क्षितिः।
मांसं शय्यासनं धान्यं प्रत्याख्येयं न वारि च॥

२१३ अयाचिताहृतं ग्राह्यमपि दुष्कृतकर्मणः।
अन्यत्र कुलटाषण्ढपतितेभ्यस्तथा द्विषः॥

२१४ सुरातिथ्यर्चनकृते गुरुभृत्यार्थमेव च।
सर्वतः प्रतिगृह्णीयादात्मवृत्त्यर्थमेव च॥

॥ इति दानप्रकरणम्॥

Brahma, that is, the Veda, which consists of all the dharmas, is greater than those gifts. Therefore, by gifting it a man obtains the world of Brahma, himself remaining imperishable. 210

When a man, although eligible to receive donations, does not accept them, he obtains the opulent worlds reserved for those who are devoted to giving gifts. 211

*Kuśa* grass, vegetables, milk, fish, perfumes, flowers, curd, earth, meat, bed, seat, and grain should not be refused, as also water. 212

What has been brought without being requested should be accepted even from a man of evil conduct, with the exception of a promiscuous woman, a eunuch, and a man fallen from his caste, as also an enemy. 213

In order to pay honor to gods and guests and for the sake of teacher and dependents, he may accept gifts from anyone, as also for the sake of sustaining himself. 214

## ॥ अथ श्राद्धप्रकरणम् ॥

२१५ अमावास्याष्टका वृद्धिः कृष्णपक्षोऽयनद्वयम् ।
द्रव्यब्राह्मणसंपत्तिर्विषुवत्सूर्यसंक्रमः ॥

२१६ व्यतीपातो गजच्छाया ग्रहणं चन्द्रसूर्ययोः ।
श्राद्धं प्रति रुचिश्चैव श्राद्धकालाः प्रकीर्तिताः ॥

२१७ अग्र्यः सर्वेषु वेदेषु श्रोत्रियो वेदविद्युवा ।
वेदार्थविज्ज्येष्ठसामा त्रिमधुस्त्रिसुपर्णकः ॥

२१८ स्वस्रीयऋत्विग्जामातृयाज्यश्वशुरमातुलाः ।
त्रिणाचिकेतदौहित्रशिष्यसंबन्धिबान्धवाः ॥

२१९ कर्मनिष्ठतपोनिष्ठपञ्चाग्निब्रह्मचारिणः ।
पितृमातृपराश्चैव ब्राह्मणाः श्राद्धसंपदः ॥

## TOPIC 10: ANCESTRAL OFFERINGS

The new-moon day, the eighth day,[92] a prosperous occasion, the dark half of the month, the two solstices, the availability of excellent material and Brahmans, the equinox, the days when the sun moves from one sign of the zodiac to another, the special new-moon day, the elephant's shadow, the eclipse of the moon and sun, and when one longs to perform an ancestral offering—these are declared to be the times for the performance of ancestral offerings.[93] 215–216

A man of preeminence in all the Vedas, a Vedic scholar, one who knows the Veda, a young man, one who knows the meaning of the Vedas, a singer of the *jyeṣṭhasāman,* one who knows the *trimadhu,* one who knows the *trisuparṇa,*[94] 217

a sister's son, an officiating priest, a son-in-law, a person at whose sacrifices one officiates, the father-in-law, a maternal uncle, an expert in the *triṇāciketa* fire altars, a daughter's son, a pupil, an affinal relative, a maternal relative,[95] 218

someone steadfast in ritual activities, someone steadfast in ascetic toil, someone who maintains the five sacred fires, a Vedic student, those devoted to their father and mother—these are the Brahmans who bring excellence to an ancestral offering.[96] 219

२२० रोगी हीनातिरिक्ताङ्गः काणः पौनर्भवस्तथा ।
अवकीर्णी कुण्डगोलौ कुनखी श्यावदन्तकः ॥

२२१ भृतकाध्यापकः क्रूरः कन्यादूष्यभिशस्तकः ।
मित्रध्रुक्पिशुनः सोमविक्रयी परिविन्दकः[३०] ॥

२२२ मातापितृसुतत्यागी कुण्डाशी वृषलात्मजः ।
परपूर्वापतिः स्तेनः कर्मदुष्टश्च निन्दिताः[३१] ॥

२२३ निमन्त्रयीत पूर्वेद्युर्ब्राह्मणानात्मवाञ्छुचिः ।
निमन्त्रितैश्च तैर्भाव्यं मनोवाक्कायसंयतैः ॥

२२४ अपराह्णे समभ्यर्च्य स्वागतेनागतांस्तु तान् ।
पवित्रपाणिराचान्तानासनेषूपवेशयेत् ॥

२२५ दैवे युग्मान्यथाशक्ति पित्र्येऽयुग्मांस्तथैव च ।
परिश्रिते शुचौ देशे दक्षिणाप्रवणे तथा ॥

A sick person; someone who lacks a limb or has an excess limb; a one-eyed man; someone born to a remarried woman; a Vedic student who has broken his vow of chastity; a son of an adulteress or a widow; someone with bad nails or black teeth; 220

someone who teaches for a fee; a cruel man; someone who has deflowered a virgin; a heinous sinner; someone who injures a friend; a slanderer; someone who sells *soma;* someone who marries before his older brother;[97] 221

someone who abandons his father, mother, or son; someone who eats food given by the son of an adulteress; someone whose son is a Shudra; the husband of a remarried woman; a thief; and someone doing evil deeds—these are disqualified.[98] 222

Being self-composed and pure, he should invite the Brahmans on the previous day. And those who have been invited should keep their mind, speech, and body restrained. 223

In the afternoon when they arrive, he should pay his respects to them with greetings of welcome. Then, after they have sipped water, wearing the purifying rings in his hands, he should get them to sit down in their seats[99]— 224

according to his ability, an even number for an offering to gods and an uneven number for an offering to the forefathers, and in a pure spot screened off and inclining toward the south; 225

२२६ द्वौ दैवे प्रागुदक्पित्र्ये त्रय एकैकमेव वा।
मातामहानामप्येवं तन्त्रं वा वैश्वदेविकम्॥

२२७ पाणिप्रक्षालनं दत्त्वा विष्टरार्थान्कुशानपि।
आवाहयेदनुज्ञातो विश्वेदेवास इत्यृचा॥

२२८ यवैरन्ववकीर्याथ भाजने सपवित्रके।
शं नो देव्या पयः क्षिप्त्वा यवोऽसीति यवान्क्षिपेत्॥

२२९ या दिव्या इति मन्त्रेण हस्तेष्वर्घ्यं विनिक्षिपेत्।
दत्त्वोदकं गन्धधूपमाल्यदानं सदीपकम्[३२]॥

two facing the east at an offering to gods and three facing the north at an offering to the forefathers; or else, one at each. The same procedure holds for maternal grandfathers, or the rite for All-Gods may be performed once in common. 226

After offering water to wash their hands, as well as *kuśa* grass for seats, receiving permission, he should issue the invitation with the *ṛc* verse: "All you gods, come here; hear this call of mine. Sit down here on this ritual grass."[100] 227

After sprinkling with barley, he should then put water into a vessel containing purifying *kuśa* grass, reciting: "Let the goddesses, the Waters, be luck for us to prevail, for us to drink,"[101] and then put barley, reciting: "You are barley; drive away from us foes, drive away evil spirits."[102] 228

With the mantra, "Those heavenly waters that arose on earth, those in the mid region, those on the earth—with the brilliance of all those, with the strength, I sprinkle you,"[103] he should place the welcome-water in their hands. After giving the water, there follows the offering of perfume, incense, and garlands, along with lamps.[104] 229

२३० अपसव्यं ततः कृत्वा पितॄणामप्रदक्षिणम् ।
द्विगुणांस्तु कुशान्दत्त्वा उषन्तस्त्वेत्यृचा पितॄन् ॥

२३१ आवाह्य तदनुज्ञातो जपेदायन्तु नस्ततः ।
यवार्थांस्तु तिलैः कुर्याच्छेषं त्वर्घ्यादि पूर्ववत्[३३] ॥

२३२ दत्त्वार्घ्यं संस्रवानेषां पात्रे कृत्वा विधानतः ।
पितृभ्यः स्थानमासीति न्युब्जं पात्रं करोत्यधः ॥

२३३ अग्नौ करिष्यन्नादाय पृच्छत्यन्नं घृताप्लुतम् ।
कुरुष्वेत्यभ्यनुज्ञातो हुत्वाग्नौ पितृयज्ञवत् ॥

२३४ हुतशेषं प्रदद्यात्तु भाजनेषु समाहितः ।
यथालाभोपपन्नेषु रौप्येषु तु विशेषतः ॥

Then, after placing his sacrificial cord on the right shoulder, he should offer *kuśa* grass folded double to the forefathers toward the left side, summon the forefathers with the *ṛc* verse, "Eagerly we would install you; eagerly we would kindle you. Eagerly convey the eager forefathers here, to eat the oblation,"[105] and with their permission then recite: "May our fathers, *soma* loving and tasted by the funeral fire, come along the paths of the gods. Delighting with the *svadhā* offerings in this sacrifice, may they intercede for us, may they aid us."[106] What normally requires barley, however, should be done with sesame. He should perform the remaining rites, such as the welcome-water, as before.[107] 230–231

After offering the welcome-water and gathering the water trickling down from them in a vessel according to rule, he places the inverted pot upside down saying: "You are the place for the fathers." 232

When he is about to make the offering in the fire, he should take the food soaked with ghee and make the request. When they permit him, saying, "Carry on," he should make the offering in the fire in the same way as at a sacrifice to the forefathers. 233

With a collected mind, however, he should place what remains from the offering in vessels that he may happen to have, especially in ones made of silver. 234

२३५ दत्त्वान्नं पृथिवी पात्रमिति पात्राभिमन्त्रणम् ।
कृत्वेदं विष्णुरित्यन्ने द्विजाङ्गुष्ठान्निवेशयेत् ॥

२३६ सव्याहृतिकां सावित्रीं मधु वाता इति त्र्यृचम् ।
जप्त्वा यथासुखं वाच्यं भुञ्जीरंस्तेऽपि वाग्यताः ॥

२३७ अन्नमिष्टं हविष्यं च दद्यादक्रोधनोऽत्वरः ।
आ तृप्तेस्तु पवित्राणि जप्त्वा पूर्वजपं तथा ॥

२३८ अन्नमादाय तृप्ताः स्थ शेषं चैवानुमान्य ह ।
तदन्नं प्रकिरेद्भूमौ दद्याच्चापः सकृत्सकृत् ॥

२३९ सर्वमन्नमुपादाय सतिलं दक्षिणामुखः ।
उच्छिष्टसंनिधौ पिण्डान्प्रदद्यात्पितृयज्ञवत् ॥

After offering the food and consecrating the vessels, saying, "The earth is your vessel, heaven the lid. I offer you in the mouth of Brahma. I offer you in the out-breath and the in-breath of the Brahmans. You are imperishable. Do not perish for them there, in that world," he should have a Brahman push his thumb into the food, saying: "Vishnu strode out this world; three times he laid down a step; this world is concentrated in his dusty step."[108] 235

After softly reciting the *sāvitrī* verse along with the Calls and the three verses, "Honey do the winds blow to the one who follows the truth; honey do the rivers stream. Honeyed be the plants for us. Honey by night and at dawn; honeyed is the earthly realm. Honey be Father Heaven for us. Honeyed be the tree for us, honeyed the sun. Honeyed be the cows for us,"[109] he should say: "Enjoy as you please." They too should eat in silence. 236

Without being angry or in a hurry, he should give the food that is desirable and fit for an oblation until they are satisfied, softly reciting purificatory verses, as also those he had previously recited. 237

Picking up the food, asking, "Are you satisfied?" and, after getting their permission, taking what is left over, he should spread the food on the ground and give water to each of them individually. 238

Taking all the food along with sesame seeds and facing the south, he should place balls of rice in the vicinity of the leftovers, in the same way as at the sacrifice to the forefathers. 239

२४० मातामहानामप्येवं दद्यादाचमनं ततः।
स्वस्ति वाच्य ततो दद्यादक्षय्योदकमेव च॥

२४१ दत्त्वा तु दक्षिणां शक्त्या स्वधाकारमुदाहरेत्।
वाच्यतामित्यनुज्ञातः प्रकृतेभ्यः स्वधोच्यताम्॥

२४२ ब्रूयुरस्तु स्वधेत्युक्ते भूमौ सिञ्चेत्ततो जलम्।
प्रीयन्तामिति चाहैवं विश्वेदेवा जलं ददत्[३४]॥

२४३ दातारो नो विवर्धन्तां वेदसंततिरेव च।
श्रद्धा च नो मा व्यगमद्बहु देयं च नोऽस्त्विति॥

२४४ उक्त्वोक्त्वा च प्रिया वाचः प्रणिपत्य विसर्जयेत्।
वाजे वाज इति प्रीतः पितृपूर्वं विसर्जनम्॥

२४५ यस्मिंस्ते संस्रवाः पूर्वमर्घ्यपात्रे निपातिताः।
पितृपात्रं तदुत्तानं कृत्वा विप्रान्विसर्जयेत्॥

For the maternal grandfathers also these should be performed in the same manner. Thereafter, he should give water for sipping, request them to say, "May there be well-being," and then give them the "inexhaustible water."[110] 240

After giving the sacrificial fees according to his ability, however, he should say: "I will have *svadhā* uttered," and when they give him permission with the words: "Let it be uttered," he should say, "May the *svadhā* be uttered for the forefathers to whom the offering is made." 241

They should say, "May there be *svadhā*," and when they have spoken, he should then sprinkle water on the ground and also say "May the All-Gods be pleased," while he gives water.[111] 242

"May donors thrive amidst us, may the Vedas and progeny! May the generous spirit never abandon us! And may we have a lot to give!"[112] 243

Having said this, and after saying pleasant words, he should bow to the ground and dismiss them. The dismissal is done beginning with the forefathers, being delighted and after reciting, "Help us to every prize, o prizewinners, when the stakes are set, you truth-knowing, immortal inspired poets. Drink of this honey here; make yourselves exhilarated. Satisfied, drive along the paths that lead to the gods."[113] 244

The vessel for the welcome-water into which earlier the water trickling down had been made to fall—after placing upright that vessel of the forefathers, he should dismiss the Brahmans. 245

२४६ प्रदक्षिणमनुव्रज्य भुञ्जीत पितृसेवितम् ।
ब्रह्मचारी निशां तां तु नियतात्मा सह द्विजैः[३५] ॥

२४७ एवं प्रदक्षिणं कृत्वा वृद्धौ नान्दीमुखान्पितॄन् ।
यजन्ति दधिकर्कन्धूमिश्राः पिण्डा यवैः क्रियाः ॥

२४८ एकोद्दिष्टं दैवहीनमेकार्घ्यैकपवित्रकम् ।
आवाहनाग्नौकरणरहितं ह्यपसव्यवत् ॥

२४९ उपतिष्ठतामित्यक्षय्यस्थाने विप्रविसर्जने ।
अभिरम्यतामिति वदेद्ब्रूयुस्तेऽभिरताः स्म ह ॥

After following them while keeping them to his right side, he should eat what has been served to the forefathers. He should remain celibate that night, however, keeping himself restrained, along with the Brahmans.[114] 246

On a prosperous occasion, after performing the action the same way but in a clockwise manner, they sacrifice to the joyful-faced forefathers; the balls of rice should be mixed with curd and jujube fruit, and the rites should be performed with barley. 247

An offering made to a newly deceased person is performed without offerings to gods, with a single welcome-water and a single purificatory ring, without the invitation and the fire offering, and with the sacrificial cord worn on the right shoulder. 248

In place of the "inexhaustible water," he should say, "May it reach," and in dismissing the Brahmans he should say, "May you be pleased!" And they should say, "We are pleased." 249

२५० गन्धोदकतिलैर्युक्तं कुर्यात्पात्रचतुष्टयम् ।
अर्घ्यार्थं पितृपात्रेषु प्रेतपात्रं प्रसेचयेत् ॥

२५१ ये समाना इति द्वाभ्यां शेषं त्वर्घ्यादि पूर्ववत् ।
एतत्सपिण्डीकरणमेकोद्दिष्टं स्त्रिया अपि[३६] ॥

२५२ अर्वाक्सपिण्डीकरणं यस्य संवत्सराद्भवेत् ।
तस्याप्यन्नं सोदकुम्भं दद्यात्संवत्सरं द्विजे ॥

२५३ मृताहनि च कर्तव्यं प्रतिमासं तु वत्सरम् ।
प्रतिसंवत्सरं चैव श्राद्धं वै मासिकार्थवत् ॥

२५४ पिण्डांस्तु गोऽजविप्रेभ्यो दद्यादग्नौ जलेऽपि वा ।
प्रक्षिपेत्सत्सु विप्रेषु द्विजोच्छिष्टं न मार्जयेत् ॥

He should place perfume, water, and sesame seeds in four vessels for the purpose of the welcome-water, and pour the vessel of the newly deceased into the vessels of the forefathers, reciting the two verses: "Those forefathers in Yama's world who are akin and of kindred mind—may their world, *svadhā,* homage, and sacrifice flourish among the gods. Those my own folks living among the living who are akin and of kindred mind—may their prosperity flourish in me for a hundred years in this world."[115] The rest, however, beginning with the welcome-water is performed as before. This is the rite of "making rice-ball-sharers." The offering made to a newly deceased person should be performed also for women.[116] 250–251

When the rite of "making rice-ball-sharers" has been performed for a person before the lapse of one year, even on behalf of him one should give food along with a pot of water to a Brahman for one full year. 252

On the day of death, moreover, an ancestral offering should be made every month for a year, and then every year according to the procedure of the monthly ancestral offering. 253

He should give the rice balls, however, to cows, goats, or Brahmans, or else throw them in fire or water. While the twice-born men are present, he should not clean up the leftovers. 254

२५५ हविष्यान्नेन वै मासं पायसेन तु वत्सरम् ।
मात्स्यहारिणऔरभ्रशाकुनच्छागपार्षतैः ॥

२५६ ऐणरौरववाराहशाशैर्मांसैर्यथाक्रमम् ।
मासवृद्ध्या हि तुष्यन्ति दत्तैरिह पितामहाः ॥

२५७ खड्गामिषं महाशल्कं मधु मुन्यन्नमेव च ।
लोहामिषं कालशाकं मांसं वार्ध्राणसस्य च ॥

२५८ यद्ददाति गयास्थश्च सर्वमानन्त्यमश्नुते ।
तथा वर्षे त्रयोदश्यां मघासु च न संशयः ॥

२५९ कन्यां कन्यावेदिनश्च पशून्मुख्यान्सुतानपि ।
द्यूतं कृषिवणिज्यं च द्विशफैकशफं तथा ॥

२६० ब्रह्मवर्चस्विनः पुत्रान्स्वर्णरूप्ये सकुप्यके ।
ज्ञातिश्रैष्ठ्यं सर्वकामानाप्नोति श्राद्धदः सदा ॥

२६१ प्रतिपत्प्रभृति ह्येता वर्जयित्वा चतुर्दशीम् ।
शस्त्रेण तु हता ये वै तेषां तत्र प्रदीयते ॥

The grandfathers are satisfied for a month with sacrificial food, and for a year with milk rice, whereas when the flesh of fish, common deer, sheep, birds, goat, spotted deer, *eṇa* antelope, *ruru* deer, boar, and rabbit are offered in this world, each succeeding one makes them satisfied for a month longer than each preceding.[117] 255–256

Flesh of the rhinoceros and the *mahāśalka* crustacean, honey, food of sages, flesh of the red goat, *kālaśāka* herb, flesh of *vārdhrāṇasa* horn-bill, and whatever a man staying in Gaya offers—all these are efficacious for eternity; likewise, without a doubt, what is offered on the thirteenth day of the rainy season and under the constellation *magha.*[118] 257–258

A daughter; a son-in-law; farm animals; foremost sons; success in gambling, agriculture, and trade; double-hoofed and single-hoofed animals; sons eminent in Vedic knowledge; gold and silver; base metals; preeminence among paternal relatives; and all desires—a person obtains these when he always makes ancestral offerings every day. These days begin with the first day of the fortnight, excluding the fourteenth. On that day, however, the ancestral offering is made to those who have been killed with a weapon.[119] 259–261

२६२ स्वर्गं ह्यपत्यमोजश्च शौर्यं क्षेत्रं बलं तथा।
पुत्रान्श्रैष्ठ्यं ससौभाग्यमपत्यं मुख्यतां सुतान्[३७]॥

२६३ प्रवृत्तचक्रतां पुत्राञ्ज्ञातिभ्यः प्रभुतां तथा।
अरोगित्वं यशो वीतशोकतां परमां गतिम्॥

२६४ धनं विद्यां भिषक्सिद्धिं कुप्यं गावो ह्यजाविकम्।
अश्वानायुश्च विधिवद्यः श्राद्धं परिवेषयेत्॥

२६५ कृत्तिकादिभरण्यन्तं स कामानाप्नुयादिमान्।
आस्तिकः श्रद्दधानश्च व्यपेतमदमत्सरः॥

२६६ वसुरुद्रादितिसुताः पितरः श्राद्धदेवताः।
प्रीणयन्ति मनुष्याणां पितॄन्श्राद्धेन तर्पिताः॥

२६७ आयुः प्रज्ञां धनं विद्यां स्वर्गं मोक्षं सुखानि च।
प्रयच्छन्ति तथा राज्यं प्रीता नृणां पितामहाः[३८]॥

॥ इति श्राद्धप्रकरणम्॥

## ॥ अथ विनायकादिकल्पप्रकरणम्॥

२६८ विनायकः कर्मविघ्नसिद्ध्यर्थं विनियोजितः।
गणानामाधिपत्याय रुद्रेण ब्रह्मणा पुरा॥

Heaven, offspring, might, valor, land, strength, sons, preeminence, good fortune, offspring, primacy, sons, enhanced sovereignty, sons, supremacy over paternal relatives, freedom from sickness, fame, freedom from sorrow, highest state, wealth, knowledge, success in medical practice, base metal, cows, goats and sheep, horses, and long life—he who performs an ancestral offering according to rule beginning with the constellation *kṛttikā* and ending at the constellation *bharaṇī* attains these desires if he is a man of faith, is imbued with a spirit of generosity, and is free from pride and rancor.[120] 262–265

The Vasus, Rudras, and Adityas are the forefathers who are the divinities of an ancestral offering. When they have been sated by an ancestral offering, they gratify the forefathers of humans. 266

The grandfathers of humans, being gratified, bestow long life, intelligence, wealth, knowledge, heaven, liberation, and delights, as also royal power.[121] 267

## TOPIC 11: RULES FOR THE WORSHIP OF VINAYAKA AND OTHERS

Vinayaka was formerly appointed by Rudra and Brahma to be the lord of *gaṇas*, the divine troops, for establishing obstacles to ritual activities.[122] 268

२६९ तेनोपसृष्टो यस्तस्य लक्षणानि निबोधत।
स्वप्ने ऽवगाहतेऽत्यर्थं जलं मुण्डांश्च पश्यति॥

२७० काषायवाससश्चैव क्रव्यादांश्चाधिरोहति।
अन्त्यजैर्गर्दभैरुष्ट्रैः सहैकत्रावतिष्ठते॥

२७१ व्रजमानस्तथात्मानं मन्यतेऽनुगतं परैः।
विमना विफलारम्भः संसीदत्यनिमित्ततः॥

२७२ तेनोपसृष्टो लभते न राज्यं राजनन्दनः।
कुमारी न च भर्तारमपत्यं गर्भमेव च[३९]॥

२७३ आचार्यत्वं श्रोत्रियः सन्न शिष्योऽध्ययनं तथा।
वणिग्लाभं न चाप्नोति कृषिं चैव कृषीवलः॥

२७४ स्नपनं तस्य कर्तव्यं पुण्येऽह्नि विधिपूर्वकम्।
गौरसर्षपकल्केन साज्येनोच्छादितस्य तु[४०]॥

२७५ सर्वौषधैः सर्वगन्धैर्विलिप्तशिरसस्तथा।
भद्रासनोपविष्टस्य स्वस्ति वाच्य द्विजाञ्छुभान्॥

२७६ अश्वस्थानाद्गजस्थानाद्वल्मीकात्संगमाद्ध्रदात्।
मृत्तिकां रोचनां गन्धान्गुल्गुलुं चाप्सु संक्षिपेत्॥

२७७ या आहृता एकवर्णैश्चतुर्भिः कलशैर्ह्रदात्।
चर्मण्यानडुहे रक्ते स्थाप्यं भद्रासनं तथा॥

Listen to the signs of someone who has been possessed by him. In his dreams, he plunges into deep water; sees shaven-headed men, as well as men wearing ochre clothes; climbs on carnivorous animals; and dwells in the same place with lowest-born persons, donkeys, and camels. 269–270

Likewise, he imagines that while he is walking he is being followed by enemies. Out of his mind and unsuccessful in his enterprises, he becomes dejected without cause. 271

Possessed by him, a man who is the king's favorite son does not obtain the kingdom, a maiden does not find a husband, and a woman fails to get offspring and to conceive;[123] 272

a man fails to attain the status of teacher even though he is a Vedic scholar; a student does not master his lessons; a merchant does not realize a profit; and a farmer does not reap a harvest. 273

His bathing should be carried out according to rule on an auspicious day, after his body has been rubbed with a newly prepared paste of white mustard.[124] 274

As he is seated on a splendid seat, his head anointed with all kinds of herbs and perfumes, one should get auspicious Brahmans to say: "May there be well-being." 275

He should throw these in water that has been brought from a lake in four pots of the same color: earth brought from a horse stable, an elephant stable, an anthill, a confluence of rivers, and a lake; yellow bile; perfume; and bdellium. A splendid seat, likewise, should be placed upon the skin of a red ox. 276–277

२७८ सहस्राक्षं शतधारमृषिभिः पावनं कृतम् ।
तेन त्वामभिषिञ्चामि पावमानीः पुनन्तु ते ॥

२७९ भगं ते वरुणो राजा भगं सूर्यो बृहस्पतिः ।
भगमिन्द्रश्च वायुश्च भगं सप्तर्षयो ददुः ॥

२८० यत्ते केशेषु दौर्भाग्यं सीमन्ते यच्च मूर्धनि ।
ललाटे कर्णयोरक्ष्णोरापस्तद्घ्नन्तु ते सदा ॥

२८१ स्नातस्य सार्षपं तैलं स्रुवेणौदुम्बरेण तु ।
जुहुयान्मूर्धनि कुशान्सव्येन परिगृह्य च ॥

२८२ मितश्च संमितश्चैव तथा सालकटङ्कटः ।
कूश्माण्डराजपुत्रश्च जपेत्स्वाहासमन्वितान् ॥

२८३ नामभिर्बलिमन्त्रैश्च नमस्कारसमन्वितैः ।
दद्याच्चतुष्पथे शूर्पे कुशानास्तीर्य सर्वतः ॥

२८४ कृताकृतांस्तण्डुलांश्च पललौदनमेव च ।
मत्स्यान्पक्वांस्तथैवामान्मांसमेतावदेव तु ॥

२८५ पुष्पं चित्रं सुगन्धं च सुरां च त्रिविधामपि ।
मूलकं पूरिकापूपांस्तथैवोड्डेरकस्रजम्[४१] ॥

२८६ दूर्वासर्षपकल्केन दत्त्वार्घ्यं पूर्णमञ्जलिम् ।
विनायकस्य जननीमुपतिष्ठेत्ततोऽम्बिकाम् ॥

"The seers have made the one with a thousand eyes and a hundred streams the means of purification. With that I sprinkle you. May the purifying waters purify you. 278

May King Varuna grant you fortune! May Sun and Brihaspati grant you fortune! May Indra and Wind grant you fortune! May the seven seers grant you fortune! 279

Whatever misfortune resides in your hairs; whatever in the parting of your hair and in the crown of your head; whatever in your forehead, ears, eyes—may the waters always wipe them out." 280

After he has bathed, one should offer mustard oil with a *sruva* ladle made of *udumbara* fig wood on the crown of his head holding blades of *kuśa* grass in his left hand. 281

*Mita, saṃmita, sālakaṭaṅkaṭa,* and *kūśmāṇḍarājaputra*—he should softly recite these along with *svāhā.*[125] 282

With these names and with the mantras associated with Bali offerings and containing the word "Homage," he should offer the following in a winnowing basket at a crossroads after spreading *kuśa* grass all around—husked and unhusked rice kernels, rice cooked with ground sesame, fish both cooked and raw, meat of the same sort, sweet smelling flowers of various colors, three kinds of *surā* liquor, root vegetable, *pūrikā* bread, *apūpa* cake, and a garland of flour balls.[126] 283–285

After giving a hand-full of the welcome water[127] mixed with a paste of *dūrvā* grass and mustard, he should then worship Ambika, the mother of Vinayaka.[128] 286

२८७ रूपं देहि यशो देहि भगं भवति देहि मे ।
पुत्रान्देहि श्रियं पुण्यान्सर्वकामांश्च देहि मे[४२] ॥

२८८ शुक्लाम्बरधरः शुक्लमाल्यगन्धानुलेपनः ।
ब्राह्मणान्भोजयेद्दद्याद्वस्त्रयुग्मं गुरोरपि ॥

२८९ एवं विनायकं पूज्य ग्रहांश्चैव विधानतः ।
कर्मणां फलमाप्नोति श्रियं चाप्नोत्यनुत्तमाम् ॥

२९० आदित्यस्य सदा पूजां तिलकस्वामिनस्तथा ।
महागणपतेश्चैव कुर्वन्सिद्धिमवाप्नुयात्[४३] ॥

॥ इति विनायकादिकल्पप्रकरणम् ॥

## ॥ अथ ग्रहशान्तिप्रकरणम् ॥

२९१ श्रीकामः शान्तिकामो वा ग्रहयज्ञं समारभेत् ।
वृष्ट्यायुःपुष्टिकामो वा तथैवाभिचरन्पुनः ॥

२९२ सूर्यः सोमो महीपुत्रः सोमपुत्रो बृहस्पतिः ।
शुक्रः शनैश्चरो राहुः केतुश्चेति ग्रहाः स्मृताः ॥

२९३ ताम्रिकात्स्फटिकाद्रक्तचन्दनात्स्वर्णकादुभौ ।
रजतादयसः सीसाद्ग्रहाः कार्याः क्रमादिमे ॥

२९४ स्ववर्णैर्वा पटे लेख्या गन्धमण्डलकेषु वा ।
यथावर्णं प्रदेयानि वासांसि कुसुमानि च ॥

"Grant me beauty! Grant me fame! Grant me fortune, O Lady! Grant me sons, prosperity, and merits! Grant me all my wishes!"[129] 287

Wearing white clothes and a white garland and daubed with perfumes, he should feed the Brahmans and also present his teacher with a pair of garments. 288

By thus worshiping Vinayaka and the planets according to rule, he obtains the fruits of his actions, as well as unsurpassed prosperity. 289

By always performing the worship of the sun, Skanda, and Great Ganapati, he obtains success.[130] 290

## TOPIC 12: PACIFICATION OF PLANETS

A person desiring prosperity or pacification should offer a sacrifice to the planets; so also a person who desires rain, long life, or affluence, as well as someone who intends to perform sorcery. 291

Sun, Moon, Mars, Mercury, Jupiter, Venus, Saturn, Rahu, and Ketu—these are said to be the planets.[131] 292

These planets should be made of copper, crystal, red sandalwood, next two gold, silver, iron, and lead.[132] 293

Alternatively, they should be written on a piece of cloth, each with his respective color, or on circles of perfume. And they should be offered garments and flowers, each according to his respective color. 294

२९५ गन्धाश्च बलयश्चैव धूपो देयः सगुल्गुलुः ।
कर्तव्यास्तन्त्रवन्तश्च चरवः प्रतिदैवतम् ॥

२९६ आकृष्णेन इमं देवा अग्निर्मूर्धा दिवः ककुत् ।
उद्बुध्यस्वेति च ऋचो यथासंख्यं प्रकीर्तिताः ॥

Further, perfumes, bracelets, and incense should be given, along with bdellium. And offerings of milk rice should be made to each deity individually with the common rites performed just once: 295

"Turning hither through the black realm, bringing to rest the immortal and the mortal, with his golden chariot Savitar the god drives here, gazing upon the creatures."[133] 296

"This man, impel him, Oh gods, to be unrivalled—
to great command, to great lordship, to rule over men,
to Indra's might. This man, the son of that man, the son of that woman, of such a clan—he is your king!
Soma is the king of us, Brahmans."[134]

"Agni is the head, the peak of heaven; this Agni here is lord of the earth. He quickens the spawn of the waters."[135]

"Awake, Oh Agni, and be vigilant. May you and this man create together sacrifice and donation.
On this higher seat may All Gods and the sacrificer sit down."[136]

These *ṛc* verses are declared according to the proper number;[137]

२९७ बृहस्पते अति यदर्यस्तथैवान्नात्परिस्रुतः।
शंनो देवीस्तथा काण्डात्केतुं कृण्वन्निमा अपि॥

२९८ अर्कः पलाशखदिरावपामार्गोऽथ पिप्पलः।
उदुम्बरः शमी दूर्वा कुशाश्च समिधः क्रमात्॥

२९९ एकैकस्यात्राष्टशतमष्टाविंशतिरेव वा।
होतव्या मधुसर्पिर्भ्यां दध्ना चैव समन्विताः[४४]॥

as also these: 297

"Brihaspati! That which will be worth more than what belongs to the stranger, that which will radiate among the peoples with brilliance and purpose, and that which will shine by means of your power, o you born through the truth—set that shimmering possession among us."[138]

"From food, the flowing liquor, Prajapati drank the sap by means of brahman; he drank the royal-power, the milk, the *soma*."[139]

"Let the goddesses, the Waters, be luck for us to prevail, for us to drink. Let them flow to us for luck and life."[140]

"Shooting forth joint by joint, knot by knot, Oh *dūrvā* grass, do indeed extend us by a thousand and by a hundred."[141]

"You young men—making a beacon for that without beacon and an ornament for that without ornament, you were born together with the dawns."[142]

*Arka* madder, *palāśa* fig, *khadira* catechu, *apāmārga* devil's horse-whip, *pippala* fig, *udumbara* fig, *śamī* shrub, *dūrvā* grass, and *kuśa* grass—the kindling sticks are made from these in due order.[143] 298

For each planet eight hundred of these, or just twenty-eight, dipped in honey, ghee, and curd, should be offered.[144] 299

३०० गुलौदनं पायसं च हविष्यं क्षीरषाष्टिकम् ।
दध्योदनं हविः पूपान्मांसं चित्रान्नमेव च ॥

३०१ दद्याद्ग्रहक्रमादेतद्द्विजेभ्यो भोजनं बुधः ।
शक्तितो वा यथालाभं सत्कृत्य विधिपूर्वकम् ॥

३०२ धेनुं शङ्खमनड्वाहं काञ्चनं वसनं हयम् ।
कृष्णां गामायसं छागं प्रदद्याद्दक्षिणाः क्रमात् ॥

३०३ यश्च यस्य यदा दुःस्थः स तं यत्नेन पूजयेत् ।
ब्रह्मणैषां वरो दत्तः पूजिताः पूजयिष्यथ ॥

३०४ ग्रहाधीना नरेन्द्राणामुच्छ्रायाः पतनानि च ।
भावाभावौ च जगतस्तस्मात्पूज्यतमा ग्रहाः ॥

॥ इति ग्रहशान्तिप्रकरणम् ॥

Jaggery rice, milk rice, sacrificial food, sixty-day rice with milk, curd rice, sacrificial oblation, cakes, meat, and colored rice—a wise man should present this meal in the order of the planets to twice-born men, or else whatever he may get according to his ability, after paying them honor and according to rule.[145] 300–301

A milch cow, a conch, an ox, gold, a garment, a horse, a black cow, iron, and a goat—he should give these in the proper order as sacrificial fees. 302

Whichever planet is unfavorably disposed toward a particular person, he should assiduously worship that planet. Brahma has given this boon to them: "You will worship those who worship you." 303

The upturns and downturns of great kings are dependent on the planets, as also the fortune and misfortune of creatures. Therefore, planets are most worthy of worship. 304

## ॥ अथ राजधर्मप्रकरणम् ॥

३०५ महोत्साहः स्थूललक्षः कृतज्ञो वृद्धसेविता ।
विनीतः सत्त्वसंपन्नः कुलीनः सत्यवाक्छुचिः ॥

३०६ अदीर्घसूत्रः स्मृतिमानक्षुद्रपरिषत्तथा ।
धार्मिको दृढभक्तिश्च प्राज्ञः शूरो रहस्यवित्[४५] ॥

३०७ स्वरन्ध्रगोप्तान्वीक्षिक्यां दण्डनीत्यां तथैव च ।
विनीतस्त्वथ वार्तायां त्रय्यां चैव नराधिपः ॥

३०८ स मन्त्रिणः प्रकुर्वीत प्राज्ञान्मौलान्स्थिराञ्छुचीन् ।
तैः सार्धं चिन्तयेत्कार्यं विप्रेणाथ ततः स्वयम्[४६] ॥

३०९ पुरोहितं च कुर्वीत दैवज्ञमुदितोदितम् ।
दण्डनीत्यां च कुशलमथर्वाङ्गिरसे तथा ॥

३१० श्रौतस्मार्तक्रियाहेतोर्वृणुयादृत्विजस्तथा ।
यज्ञांश्चैव प्रकुर्वीत विधिवद्भूरिदक्षिणान् ॥

३११ भोगांश्च दद्याद्विप्रेभ्यो वसूनि विविधानि च ।
अक्षयोऽयं निधी राज्ञां यद्विप्रेषूपपादितम् ॥

## TOPIC 13: DHARMA OF KINGS

Possessing immense energy, generous, grateful, attending to elders, well-trained, endowed with spirit, coming from a noble family, truthful, honest, not given to procrastination, having a good memory, possessing a council that is not petty, righteous, firmly loyal, intelligent, brave, knowing secrets, guarding his own vulnerable points, and well-trained in critical inquiry and government, as well as in economics and the triple Veda—such is a king.[146] 305–307

He should appoint counselors who are intelligent, natives of the land, resolute, and honest. With them he should confer about what has to be done, then with the Brahman, and finally by himself.[147] 308

He should also appoint a chaplain who is knowledgeable about divine omens, comes from a very distinguished family, and is an expert in government, as also in *atharva-aṅgirasa*. 309

Likewise, for the purpose of carrying out rites prescribed in the Vedas and in texts of recollection, he should choose officiating priests. And he should perform sacrifices according to rule accompanied by lavish sacrificial fees. 310

Further, he should give luxuries and various kinds of property to Brahmans. This is the inexhaustible treasure of kings, namely, what has been presented to Brahmans. 311

३१२ अस्कन्नमव्यथं चैव प्रायश्चित्तैरदूषितम्।
अग्नेः सकाशाद्विप्राग्नौ हुतं श्रेष्ठमिहोच्यते॥

३१३ अलब्धं लब्धुमीहेत लब्धं यत्नेन पालयेत्।
पालितं वर्धयेन्नित्यं वृद्धं पात्रेषु निक्षिपेत्[४७]॥

३१४ दत्त्वा भूमिं निबन्धं वा कृत्वा लेख्यं तु कारयेत्।
आगामिक्षुद्रनृपतिपरिज्ञानाय पार्थिवः[४८]॥

३१५ पटे वा ताम्रपट्टे वा स्वमुद्रापरिचिह्नितम्।
अभिलेख्यात्मनो वंश्यानात्मानं च महीपतिः॥

३१६ प्रतिग्रहपरीमाणं दानच्छेदोपवर्णनम्।
स्वहस्तकालसंपन्नं शासनं कारयेत्स्थिरम्॥

३१७ रम्यं पशव्यं स्वाजीव्यं जाङ्गलं देशमाश्रयेत्।
तत्र दुर्गाणि कुर्वीत जनकोशात्मवृद्धये॥

३१८ तत्र तत्र च निष्णातानध्यक्षान्कुशलाञ्छुचीन्।
प्रकुर्यादायकर्मान्तव्ययकर्मसु चोद्यतान्॥

३१९ नातः परतरो धर्मो नृपाणां यद्रणार्जितम्।
विप्रेभ्यो दीयते द्रव्यं प्रजाभ्यश्चाभयं सदा॥

३२० य आहवेषु वध्यन्ते भूम्यर्थमपराङ्मुखाः।
अकूटैरायुधैर्यान्ति ते स्वर्गं योगिनो यथा॥

It does not spill, it does not fail, and it is not marred by expiatory penances. What is offered in the fire of a Brahman is here declared to be superior to what is offered in the presence of a ritual fire. 312

He should seek to acquire what has not been acquired, protect assiduously what has been acquired, increase constantly what has been protected, and deposit what has been increased in worthy recipients.[148] 313

After giving a piece of land or creating an endowment, however, the king should get a document executed in order to inform avaricious future kings.[149] 314

The king should execute a lasting edict on a cloth or a copper plate marked with his seal, writing down his own name and the names of his ancestors, the extent of the donation, and the description and boundaries of the grant, and bearing his signature and date. 315–316

He should settle in a region that is beautiful, suitable for animal husbandry, providing an easy living, and dry. There he should build forts for the advancement of the people, treasury, and himself. 317

And he should appoint to various spheres clever, skilled, and honest superintendents, and those who are diligent to activities relating to income, factories, and expenditure. 318

For kings there is no dharma greater than this—always giving the wealth won in battle to Brahmans and granting safety to his subjects. 319

When, without turning back, they are killed in battles for the sake of land with weapons that are not treacherous, they go to heaven just like yogis. 320

३२१ पदानि क्रतुतुल्यानि भग्नेष्वविनिवर्तताम् ।
राजा सुकृतमादत्ते हतानां विपलायताम् ॥

३२२ तवाहंवादिनं क्लीबं निर्हेतिं परसंगतम् ।
न हन्याद्विनिवृत्तं च युद्धप्रेक्षकमेव च ॥

३२३ कृतरक्षः समुत्थाय पश्येदायव्ययौ स्वयम् ।
व्यवहारांस्ततो दृष्ट्वा स्नात्वा भुञ्जीत कामतः ॥

३२४ हिरण्यं व्यापृतानीतं भाण्डागारे न्यसेत्ततः ।
पश्येच्चारांस्ततो दूतान्प्रेषयेन्मन्त्रिसंगतः ॥

३२५ ततः स्वैरविहारी स्यान्मन्त्रिभिर्वा समागतः ।
बलानां दर्शनं कृत्वा सेनान्या सह चिन्तयेत् ॥

३२६ संध्यामुपास्य शृणुयाच्चाराणां गूढभाषितम् ।
गीतनृत्यैश्च भुञ्जीत पठेत्स्वाध्यायमेव च ॥

३२७ संविशेत्तूर्यघोषेण सुप्त्वा बुध्येत्तथैव च ।
शास्त्राणि चिन्तयेद्बुद्ध्वा सर्वकर्तव्यतास्तथा[४९] ॥

The steps of those who do not turn back when their ranks are broken are equal to sacrifices. The king takes the good works of those who are killed while they are fleeing. 321

He should not kill a person who declares, "I am yours," who is effeminate, who is without a weapon, or who is engaged in battle with someone else, as also a man who is fleeing or who is a spectator of the battle. 322

Once the defenses have been arranged, he should, after rising up, himself look into income and expenditure. Then, having tried lawsuits, he should bathe and eat at his pleasure. 323

Then, he should deposit in the treasury gold brought by his officials. He should see his secret agents, and then, in the company of his counselors, he should dispatch envoys. 324

Thereafter, he should engage in recreational activities on his own or in the company of his counselors. After inspecting his armed forces, he should confer with his military chief. 325

After performing the twilight worship, he should listen to clandestine reports of his secret agents. He should eat to the accompaniment of songs and dance and carry out his Vedic recitation. 326

He should retire to the sound of music and, after sleeping, wake up in the same manner. After waking up, he should ponder over scientific treatises, as well as all the activities that need to be carried out.[150] 327

३२८ प्रेषयेत ततश्चारान्स्वेष्वन्येषु च सादरम् ।
ऋत्विक्पुरोहिताचार्यैराशीर्भिरभिनन्दितः ॥

३२९ दृष्ट्वा ज्योतिर्विदो वैद्यान्दत्वा गां कनकं महीम् ।
नैवेशिकानि च तथा श्रोत्रियाणां गृहाणि च ॥

३३० ब्राह्मणेषु क्षमी स्निग्धेष्वजिह्मः क्रोधनोऽरिषु ।
स्याद्राजा भृत्यवर्गेषु प्रजाभ्यश्च यथा पिता ॥

३३१ पुण्यात्षड्भागमादत्ते न्यायेन परिपालयन् ।
सर्वदानाधिकं यस्मान्न्यायेन परिपालनम्[५०] ॥

३३२ चाटतस्करदुर्वृत्तमहासाहसिकादिभिः ।
पीड्यमानाः प्रजा रक्ष्याः कायस्थैश्च विशेषतः ॥

३३३ अरक्ष्यमाणाः कुर्वन्ति यत्किंचित्किल्बिषं प्रजाः ।
तस्मात्तु नृपतेरर्धं यस्माद्गृह्णात्यसौ करान् ॥

३३४ ये राष्ट्राधिकृतास्तेषां चारैर्ज्ञात्वा विचेष्टितम् ।
साधून्संमानयेन्नित्यं विपरीतांस्तु घातयेत्[५१] ॥

३३५ उत्कोचजीविनो द्रव्यहीनान्कृत्वा विवासयेत् ।
सदानमानसत्कारैः श्रोत्रियान्वासयेत्सदा ॥

३३६ अन्यायेन नृपो राष्ट्रात्स्वकोशं योऽभिवर्धयेत् ।
सोऽचिराद्विगतश्रीको नाशमेति सबान्धवः ॥

Then he should dispatch diligently secret agents among his own people and to outsiders—after he has been gladdened by the blessings of officiating priests, chaplain, and teacher; seen the astrologers and doctors; and presented a cow, gold, land, as well as wedding gifts and houses to Vedic scholars. 328–329

The king should act with forbearance toward Brahmans, without guile toward loved ones, with anger toward enemies, and like a father toward his various dependents and his subjects. 330

He takes a sixth portion of the merits by providing protection justly, because providing protection justly is greater than all gifts.[151] 331

He should protect his subjects when they are being harassed by rogues, thieves, evildoers, extremely violent men, and the like, and especially by scribes. 332

Whatever evil his subjects commit when they are not being protected, half of that falls on the king, because he collects taxes.[152] 333

Finding out through secret agents the activities of those who are appointed to administer his kingdom, he should always honor those who are righteous, but execute those who are not.[153] 334

Having confiscated all the property of those who live by taking bribes, he should expel them from his territory, and always induce Vedic scholars to dwell there, offering them gifts, honors, and reverence. 335

When a king increases his treasury by taking unjustly from his kingdom, before long, bereft of sovereignty, he will perish along with his relatives. 336

३३७ प्रजापीडनसंतापसमुद्भूतो हुताशनः।
राज्ञः कुलं श्रियं प्राणान्नादग्ध्वा विनिवर्तते॥

३३८ य एव धर्मो नृपतेः स्वराष्ट्रपरिपालने।
तमेव कृत्स्नमाप्नोति परराष्ट्रं वशं नयन्॥

३३९ यस्मिन् यस्मिन्य आचारो व्यवहारः कुले स्थितिः।
तथैव परिपाल्योऽसौ यदा वशमुपागतः॥

३४० मन्त्रमूलं यतो राज्यमतो मन्त्रं सुरक्षितम्।
कुर्याद्यथास्य न विदुः कर्मणामाफलोदयात्॥

३४१ अरिर्मित्रमुदासीनोऽनन्तरस्तत्परः परः।
क्रमशो मण्डलं चिन्त्यं सामादिभिरुपक्रमैः॥

३४२ उपायाः साम दानं च भेदो दण्डस्तथैव च।
सम्यक्प्रयुक्ताः सिध्येयुर्दण्डस्त्वगतिका गतिः॥

३४३ संधिं सविग्रहं यानमासनं संश्रयं तथा।
द्वैधीभावं गुणानेतान्यथावत्परिकल्पयेत्॥

The fire set ablaze by the intense heat from the oppression of his subjects will not turn back without burning up the king's family, sovereignty, and life. 337

The merit that a king obtains by properly protecting his own kingdom, that same merit he obtains completely by bringing the kingdom of his enemy under his power. 338

Whatever practice, convention, and family custom are found in a particular region, he should govern that region in accordance with them when he brings it under his power.[154] 339

Because a kingdom is founded on counsel, he must, therefore, keep his counsel well guarded, such that they do not find out about it until his activities have borne fruit. 340

He should make plans concerning the circle consisting of the enemy, the ally, and the neutral—who are the immediate neighbor, the one beyond him, and the one beyond the latter, respectively—through strategies beginning with conciliation.[155] 341

The strategies are conciliation, gifts, fomenting dissension, and force. When they are properly deployed, they bring success, but force should only be the last resort. 342

Peace pact, initiating hostilities, marching into battle, remaining stationary, seeking refuge, and double stratagem—he should employ these tactics as suitable.[156] 343

३४४ यदासम्यग्गुणोपेतं परराष्ट्रं तदा व्रजेत्।
परश्च हीन आत्मा च हृष्टवाहनपूरुषः[५२] ॥

३४५ दैवे पुरुषकारे च द्वये सिद्धिः प्रतिष्ठिता।
तत्र दैवमभिव्यक्तं पौरुषं पौर्वदेहिकम् ॥

३४६ केचिद्दैवाद्धटात्केचित्केचित्पुरुषकारतः।
सिध्यन्त्यर्था मनुष्याणां तेषां योनिस्तु पौरुषम्[५३] ॥

३४७ यथा ह्येकेन चक्रेण रथस्य न गतिर्भवेत्।
एवं पुरुषकारेण विना दैवं न सिध्यति ॥

३४८ हिरण्यभूमिलाभेभ्यो मित्रलब्धिर्वरा यतः।
अतो यतेत तत्प्राप्तौ सत्यं रक्षेत्समाहितः ॥

३४९ स्वाम्यमात्यो जनो दुर्गं कोशो दण्डस्तथैव च।
मित्राण्येताः प्रकृतयो राज्यं सप्ताङ्गमुच्यते ॥

३५० तदवाप्य नृपो दण्डं दुर्वृत्तेषु निपातयेत्।
धर्मो हि दण्डरूपेण ब्रह्मणा निर्मितः पुरा ॥

३५१ न स नेतुमतः शक्यो लुब्धेनाकृतबुद्धिना।
सत्यसंधेन शुचिना सुसहायेन धीमता[५४] ॥

३५२ यथाशास्त्रं प्रयुक्तः सन्सदेवासुरमानवम्।
जगदानन्दयेत्कृत्स्नमन्यथा तु प्रकोपयेत् ॥

When the enemy's kingdom lacks the proper strategic advantages, then he should march, as also when the enemy is weak and he himself has mounts and men in excellent spirits.[157] 344

Fate and human effort—on these two rests success. Of these, fate is the manifestation of human effort undertaken in a past life. 345

Some aims of human beings succeed through fate, some through predetermination, and some through human effort. But they are all rooted in human effort.[158] 346

As a chariot cannot move with just one wheel, so fate cannot succeed without human effort.[159] 347

Gaining an ally is better than gaining gold or land. Therefore, he should strive to gain an ally and, self-possessed, guard his troth. 348

Lord, minister, countryside, fort, treasury, army, and allies: these are the constituent parts—a kingdom is said to have seven limbs.[160] 349

Having obtained that kingdom, the king should inflict punishment on evildoers, for dharma was formerly created by Brahma in the shape of punishment. 350

It cannot be wielded, therefore, by someone who is greedy and whose mind is not developed, but only by a man who is true to his word and honest, has good assistants, and is wise.[161] 351

When it is wielded according to the dictates of authoritative texts, he gladdens the entire world of gods, demons, and humans; otherwise, he will cause it to revolt. 352

३५३ अधर्मदण्डनं लोकस्वर्गकीर्त्तिविनाशनम्।
सम्यक्तु दण्डनं राज्ञः स्वर्गकीर्त्तिजयावहम्॥

३५४ अपि भ्राता सुतोऽर्घ्यो वा श्वशुरो मातुलोऽपि वा।
नादण्ड्यो नाम राज्ञोऽस्ति धर्माद्विचलितः स्वकात्॥

३५५ यो दण्ड्यान्दण्डयेद्राजा सम्यग्वध्यांश्च घातयेत्।
इष्टं स्यात्क्रतुभिस्तेन सहस्रशतदक्षिणैः[५५]॥

३५६ इति संचिन्त्य नृपतिः क्रतुतुल्यफलं पृथक्।
व्यवहारान्स्वयं पश्येत्सभ्यैः परिवृतोऽन्वहम्॥

३५७ जालसूर्यमरीचिस्थं त्रसरेणू रजः स्मृतम्।
तेऽष्टौ लिक्षा तु तास्तिस्रो राजसर्षप उच्यते॥

३५८ गौरस्तु ते त्रयः षट् ते यवो मध्यस्तु ते त्रयः।
कृष्णलः पञ्च ते माषस्ते सुवर्णस्तु षोडश॥

३५९ पलं सुवर्णाश्चत्वारः पञ्च वापि प्रकीर्तितम्।
द्विकृष्णलो रौप्यमाषो धरणं षोडशैव ते॥

३६० शतमानं तु दशभिर्धरणैः पलमेव तत्।
निष्कं सुवर्णाश्चत्वारः कार्षिकस्ताम्रिकः पणः॥

३६१ साशीतिः पणसाहस्री दण्ड उत्तमसाहसः।
तदर्धं मध्यमः प्रोक्तस्तदर्धमधमः स्मृतः॥

Inflicting unjust punishment is destructive of the world, heaven, and fame. Inflicting punishment properly, however, brings heaven, fame, and victory to the king. 353

There is no one who is not subject to the king's punishment when a man deviates from the dharma specific to him, whether it is his brother, son, person deserving honor, father-in-law, or maternal uncle. 354

When a king punishes those who deserve to be punished and properly executes those who deserve to be executed, he has thereby offered sacrifices provided with one hundred thousand in sacrificial fees.[162] 355

After considering in this manner the distinct fruits equal to sacrifices, he should try lawsuits by himself every day surrounded by assessors.[163] 356

The fleck of dust seen when the sun shines through a lattice is said to be a *trasareṇu.* Eight of those constitute a *likṣā,* and three of those are said to be a *rājasarṣapa.*[164] 357

Three of those make a *gaurasarṣapa;* six of those, a middling *yava;* three of those, a *kṛṣṇala;* five of those, a *māṣa;* and sixteen of those, a *suvarṇa.*[165] 358

Four *suvarṇas*—or else five—are said to be a *pala.* Two *kṛṣṇalas* make one silver *māṣa,* and sixteen of those make a *dharaṇa.* 359

Ten *dharaṇas* make one *śatamāna,* which is the same as a *pala.* Four *suvarṇas* make one *niṣka.* A *kārṣika* is the same as a copper *paṇa.*[166] 360

The highest seizure-fine is 1,080 *paṇas.* The middle is said to be half that amount, and the lowest is given as half the latter amount.[167] 361

३६२ वाग्दण्डस्त्वथ धिग्दण्डो धनदण्डो वधस्तथा ।
योज्या व्यस्ताः समस्ता वाप्यपराधबलादिमे ॥

३६३ ज्ञात्वापराधं देशं च कालं बलमथापि च ।
वयः कर्म च वित्तं च ज्ञात्वा दण्डं प्रकल्पयेत् ॥

॥ इति राजधर्मप्रकरणम् ॥

॥ इति याज्ञवल्कीये धर्मशास्त्रे आचाराख्यः प्रथमोऽध्यायः ॥

Verbal reprimand, public denunciation, monetary fine, and corporal punishment—these should be imposed individually or collectively according to the magnitude of the crime. 362

Taking into consideration the crime, place, time, and magnitude, as well as age, occupation, and wealth, he should fix a punishment. 363

# व्यवहाराध्यायः

## ॥ अथ सामान्यन्यायप्रकरणम् ॥

१ व्यवहारान्नृपः पश्येद्विद्वद्भिर्ब्राह्मणैः सह ।
धर्मशास्त्रानुसारेण क्रोधलोभविवर्जितः ॥

२ श्रुताध्ययनसंपन्नाः कुलीनाः सत्यवादिनः ।
राज्ञा सभासदः कार्या रिपौ मित्रे च ये समाः[1] ॥

३ अपश्यता कार्यवशाद्व्यवहारान्नृपेण तु ।
सभ्यैः सह नियोक्तव्यो ब्राह्मणः सर्वधर्मवित् ॥

४ रागाद्द्वेषाद्भयाद्वापि स्मृत्यपेतादिकारिणः ।
सभ्याः पृथक्पृथग्दण्ड्या विवादद्विगुणं धनम्[2] ॥

५ स्मृत्याचारव्यपेतेन मार्गेणाधर्षितः परैः ।
आवेदयति चेद्राज्ञे व्यवहारपदं हि तत् ॥

६ प्रत्यर्थिनोऽग्रतो लेख्यं यथावेदितमर्थिना ।
समामासतदर्धाहोनामजात्यादिचिह्नितम् ॥

# 2 *Legal Procedure*

## TOPIC 14: COMMON RULES OF PROCEDURE

The king should try lawsuits accompanied by learned Brahmans, in conformity with treatises on dharma and free from anger and greed. 1

The king should appoint as court officers individuals who possess erudition and Vedic learning, belong to distinguished families, speak the truth, and treat both friend and foe alike.[1] 2

When the king is unable to try lawsuits because of the pressure of work, however, he should assign a Brahman who is learned in every facet of dharma, along with assessors. 3

Assessors who act contrary to what is given in texts of recollection or in a similar manner out of love, hatred, or fear should be fined individually a sum equal to twice the amount under litigation.[2] 4

When someone suffers an injury at the hands of others in a manner contrary to texts of recollection or normative practice and reports it to the king, it is a subject of litigation. 5

In the presence of the defendant, the charge should be written down exactly as reported by the plaintiff, recording the year, month, fortnight, day, name, caste, and the like. 6

७ श्रुतार्थस्योत्तरं लेख्यं पूर्वावेदकसंनिधौ ।
ततोऽर्थी लेखयेत्सद्यः प्रतिज्ञातार्थसाधनम् ॥

८ तत्सिद्धौ सिद्धिमाप्नोति विपरीतमतोऽन्यथा ।
चतुष्पाद्व्यवहारोऽयं विवादेषूपदर्शितः ॥

९ अभियोगमनिस्तीर्य नैनं प्रत्यभियोजयेत् ।
न चाभियुक्तमन्येन नोक्तं विप्रकृतिं नयेत् ॥

१० कुर्यात्प्रत्यभियोगं तु कलहे साहसेषु च ।
उभयोः प्रतिभूर्ग्राह्यः समर्थः कार्यनिर्णये ॥

११ निह्नवे भावितो दद्याद्धनं राज्ञे च तत्समम् ।
मिथ्याभियोगी द्विगुणमभियोगाद्धनं वहेत् ॥

१२ साहसस्तेयपारुष्यगोऽभिशापात्यये स्त्रियः ।
विवादयेत्सद्य एव कालोऽन्यत्रेच्छया भवेत् ॥

After the defendant has heard the plaint, his plea should be written down in the presence of the plaintiff. Immediately thereafter, the plaintiff should have the evidence written down, evidence he will use to prove what is alleged in his plaint. 7

If the evidence proves successful, he obtains success; the opposite, if it is otherwise. In litigations, this legal procedure has been shown to have four feet.[3] 8

Until the accusation has been disposed of, the defendant may not file a counter-accusation against the plaintiff; no one else may file an accusation against the accused; and what has been stated may not be altered. 9

The defendant, however, may file a counter-accusation in cases involving brawls and violence. From each of the two parties a surety should be secured capable of satisfying the verdict.[4] 10

When, after a denial, the charge against him has been proven, he should give the sum claimed and an equal amount to the king. A man who files a false accusation should pay twice the sum listed in the accusation. 11

In cases involving violence, theft, assault, cows, calumny, and an urgent matter, as well as one involving a woman, he should make the defendant enter a plea immediately; in other cases a delay may be allowed as desired. 12

१३ देशाद्देशान्तरं याति सृक्कणी परिलेढि च ।
ललाटं स्विद्यते चास्य मुखं वैवर्ण्यमेति च ॥

१४ परिशुष्यत्स्खलद्वाक्यो विरुद्धं बहु भाषते ।
वाक्चक्षुः पूजयति नो तथौष्ठौ निर्भुजत्यपि ॥

१५ स्वभावाद्विकृतिं गच्छेन्मनोवाक्कायकर्मभिः ।
अभियोगे च साक्ष्ये च स दुष्टः परिकीर्तितः ॥

१६ संदिग्धार्थं स्वतन्त्रो यः साधयेद्यश्च निष्पतेत् ।
न चाहूतो वदेत्किंचिद्धीनो दण्ड्यश्च स स्मृतः ॥

१७ साक्षिषूभयतः सत्सु साक्षिणः पूर्ववादिनः ।
पूर्वपक्षेऽधरीभूते भवन्त्युत्तरवादिनः ॥

१८ सपणश्चेद्विवादः स्यात्तत्र हीनं तु दापयेत् ।
दण्डं च स्वपणं चैव धनिने धनमेव च ॥

१९ छलं निरस्य भूतेन व्यवहारान्नयेन्नृपः ।
भूतमप्यनुपन्यस्तं हीयते व्यवहारतः ॥

२० निह्नुते लिखितोऽनेकमेकदेशविभावितः ।
दाप्यः सर्वान्नृपेणार्थान्न ग्राह्यस्त्वनिवेदितः ॥

A person who moves from place to place; who licks the corners of his mouth; whose forehead perspires; whose face changes color; who speaks in a stumbling and stuttering manner; whose speech is inconsistent and rambling; who is unresponsive when spoken to or looked at; who bites his lips; and who displays a change in his natural condition through acts of mind, speech, and body—in filing an accusation or giving testimony, such a person is declared to be deceitful. 13–15

When someone seeks to prove a doubtful legal matter independently, absconds, or does not say anything when summoned, he is said to be both defeated and subject to punishment.[5] 16

When witnesses are available for both parties, the witnesses of the appellant are to be deposed first; but if the plaintiff's claim has been superseded, then the witnesses of the respondent.[6] 17

If the litigation includes a wager, then the court should make the defeated party pay both the fine and the wager, as well as return the sum claimed to the creditor.[7] 18

Discarding subterfuge, the king should conduct judicial proceedings in accordance with the facts; for even what is factual that is not properly presented may suffer defeat through a judicial proceeding.[8] 19

In case someone denies a written plaint containing several parts and the plaint is later proven with regard to one of its parts, the king should make him pay all the claims; he may not, however, recover a claim not recorded in the plaint. 20

२१ स्मृतेर्विरोधे न्यायस्तु बलवान्व्यवहारतः।
अर्थशास्त्रात्तु बलवद्धर्मशास्त्रमिति स्थितिः[3] ॥

२२ प्रमाणं लिखितं भुक्तिः साक्षिणश्चेति कीर्तितम्।
एषामन्यतमाभावे दिव्यान्यतममुच्यते ॥

२३ सर्वेष्वेव विवादेषु बलवत्युत्तरा क्रिया।
आधौ प्रतिग्रहे क्रीते पूर्वा तु बलवत्तरा[4] ॥

२४ पश्यतोऽब्रुवतो भूमेर्हानिर्विंशतिवार्षिकी।
परेण भुज्यमानाया धनस्य दशवार्षिकी ॥

२५ आधिसीमोपनिक्षेपजडबालधनैर्विना।
तथोपनिधिराजस्त्रीश्रोत्रियाणां धनैरपि ॥

२६ आध्यादीनां हि हर्तारं धनिने दापयेद्धनम्।
दण्डं च तत्समं राज्ञे शक्त्यपेक्षमथापि वा ॥

२७ आगमोऽभ्यधिको भुक्तेर्विना पूर्वक्रमागतात्।
आगमेऽपि बलं नैव भुक्तिः स्तोकापि यत्र नो ॥

When there is a conflict with a text of recollection, however, an edict has greater force within the context of legal procedure, and a treatise on dharma has greater force than a treatise on political science—that is the rule.[9] 21

A document, enjoyment, and witnesses, it is declared, constitute evidence; and, in the absence of any of these, one of the ordeals.[10] 22

In all litigations, evidence relating to a later transaction has greater force; in the case of a pledge, gift, or purchase, however, evidence relating to an earlier transaction has greater force.[11] 23

When a man looks on without speaking up while his land is being enjoyed by someone else, he loses his title to it in twenty years; in the case of movable property, in ten years—with the exception of a pledge, a boundary, an open deposit, and the property of the mentally incompetent and children, as well as a sealed deposit and the property of the king, women, and Vedic scholars. 24–25

A man who purloins a pledge and the like should indeed be made to give the property to the owner, and a fine equal to its value or proportionate to his ability to the king.[12] 26

Title has greater force than enjoyment, except when it has come down through successive generations. Even title has no force at all in the absence of even a modicum of enjoyment. 27

२८ आगमस्तु कृतो येन सोऽभियुक्तस्तमुद्धरेत्।
न तत्सुतस्तत्सुतो वा भुक्तिस्तत्र गरीयसी॥

२९ आगमेन विशुद्धेन भोगो याति प्रमाणताम्।
अविशुद्धागमो भोगः प्रामाण्यं नाधिगच्छति[५]॥

३० योऽभियुक्तः परेतः स्यात्तस्य रिक्थी तमुद्धरेत्।
न तत्र कारणं भुक्तिरागमेन विना कृता॥

३१ नृपोऽर्थाधिकृताः पूगाः श्रेणयोऽथ कुलानि च।
पूर्वं पूर्वं गुरु ज्ञेयं व्यवहारविधौ नृणाम्[६]॥

३२ बलोपधिविनिर्वृत्तान्व्यवहारान्निवर्तयेत्।
स्त्रीनक्तमन्तरागारबहिःशत्रुकृतांस्तथा॥

३३ मत्तोन्मत्तार्तव्यसनिबालभीतप्रयोजितः।
असंबन्धकृतश्चैव व्यवहारो न सिध्यति॥

३४ कुलानि जातयः श्रेण्यो गणाञ्जानपदानपि।
स्वधर्माच्चलितान्राजा विनीय स्थापयेत्पथि[७]॥

३५ प्रनष्टाधिगतं देयं नृपेण धनिने धनम्।
विभावयेन्न चेल्लिङ्गैस्तत्समं दण्डमर्हति॥

When a man who has drawn up the title is sued, however, he should produce it; but not his son or his son's son— in their case, enjoyment has greater force. 28

Enjoyment constitutes probative evidence by means of a clear title; enjoyment without a clear title does not represent probative evidence.[13] 29

If the person sued happens to die, his heir should produce the title—in that case, enjoyment is no proof when it has been carried out without proper title. 30

King, officials authorized to adjudicate lawsuits, associations, guilds, and families—of these, each preceding one should be recognized as having greater authority with respect to legal proceedings among men.[14] 31

He should annul legal actions carried out by force or fraud, as also those executed by women, at night, within a house, outside, or by an enemy.[15] 32

A legal action carried out by someone who is intoxicated, mad, afflicted, in distress, a child, or frightened, as well as one executed by an unrelated person, is invalid. 33

Families, castes, guilds, companies, and also people in the countryside—when these stray from the dharma specific to them, the king should discipline them and set them on the right path.[16] 34

When lost property is found, the king should return it to the owner. If he is unable to identify it through its specific marks, he is subject to a fine equal to its value. 35

३६ राजा लब्ध्वा निधिं दद्याद्द्विजेभ्योऽर्धं द्विजः पुनः ।
विद्वानशेषमादद्यात्स सर्वस्य प्रभुर्यतः ॥

३७ इतरेण निधौ लब्धे राजा षष्ठांशमाहरेत् ।
अनिवेदितविज्ञातो दाप्यस्तद्दण्डमेव च ॥

३८ देयं चोरहृतं द्रव्यं राज्ञा जनपदाय तु ।
अददद्धि समाप्नोति किल्बिषं तस्य यस्य तत् ॥

इति सामान्यन्यायप्रकरणम् ।

## अथ ऋणादानप्रकरणम् ।

३९ अशीतिभागो वृद्धिः स्यान्मासि मासि सबन्धके ।
वर्णक्रमाच्छतं द्वित्रिचतुष्पञ्चकमन्यथा ॥

४० संततिस्तु पशुस्त्रीणां रसस्याष्टगुणा परा ।
वस्त्रधान्यहिरण्यानां चतुस्त्रिद्विगुणा तथा[8] ॥

When the king finds a treasure-trove, he should give half of it to Brahmans. A learned Brahman, on the other hand, may keep the whole of it, because he is the master of all. 36

When a treasure-trove is found by anyone else, the king should take one-sixth of it. If the finder fails to inform and is discovered, he should be forced to hand it over and also to pay a fine. 37

The king, however, should return to a man within his country property stolen by a thief, for if he fails to return it, he assumes the same sin as the thief. 38

## TOPIC 15: NON-PAYMENT OF DEBTS

One-eightieth part per month is the interest rate for a secured loan; otherwise, it is 2, 3, 4, and 5 percent, respectively, according to the direct order of social class.[17] 39

In the case of farm animals and women, however, the interest is their offspring. In the case of liquids, the highest level that interest may accrue is eight times the principal, while in the case of clothes, grains, and gold, it is four times, three times, and two times, respectively.[18] 40

४१ कान्तारगास्तु दशकं सामुद्रा विंशकं शतम्।
दद्युर्वा स्वकृतां वृद्धिं सर्वे सर्वासु जातिषु॥

४२ प्रपन्नं साधयानोऽर्थं न वाच्यो नृपतेर्भवेत्।
साध्यमानो नृपं गच्छेद्दण्ड्यो दाप्यश्च तद्धनम्॥

४३ गृहीतानुक्रमाद्दद्याद्धनिनामधमर्णिकः।
दद्यात्तु ब्राह्मणायाग्रे नृपाय तदनन्तरम्॥

४४ राज्ञाधमर्णिको दाप्यः साधिताद्दशकं शतम्।
पञ्चकं तु शतं दाप्यः प्राप्तार्थो ह्युत्तमर्णिकः॥

४५ हीनजातिं परिक्षीणमृणार्थं कर्म कारयेत्।
ब्राह्मणस्तु परिक्षीणः शनैर्दाप्यो यथोदयम्॥

४६ दीयमानं न गृह्णीत प्रयुक्तं यत्स्वकं धनम्।
मध्यस्थस्थापितं तत्स्याद्वर्धते न ततः परम्॥

४७ रिक्थग्राह ऋणं दद्याद्योषिद्ग्राहस्तथैव च।
पुत्रोऽनन्याश्रितद्रव्यः पुत्रहीनस्य रिक्थिनः[१]॥

Persons traveling through forests, on the other hand, should pay 10 percent, and those traveling by sea, 20 percent. Alternatively, all persons of all castes should pay the rate of interest they themselves have set. 41

The king must not censure a person when he recovers an acknowledged loan. If the person from whom the debt is being recovered resorts to the king, he should be fined and made to return that property. 42

A debtor should repay the creditors in the order in which he took out the loans. He should, however, repay a Brahman first and right after that the king. 43

The king should make the debtor pay him 10 percent of the amount recovered, while the creditor who has recovered his loan should be made to pay 5 percent. 44

He should make an insolvent low-caste person do manual labor to satisfy his debt. An insolvent Brahman, on the other hand, should be made to pay it off in installments proportionate to his income. 45

If someone does not accept the property he has loaned when it is being returned, it is to be deposited with a neutral third party. From that time forward it ceases to accrue interest. 46

The man who takes someone's inheritance should pay his debt, as also the man who takes his wife; his son, when the property has not gone to another person; and if he has no son, the heirs.[19] 47

४८ अविभक्तैः कुटुम्बार्थे यदृणं तु कृतं भवेत्।
दद्युस्तद्रिक्थिनः प्रेते प्रोषिते वा कुटुम्बिनि॥

४९ न योषित्पतिपुत्राभ्यां न पुत्रेण कृतं पिता।
दद्यादृते कुटुम्बार्थान्न पतिः स्त्रीकृतं तथा॥

५० गोपशौण्डिकशैलूषरजकव्याधयोषिताम्।
ऋणं दद्यात्पतिस्तासां यस्माद्वृत्तिस्तदाश्रया॥

५१ प्रतिपन्नं स्त्रिया देयं पत्या वा सह यत्कृतम्।
स्वयं कृतमृणं वापि नान्यत्स्त्री दातुमर्हति॥

५२ पितरि प्रोषिते प्रेते व्यसनाभिप्लुतेऽपि वा।
पुत्रपौत्रैर्ऋणं देयं निह्नवे साक्षिभावितम्॥

५३ सुराकामद्यूतकृतं दण्डशुल्कावशिष्टकम्।
वृथादानं तथैवेह पुत्रो दद्यान्न पैतृकम्॥

५४ भ्रातॄणामथ दम्पत्योः पितुः पुत्रस्य चैव हि।
प्रातिभाव्यमृणं साक्ष्यमविभक्ते न तु स्मृतम्॥

When a debt is entered into by undivided coparceners for the benefit of the family, however, the heirs should repay it when the head of the family has died or gone abroad.[20] 48

A wife is not obliged to pay a debt incurred by her husband or son, a father a debt incurred by his son, or a husband a debt incurred by his wife, unless it was incurred for the benefit of the family. 49

When a debt has been incurred by wives of herdsmen, liquor merchants, actors, washermen, and hunters, their husbands are obliged to pay it, because they are dependent on their wives for their livelihood. 50

A wife has to repay a debt to which she consented, one that she incurred together with her husband, and one that she incurred herself; a wife is not obliged to repay anything else. 51

When the father has gone abroad or died, or is overwhelmed by misfortune, a debt of his should be paid by his sons or grandsons—in case they deny it, when it has been established through witnesses. 52

A son is here not obliged to pay a debt that his father incurred for the sake of liquor, lust, or gambling; the unpaid balance of a fine or toll levied on him; or a frivolous gift he has pledged. 53

Brothers, husband and wife, and father and son—their ability to act as surety for each other, to incur debts from each other, or to be witnesses for each other is not recognized as long as they remain undivided coparceners. 54

५५ दर्शने प्रत्यये दाने प्रातिभाव्यं विधीयते ।
आद्यौ तु वितथे दाप्यावितरस्य सुता अपि ॥

५६ दर्शनप्रतिभूर्यत्र मृतः प्रात्ययिकोऽपि वा ।
न तत्पुत्रा ऋणं दद्युर्दद्युर्दानाय यः स्थितः ॥

५७ बहवः स्युर्यदि स्वांशैर्दद्युः प्रतिभुवो धनम् ।
एकच्छायास्थितेष्वेषु धनिकस्य यथारुचि ॥

५८ प्रतिभूर्दापितो यत्र प्रकाशं धनिने धनम् ।
द्विगुणं प्रतिदातव्यमृणिकैस्तस्य तद्धनम् ॥

५९ ससंतति स्त्रीपशव्यं धान्यं त्रिगुणमेव तु ।
वस्त्रं चतुर्गुणं देयं रसश्चाष्टगुणस्तथा ॥

६० आधिः प्रणश्येद्द्विगुणे धने यदि न मोक्ष्यते ।
काले कालकृतो नश्येत्फलभोग्यो न नश्यति ॥

६१ गोप्याधिभोगे नो वृद्धिः सोपकारेऽथ भाविते ।
नष्टो देयो विनष्टो वा दैवराजकृताद्दते ॥

The law enjoins a surety for appearance, for trustworthiness, and for payment. In case of deceit, however, the first two should be made to pay, and even the sons of the third.[21] 55

When a surety for appearance or even a surety for trustworthiness dies, his sons are not obliged to pay the debt, whereas the sons of one who stands as surety for payment are obliged to pay. 56

If there are several sureties, then each should repay the loan proportionate to his share; when they have assumed individual liability for the whole debt, according to the wishes of the creditor.[22] 57

When a surety has been forced to repay the loan publicly to a creditor, the debtors are obligated to pay that surety twice the amount of that loan—also to be returned are women and domestic animals along with their offspring; three times the amount of grain; four times the amount of clothes; and eight times the amount of liquids.[23] 58–59

A pledge is forfeited if it is not redeemed before the loan has doubled; a pledge given for a set period of time is forfeited if it is not redeemed before the end of that period; whereas a pledge from which a benefit is derived is never forfeited.[24] 60

When a benefit is derived from a pledge that is to be safeguarded, no interest accrues, as also when it is proven that a pledge has been used. If a pledge is lost or destroyed, compensation should be paid, unless it was caused by an act of god or the king.[25] 61

६२ आधेः स्वीकरणात्सिद्धी रक्ष्यमाणोऽप्यसारताम् ।
यातश्चेदन्य आधेयो धनं वा धनिने वहेत् ॥

६३ चरित्रबन्धककृतं सवृद्धं दापयेद्धनम् ।
सत्यंकारकृतं द्रव्यं द्विगुणं प्रतिदापयेत् ॥

६४ उपस्थितस्य मोक्तव्य आधिर्दण्ड्योऽन्यथा भवेत् ।
प्रयोजकेऽसति धनं कुले न्यस्याधिमाप्नुयात्[10] ॥

६५ तत्कालकृतमूल्यो वा तत्र तिष्ठेदवृद्धिकः ।
विना धारणकाद्वापि विक्रीणीत ससाक्षिकम् ॥

६६ यदा तु द्विगुणीभूतमृणमाधौ तदा खलु ।
मोच्य आधिस्तदुत्पन्ने प्रविष्टे द्विगुणे धने ॥

॥ इति ऋणादानप्रकरणम् ॥

A pledge comes into force by its appropriation. If it loses its value even though it is well guarded, he should give another pledge or return the loan to the creditor.[26] 62

He should make a loan secured by character to be repaid with interest, whereas when a loan is given with an earnest, he should make him return double the amount.[27] 63

The creditor should release the pledge when the debtor comes for it; otherwise he becomes subject to punishment. If the creditor is absent, the debtor may deposit the loan with his family and retrieve the pledge.[28] 64

Alternatively, after its value at that time has been determined, the pledge should remain there without accruing interest. Or else, if the debtor is absent, it may be sold in the presence of witnesses. 65

When the debt guaranteed by a pledge has doubled, however, the pledge should be released once double the amount loaned is received through profits realized from the pledge. 66

## ॥ अथोपनिधिप्रकरणम् ॥

६७ भाजनस्थमनाख्याय हस्तेऽन्यस्य यदर्प्यते ।
द्रव्यं तदौपनिधिकं प्रतिदेयं तथैव तत्[११] ॥

६८ न दाप्योऽपहृतं तत्तु राजदैविकतस्करैः ।
भ्रेषश्चेन्मार्गितेऽदत्ते दाप्यो दण्डं च तत्समम्[१२] ॥

६९ आजीवन्स्वेच्छया दण्ड्यो दाप्यस्तच्चापि सोदयम् ।
याचितान्वाहितन्यासनिक्षेपेष्वप्ययं विधिः ॥

॥ इत्युपनिधिप्रकरणम् ॥

## TOPIC 16: SEALED DEPOSITS

When someone hands over to another person an article placed within a box without disclosing it, it is a sealed deposit, and it should be returned in the very same manner.[29] 67

He should not be forced to pay restitution when it has been taken away by the king, by an act of god, or by thieves. If the loss happened after the pledge had been requested and not returned, then he should be made to pay restitution, as well as a fine equal to it.[30] 68

If he uses the proceeds from the pledge of his own accord, he should be fined and forced to return it along with the earnings. This rule applies also to what is solicited, to what has been entrusted to a third party, to consignments, and to open deposits. 69

## ॥ अथ साक्षिप्रकरणम् ॥

७० तपस्विनो दानशीलाः कुलीनाः सत्यवादिनः ।
धर्मप्रधाना ऋजवः पुत्रवन्तो धनान्विताः ॥

७१ त्र्यवराः साक्षिणो ज्ञेयाः पञ्चयज्ञक्रियारताः ।
यथाजाति यथावर्णं सर्वे सर्वासु वा पुनः[१३] ॥

७२ स्त्रीवृद्धबालकितवमत्तोन्मत्ताभिशस्तकाः ।
रङ्गावतारिपाषण्डिकूटकृद्विकलेन्द्रियाः ॥

७३ पतिताप्तार्थसंबन्धिसहायरिपुतस्कराः ।
साहसी दृष्टदोषश्च निर्धूतश्चेत्यसाक्षिणः ॥

७४ उभयानुमतः साक्षी भवत्येकोऽपि धर्मवित् ।
सर्वः संग्रहणे साक्षी चौर्यपारुष्यसाहसे[१४] ॥

७५ अब्रुवन्हि नरः साक्ष्यमृणं सदशबन्धकम् ।
राज्ञा सर्वं प्रदाप्यः षट्चत्वारिंशत्तमेऽहनि ॥

७६ न ब्रवीति हि यः साक्ष्यं जानन्नपि नराधमः ।
स कूटसाक्षिणां पापैस्तुल्यो दण्डेन चैव हि[१५] ॥

## TOPIC 17: WITNESSES

Individuals who are given to ascetic toil, are inclined to gift giving, come from distinguished families, speak the truth, place dharma at the forefront, are upright, have sons, and possess wealth—a minimum of three such individuals who delight in rites associated with the five sacrifices are recognized as witnesses, each with respect to persons of the same caste or class, or else all with respect to persons of all castes and classes.[31] 70–71

A woman, an old person, a child, a gambler, a drunkard, a mad person, a heinous sinner, an actor, a person belonging to a heretical sect, a forger, an individual with impaired organs, a person fallen from caste, someone close to the litigants, someone with a stake in the lawsuit, an associate or enemy of the litigants, a thief, a violent individual, a person of ill repute, and an extreme ascetic—these are not qualified to be witnesses. 72–73

When approved by both parties, even a single person who knows dharma is qualified to be a witness. Anyone is qualified to be a witness in cases relating to sexual crimes and to theft, assault, and violence.[32] 74

When a man fails to give testimony, on the forty-sixth day the king should force him to pay the entire debt along with a penalty of one-tenth the amount.[33] 75

That vilest of men who, although he knows the facts, does not provide testimony is equal to false witnesses with respect to both the sins and the punishment. 76

७७ साक्षिणः श्रावयेद्वादिप्रतिवादिसमीपगान् ।
ये पातककृतां लोका महापातकिनां तथा ॥

७८ अग्निदानां च ये लोका ये च स्त्रीबालघातिनाम् ।
तान्सर्वान्समवाप्नोति यः साक्ष्यमनृतं वदेत् ॥

७९ यत्त्वया सुकृतं किंचिज्जन्मान्तरशतैः कृतम् ।
तत्सर्वं तस्य जानीहि पराजयसि यं मृषा ॥

८० साक्षिद्वैधे प्रभूतानां समेषु गुणिनां तथा ।
गुणिद्वैधे तु वचनं ग्राह्यं यद्गुणवत्तरम् ॥

८१ यस्याहुः साक्षिणः सत्यां प्रतिज्ञां स जयी भवेत् ।
अन्यथावादिनो यस्य ध्रुवस्तस्य पराजयः ॥

८२ उक्तेऽपि साक्षिभिः साक्ष्ये यद्यन्ये गुणवत्तराः ।
द्विगुणा वान्यथा ब्रूयुः कूटाः स्युः पूर्वसाक्षिणः ॥

८३ पृथक्पृथग्दण्डनीयाः कूटकृत्साक्षिणस्तथा ।
विवादद्विगुणं द्रव्यं विवास्यो ब्राह्मणो भवेत् ॥

When the witnesses have come into the presence of the plaintiff and defendant, he should make them give testimony, saying: "The worlds that await those who commit sins causing loss of caste, as well as those who commit the grievous sins causing loss of caste;[34] the worlds that await arsonists and slayers of women and children—all those worlds will a man obtain who gives false testimony. 77–78

Whatever good deed you have performed over hundreds of lifetimes, all that, you should know, will go to the man whom you defeat by your false testimony." 79

When witnesses are in disagreement, the testimony of the majority should be accepted; when they are equally divided, the testimony of quality witnesses; when quality witnesses are in disagreement, the testimony supported by those with superior qualities. 80

The person whose plaint the witnesses affirm to be true is the victor, whereas when they state otherwise, that person suffers certain defeat. 81

Even after the witnesses have given their testimony, if other witnesses with superior qualities or double the original number state otherwise, then the earlier witnesses are deemed false. 82

The person who suborned perjury, as well as the witnesses, should be fined individually twice the amount under litigation; if it is a Brahman, he should be sent into exile. 83

८४ यः साक्ष्यं श्रावितोऽन्येन निह्नुते तत्तमोवृतः ।
स दाप्योऽष्टगुणं द्रव्यं ब्राह्मणं तु विवासयेत् ॥

८५ वर्णिनां तु वधो यत्र तत्र साक्ष्यनृतं वदेत् ।
तत्पावनाय निर्वाप्यश्चरुः सारस्वतो द्विजैः ॥

॥ इति साक्षिप्रकरणम् ॥

## ॥ अथ लिखितप्रकरणम् ॥

८६ यः कश्चिदर्थो निष्णातः स्वरुच्या तु परस्परम् ।
लेख्यं वा साक्षिमत्कार्यं तस्मिन्धनिकपूर्वकम् ॥

८७ समामासतदर्धाहोवासजातिसगोत्रकैः ।
सब्रह्मचारिकात्मीयपितृनाम्ना च चिह्नितम् ॥

८८ समाप्तेऽर्थे ऋणी नाम स्वहस्तेन निवेशयेत् ।
मतं मेऽमुकपुत्रस्य यदत्रोपरि लेखितम् ॥

८९ साक्षिणश्च स्वहस्तेन पितृनामकपूर्वकम् ।
अत्राहममुकः साक्षी लिखेयुरिति तेऽसमाः[१६] ॥

When a person who has been produced to give testimony by either party, engulfed by delusion, disavows it, he should be made to pay eight times the amount; if it is a Brahman, however, he should be sent into exile. 84

One may, however, give false testimony in a case where a person of an upper class is subject to execution. To expiate that, twice-born individuals should offer an oblation of milk rice dedicated to Sarasvati, the goddess of speech. 85

## TOPIC 18: DOCUMENTS

When any transaction has been concluded by mutual agreement, however, a document with witnesses should be executed with regard to it, noting at the beginning the name of the creditor, and recording the year, month, fortnight, and day; his residence, caste, and lineage; and his Vedic affiliation and the name of his father. 86–87

Once the transaction has been completed, the debtor should write his name in his own hand: "I, the son of NN., agree to what has been written above in this document." 88

The witnesses—who should constitute an uneven number—should also write in their own hand: "I, NN., am a witness to this document," preceded by the names of their fathers.[35] 89

९० अलिपिज्ञ ऋणी यः स्यात्स्वमतं लेखयेत्तु सः ।
साक्षी वा साक्षिणान्येन सर्वसाक्षिसमीपगः[१७] ॥

९१ उभयाभ्यर्थितेनेदं मया ह्यमुकसूनुना ।
लिखितं त्वमुकेनेति लेखकस्त्वन्ततो लिखेत् ॥

९२ विनापि साक्षिभिर्लेख्यं स्वहस्तलिखितं तु यत् ।
तत्प्रमाणं स्मृतं सर्वं बलोपधिकृतादृते ॥

९३ ऋणं लेख्यगतं देयं पुरुषैस्त्रिभिरेव तु ।
आधिस्तु भुज्यते तावद्यावत् तन्न प्रदीयते ॥

९४ देशान्तरस्थे दुर्लेख्ये नष्टोन्मृष्टे हृते तथा ।
छिन्ने भिन्ने तथा दग्धे लेख्यमन्यत्तु कारयेत् ॥

९५ संदिग्धार्थविशुद्ध्यर्थं स्वहस्तलिखितं तु यत् ।
युक्तिप्राप्तिक्रियाचिह्नसंबन्धागमहेतुभिः ॥

९६ लेख्यस्य पृष्ठेऽभिलिखेत्प्रविष्टमधमर्णिकात् ।
धनी वोपगतं दद्यात्स्वहस्तपरिचिह्नितम्[१८] ॥

९७ दत्त्वर्णं पाटयेल्लेख्यं शुद्ध्यै वान्यत्तु कारयेत् ।
साक्षिमच्च भवेद्यत्तु दातव्यं तत्ससाक्षिकम् ॥

॥ इति लिखितप्रकरणम् ॥

Should the debtor be illiterate, however, he should have his view written down; so also should an illiterate witness through another witness in the presence of all the witnesses.[36] 90

The scribe, on the other hand, should write at the end: "At the request of both parties, I, NN., the son of NN., have written this." 91

When a document has been written in one's own hand, however, all of it is said to be authoritative even without witnesses, except when it is done through force or fraud. 92

A debt attested by a document, however, has to be repaid by three generations, while a pledge may be made use of so long as the debt remains unpaid. 93

When a document is located in another country, badly written, lost, erased, stolen, cut, torn, or burned, he should get another one executed. 94

In order to authenticate a dubious point, one should look at a writing sample from the man's own hand or resort to reasoning, implication, evidence, peculiar marks, connection, title, and inference.[37] 95

He should write on the back of the document any payment received from the debtor. Alternatively, the creditor should give a receipt signed in his own hand.[38] 96

After paying back the debt, he should tear up the document; or he should have another executed as acquittance. A debt contracted in the presence of witnesses should be repaid also in the presence of witnesses. 97

## ॥ अथ दिव्यप्रकरणम् ॥

९८ तुलाग्न्यापो विषं कोशो दिव्यानीह विशुद्धये ।
महाभियोगेष्वेतानि शीर्षकस्थेऽभियोक्तरि ॥

९९ रुच्या वान्यतरः कुर्यादितरो वर्तयेच्छिरः ।
विनापि शीर्षकात्कुर्याद्राजद्रोहेऽथ पातके ॥

१०० नासहस्रपरं फालं न तुला न विषं तथा ।
नृपार्थेष्वभियोगेषु वहेयुः शुचयः सदा[१९] ॥

१०१ सहस्रार्थे तुलादीनि कोशमल्पेऽपि कारयेत् ।
पञ्चाशद्दापयेच्छुद्धमशुद्धो दण्डभाग्भवेत् ॥

१०२ सचेलस्नातमाहूय सूर्योदय उपोषितम् ।
कारयेत्सर्वदिव्यानि नृपब्राह्मणसंनिधौ ॥

## TOPIC 19:
## ORDEALS

Balance, fire, water, poison, and holy water are the ordeals given here for establishing innocence. They are employed in cases of serious accusations when the accuser has accepted to be subject to punishment. 98

Or, either of the parties, if they so wish, may undergo it, while the other accepts to be subject to punishment. One must undergo it even without the acceptance to be subject to punishment in cases involving treason against the king or a sin causing loss of caste. 99

When the amount is less than one thousand, the plowshare ordeal should not be employed, nor the ordeals of balance and poison. In accusations involving royal property, people should always undergo them after they have purified themselves.[39] 100

When the property amounts to one thousand, the balance and so forth should be employed, while holy water may be used for even a small amount. A person judged innocent should be made to pay fifty, while a person who is guilty is subject to punishment. 101

He should summon at sunrise the man, who has taken a bath with his clothes on and fasted, and make him undergo any of the ordeals in the presence of the king and Brahmans. 102

१०३ तुला स्त्रीबालवृद्धार्तपङ्गुब्राह्मणरोगिणाम् ।
अग्निर्जलं वाशूद्रस्य यवाः सप्त विषस्य वा[20] ॥

१०४ तुलाधारणविद्वद्भिरभियुक्तस्तुलाश्रितः ।
प्रतिमानसमीभूतो लेखाः कृत्वावतारितः ॥

१०५ त्वं तुले सत्यधामासि पुरा देवैर्विनिर्मिता ।
तत्सत्यं वद कल्याणि संशयान्मां विमोचय ॥

१०६ यद्यस्मि पापकृन्मातस्ततो मां त्वमधो नय ।
शुद्धश्चेद्गमयोर्ध्वं मां तुलामित्यभिमन्त्रयेत् ॥

१०७ करौ विमृदितव्रीहेर्लक्षयित्वा ततो न्यसेत् ।
सप्ताश्वत्थस्य पत्राणि तावत्सूत्रेण वेष्टयेत् ॥

१०८ त्वमग्ने सर्वभूतानामन्तश्चरसि पावक ।
साक्षिवत्पुण्यपापेभ्यो ब्रूहि सत्यं कवे मम ॥

१०९ तस्येत्युक्तवतो लोहं पञ्चाशत्पलिकं समम् ।
अग्निवर्णं न्यसेत्क्षिप्रं हस्तयोरुभयोरपि ॥

११० स तमादाय सप्तैव मण्डलानि शनैर्व्रजेत् ।
षोडशाङ्गुलिकं ज्ञेयं मण्डलं तावदन्तरम् ॥

The balance ordeal is for women, children, the elderly, the afflicted, cripples, Brahmans, and the sick; the fire or the water ordeal is for a non-Shudra; and seven grains of poison for a Shudra.[40] 103

Individuals skilled in the use of balances should place the accused in the balance, make the balance even by using weights, mark lines, and take him down. 104

"You, Oh Balance, are the abode of truth formerly created by the gods. Therefore, Lovely One, speak the truth! Free me from suspicion. If I have committed the crime, Oh Mother, then push me down. If I am innocent, raise me up." So should he address the balance. 105–106

After both hands of the man have been rubbed with unhusked rice, he should make marks, and then he should place seven pipal leaves on them, and bind them with a string, wrapping around the same number of times.[41] 107

"You, Oh Fire, moves about in the interior of all beings, Oh Purifier. Like a witness, Oh Sage, speak the truth about my good and evil deeds." 108

After the man has said this, he should quickly place in both his hands a smooth red-hot iron ball weighing 50 *palas*.[42] 109

Taking it, the man should walk slowly across all seven circles. One should know that each circle has a diameter of 16 *aṅgulas*, with the same distance between any two of them.[43] 110

१११ मुक्ताग्निर्मृदितव्रीहिरदग्धः शुद्धिमाप्नुयात् ।
अन्तरा पतिते पिण्डे संदेहे वा पुनर्हरेत् ॥

११२ सत्येन माभिरक्षस्व वरुणेत्यभिशाप्य कम् ।
नाभिदघ्नोदकस्थस्य गृहीत्वोरू जलं विशेत् ॥

११३ समकालमिषुं मुक्तमानयेद्यो जवी नरः ।
गतेऽन्यस्मिन्निमग्नाङ्गं पश्येच्चेच्छुद्धिमाप्नुयात् ॥

११४ त्वं विष ब्रह्मणः पुत्र सत्यधर्मव्यवस्थित ।
त्रायस्वास्मान्माभिशापात्सत्येन भव मेऽमृतम् ॥

११५ एवमुक्त्वा विषं शार्ङ्गं भक्षयेद्धिमशैलजम् ।
यस्य वेगैर्विना जीर्णं शुद्धिं तस्य विनिर्दिशेत् ॥

११६ देवानुग्रान्समभ्यर्च्य तत्स्नानोदकमाहरेत् ।
संश्राव्य पाययेत्तस्माज्जलात्तु प्रसृतित्रयम् ॥

११७ आ चतुर्दशमादह्नो यस्य नो राजदैविकम् ।
व्यसनं जायते घोरं स शुद्धः स्यान्न संशयः ॥

॥ इति दिव्यप्रकरणम् ॥

After the man has released the fiery ball and his hands have been rubbed with unhusked ricc, if he is found to be unburned, he should be judged innocent. If the ball falls along the way or if there is a doubt, he should carry it again. 111

After beseeching water: "Protect me by truth, Oh Varuna," he should submerge himself, holding on to the thighs of a man standing in water reaching up to his navel. 112

At the very same time, when the other runner has gone, a fast runner should bring back the arrow that had been discharged. If the latter sees the man with his whole body submerged, then he should be judged innocent.[44] 113

"You, Oh Poison, son of Brahma, you who abide in the true dharma, rescue me from this accusation. By truth become my ambrosia." 114

Having said that, he should consume the *śārṅga* poison originating in the Himalayas. Should he digest it without violent symptoms, one should proclaim the man's innocence.[45] 115

After worshiping the fierce deities, he should bring their bath water. After instructing the man, he should get him to drink three handfuls of that water.[46] 116

When the man does not suffer a severe calamity caused by the king or by an act of god until the fourteenth day, he is innocent without a doubt. 117

## ॥ अथ दायविभागप्रकरणम् ॥

११८ विभागं चेत्पिता कुर्यादिच्छया विभजेत्सुतान् ।
ज्येष्ठं वा श्रेष्ठभागेन सर्वे वा स्युः समांशिनः ॥

११९ यदि दद्यात्समानंशान्कार्याः पत्न्यः समांशिकाः ।
न दत्तं स्त्रीधनं यासां भर्त्रा वा श्वशुरेण वा ॥

१२० शक्तस्यानीहमानस्य किंचिद्दत्त्वा पृथक्क्रिया ।
ऊनाधिकविभक्तानां धर्मः पितृकृतः स्मृतः ॥

१२१ विभजेयुः सुताः पित्रोरूर्ध्वं रिक्थमृणं समम् ।
मातुर्दुहितरः शेषमृणात्ताभ्य ऋतेऽन्वयः ॥

१२२ पितृद्रव्याविनाशेन यदन्यत्स्वयमार्जितम् ।
मैत्रमौद्वाहिकं चैव दायादानां न तद्भवेत् ॥

१२३ सामान्यार्थसमुत्थाने विभागस्तु समः स्मृतः ।
अनेकपितृकाणां तु पितृतो भागकल्पना ॥

## TOPIC 20: PARTITION OF INHERITANCE

If the father carries out the partition, he may partition shares among his sons as he pleases. He may either present to the eldest son the preeminent share or make all his sons have equal shares. 118

If he gives them equal shares, then he should make his wives who have not been given any women's property by their husband or father-in-law also have equal shares.[47] 119

Should someone, being capable, not want anything, the partition should be carried out after giving him something or other. With respect to those who have been apportioned smaller and larger shares, the dharma is said to be instituted by the father.[48] 120

After their parents have passed on, the sons should divide the assets and the debts equally. After their mother has passed on, the daughters should divide equally what is left over after settling her debts; in the absence of daughters, her offspring. 121

Anything else that someone has acquired without using up the paternal property, as also a gift from a friend or a wedding present, do not belong to the heirs. 122

But when common property has been collectively enhanced, it is said, the partition should be carried out equally. When the children are from different fathers, however, their shares are determined according to the father. 123

१२४ भूर्या पितामहोपात्ता निबन्धो द्रव्यमेव वा।
तत्र स्यात्सदृशं स्वाम्यं पितुः पुत्रस्य चोभयोः॥

१२५ विभक्तेषु सुतो जातः सवर्णायां विभागभाक्।
दृश्याद्वा तद्विभागः स्यादायव्ययविशोधितात्॥

१२६ क्रमादभ्यागतं द्रव्यं हृतमभ्युद्धरेत यः।
दायादेभ्यो न तद्दद्याद्विद्यया लब्धमेव च[२१]॥

१२७ पितृभ्यां यस्य यद्दत्तं तत्तस्यैव धनं भवेत्।
पितुरूर्ध्वं विभजतां माताप्यंशं समाप्नुयात्[२२]॥

१२८ असंस्कृतास्तु संस्कार्या भ्रातृभिः पूर्वसंस्कृतैः।
भगिन्यश्च निजादंशाद्दत्त्वांशं तु तुरीयकम्॥

१२९ चतुस्त्रिद्व्येकभागीना वर्णशो ब्राह्मणात्मजाः।
क्षत्रजास्त्रिद्व्येकभागा वैश्यजौ द्व्येकभागिनौ॥

१३० अन्योन्यापहृतं द्रव्यं विभक्तैर्यत्तु दृश्यते।
तत्पुनस्ते समैरंशैर्विभजेरन्निति स्थितिः॥

१३१ अपुत्रेण परक्षेत्रे नियोगोत्पादितः सुतः।
उभयोरप्यसौ रिक्थी पिण्डदाता च धर्मतः॥

When a piece of land—or even an endowment or chattel— had been acquired by the grandfather, both the father and the son have equal rights of ownership in it. 124

If, even after partition has been carried out, a son is born from a wife of the same class, he is entitled to a share; alternatively, his share comes from the visible assets after adjusting for income and expenditure. 125

When someone recovers chattel that had come down the generations but had been stolen, he is not obliged to give it to the heirs; so also what someone has acquired through learning.[49] 126

Whatever property the parents give to someone belongs exclusively to him. When they partition the estate after the passing of the father, the mother also should receive a share.[50] 127

Brothers who are already married, however, should perform the marriages of their unmarried brothers and sisters, each contributing a quarter from his share of the inheritance for that purpose. 128

Shares of sons born to a Brahman are four, three, two, and one, according to their class; to a Kshatriya, three, two, or one; and to a Vaishya, two or one.[51] 129

When chattel that had been taken away by one or the other is discovered by them after the partition, however, it should be partitioned again into equal shares—that is the rule. 130

When a man without a son fathers a son on another man's wife according to the rule of levirate, according to dharma that son is the heir of both and offers rice balls to both.[52] 131

१३२ औरसो धर्मपत्नीजस्तत्समः पुत्रिकासुतः।
क्षेत्रजः क्षेत्रजातस्तु सगोत्रेणेतरेण वा॥

१३३ गृहे प्रच्छन्न उत्पन्नो गूढजस्तु सुतो मतः।
कानीनः कन्यकाजातो मातामहसुतो मतः॥

१३४ अक्षतायां क्षतायां वा जातः पौनर्भवः सुतः।
दद्यान्माता पिता वा यं स पुत्रो दत्तको भवेत्॥

१३५ क्रीतस्तु ताभ्यां विक्रीतः कृत्रिमः स्यात्स्वयंकृतः।
दत्तात्मा तु स्वयंदत्तो गर्भे विन्नः सहोढजः॥

१३६ उत्सृष्टो गृह्यते यस्तु सोऽपविद्धो भवेत्सुतः।
पिण्डदोंऽशहरश्चैषां पूर्वाभावे परः परः॥

१३७ सजातीयेष्वयं प्रोक्तस्तनयेषु मया विधिः।
जातोऽपि दास्यां शूद्रेण कामतोंऽशहरो भवेत्॥

A natural son is one born to someone's wife married according to dharma, while a son of a female son is equal to him. A son begotten on the wife, however, is one fathered on someone's wife by a man belonging to his own lineage or by another man.[53] 132

A son born in secret is said to be one born secretly in the house. A son born to an unmarried woman is one born to a girl before marriage, and he is viewed as the son of his maternal grandfather. 133

A son born to a remarried woman is one born to a woman who remarries after losing her virginity or while still a virgin. A son given in adoption is one given away by his mother or father. 134

A purchased son is one who is sold by those two. A constituted son is one whom he himself installs as his son. A son given in adoption by himself is one who gives himself on his own. A son received with marriage is one who was already conceived when she married. 135

When someone takes in a boy who has been abandoned, he becomes a son adopted after being abandoned. In the absence of each listed earlier, each subsequent one performs the ancestral offering and partakes of a share in the inheritance. 136

I have declared this rule with reference to children belonging to the same caste. Even a son fathered by a Shudra through a slave woman may receive a share of the inheritance at the pleasure of the father.[54] 137

१३८ मृते पितरि कुर्युस्तं भ्रातरस्त्वर्धभागिनम् ।
अभ्रातृको हरेत्सर्वं दुहितॄणां सुतादृते ॥

१३९ पत्नी दुहितरश्चैव पितरौ भ्रातरस्तथा ।
तत्सुता गोत्रजो बन्धुः शिष्यः सब्रह्मचारिणः ॥

१४० एषामभावे पूर्वस्य धनभागुत्तरोत्तरः ।
स्वर्यातस्य ह्यपुत्रस्य सर्ववर्णेष्वयं विधिः ॥

१४१ वानप्रस्थयतिब्रह्मचारिणां रिक्थभागिनः ।
क्रमेणाचार्यसच्छिष्यधर्मभ्रात्रेकतीर्थिनः ॥

१४२ संसृष्टिनस्तु संसृष्टी सोदरस्य च सोदरः ।
दद्याच्चापहरेच्चांशं जातस्य च मृतस्य च ॥

१४३ अन्योदर्यस्य संसृष्टी नान्योदर्यो धनं हरेत् ।
असंसृष्ट्यपि चादद्यात्सोदर्यो नान्यमातृजः[२३] ॥

१४४ पतितस्तत्सुतः क्लीबः पङ्गुरुन्मत्तको जडः ।
अन्धोऽचिकित्स्यरोगी च भर्तव्यास्तु निरंशकाः ॥

When the father has died, however, the brothers should give him half a share. If he has no brothers, he may take the entire inheritance, so long as the daughters do not have a son. 138

Wife, daughters, parents, brothers, their sons, a person of the same lineage, maternal relative, pupil, and fellow student—among these, in the absence of each listed earlier, each listed later inherits the estate of someone who has died sonless. This is the rule for all social classes. 139-140

The heirs to the estate of forest hermits, ascetics, and Vedic students are in due order: teacher, virtuous pupil, spiritual brother, and someone belonging to one's own order.[55] 141

A reunited coparcener—or a uterine brother—should give the ancestral share to a fellow coparcener—or to his uterine brother—when he is born, and he should take the ancestral share of a fellow coparcener—or of his uterine brother—when he dies. 142

A reunited coparcener who is not a uterine brother should not take the estate of a non-uterine brother; even a non-reunited coparcener who is a uterine brother may take that estate, but not a brother born from a different mother.[56] 143

A man fallen from his caste; a son of such a man; and a man who is impotent, lame, mad, mentally incompetent, blind, or afflicted with an incurable disease do not receive a share of the inheritance but should be maintained. 144

१४५ औरसक्षेत्रजास्त्वेषां निर्दोषा भागहारिणः ।
सुताश्चैषां प्रभर्तव्या यावद्वै भर्तृसात्कृताः ॥

१४६ अपुत्रा योषितश्चैषां भर्तव्याः साधुवृत्तयः ।
निर्वास्या व्यभिचारिण्यः प्रतिकूलास्तथैव च ॥

१४७ पितृमातृपतिभ्रातृदत्तमध्यग्न्युपागतम् ।
आधिवेदनिकं चैव स्त्रीधनं परिकीर्तितम्[२४] ॥

१४८ बन्धुदत्तं तथा शुल्कमन्वाधेयकमेव च ।
अप्रजायामतीतायां बान्धवास्तदवाप्नुयुः ॥

१४९ अप्रजस्त्रीधनं भर्तुर्ब्राह्मादिषु चतुर्ष्वपि ।
दुहितॄणां प्रसूता चेच्छेषेषु पितृगामि तत् ॥

१५० दत्त्वा कन्यां हरन्दण्ड्यो व्ययं दाप्यश्च सोदयम् ।
मृतायां दत्तमादद्यात्परिशोध्योभयव्ययम् ॥

१५१ दुर्भिक्षे धर्मकार्ये च व्याधौ संप्रतिरोधके ।
गृहीतं स्त्रीधनं भर्ता न स्त्रियै दातुमर्हति ॥

A natural son of theirs and a son begotten on the wife of theirs, however, are entitled to receive shares of the inheritance as long as they are free from those defects. And their daughters should be provided maintenance until husbands to provide for them have been found. 145

Further, their sonless wives should be maintained if they are of good conduct, while those who are licentious or cantankerous should be expelled. 146

What is given to her by her father, mother, husband, or brothers; what she receives at the nuptial fire; and compensation for supersession—that is declared to be women's property.[57] 147

When a woman dies without offspring, her cognate relatives obtain what she was given by her cognate relatives, as also the bride-price and what she received subsequent to her marriage. 148

The property of a woman without offspring goes to her husband in the four kinds of marriage beginning with Brahma. If she has offspring, it goes to her daughters. In the other kinds of marriage, it goes to her father.[58] 149

When someone gives a girl in marriage and then takes her back, he should be fined and made to pay back the expenses with interest. If she dies, the groom may take back what he gave after subtracting the expenses incurred by both parties. 150

When a husband takes his wife's women's property during a time of famine, to perform a religious rite, during a sickness, or when he is under confinement, he is not obliged to return it to her. 151

१५२ अधिविन्नस्त्रियै दद्यादाधिवेदनिकं समम् ।
न दत्तं स्त्रीधनं यस्या दत्ते त्वर्धं प्रकीर्तितम् ॥

१५३ विभागनिह्नवे ज्ञातिबन्धुसाक्ष्यभिलेखितैः ।
विभागभावनादेयगृहक्षेत्रकयौतकैः ॥

॥ इति दायविभागप्रकरणम् ॥

## ॥ अथ सीमाविवादप्रकरणम् ॥

१५४ सीम्नो विवादे क्षेत्रस्य सामन्ताः स्थविरा गणाः ।
गोपाः सीम्नः कृषाणोऽन्ये सर्वे च वनगोचराः ॥

१५५ नयेयुरेते सीमान्तं स्थलाङ्गारतुषद्रुमैः ।
सेतुवल्मीकनिम्नास्थिचैत्याद्यैरुपलक्षितम् ॥

१५६ सामन्ता वा समग्रामाश्चत्वारोऽष्टौ दशाथ वा ।
रक्तस्रग्वसनाः सीमां नयेयुः क्षितिधारिणः ॥

He should give to the wife who is being superseded compensation for supersession equal to the sum spent on the supersession, if she has not been given any women's property; if she has been given it, however, half the above amount is prescribed. 152

When someone denies that a partition has taken place, the proof of partition is based on paternal and maternal relatives, witnesses, and documents, as well as on the receipt of property and on separately held houses and fields. 153

## TOPIC 21: BOUNDARY DISPUTES

When there is a dispute regarding a boundary of a field, neighbors, elderly people, persons from an association, herdsmen, other farmers near the boundary, and all men roaming in the forests should ascertain the boundary revealed by mounds, charcoal, chaff, and trees, and by dikes, anthills, trenches, bones, shrines, and the like. 154–155

Alternatively, neighbors or people of the same village—four, eight, or ten in number, wearing red garlands and clothes, and putting earth on their heads—should ascertain the boundary. 156

१५७ अनृते तु पृथग्दण्ड्या राज्ञा मध्यमसाहसम् ।
अभावे ज्ञातृचिह्नानां राजा सीम्नः प्रवर्तिता ॥

१५८ आरामायतनग्रामनिपानोद्यानवेश्मसु ।
एष एव विधिर्ज्ञेयो वर्षाम्बुप्रवहेषु च ॥

१५९ मर्यादायाः प्रभेदे च क्षेत्रस्य हरणे तथा ।
सीमातिक्रमणे दण्डा ह्यधमोत्तममध्यमाः[२५] ॥

१६० न निषेध्योऽल्पबाधस्तु सेतुः कल्याणकारकः ।
परभूमिं हरेत्कूपः स्वल्पक्षेत्रो बहूदकः ॥

१६१ स्वामिने योऽनिवेद्यैव क्षेत्रे सेतुं प्रकल्पयेत् ।
उत्पन्ने स्वामिनो भोगस्तदभावे महीपतेः ॥

१६२ फालाहतमपि क्षेत्रं यो न कुर्यान्न कारयेत् ।
तं प्रदाप्याकृष्टशदं क्षेत्रमन्येन कारयेत् ॥

॥ इति सीमाविवादप्रकरणम् ॥

If they are untruthful, however, the king should punish them individually with the middle seizure-fine.[59] In the absence of people who know the boundary or of boundary markers, the king settles the boundary. 157

One should know that the very same rule applies to groves, shrines, villages, reservoirs, parks, and houses, as well as to drains for rainwater.[60] 158

For demolishing a border, for seizing a field, and for encroaching on a boundary, the punishments are the lowest, highest, and middle seizure-fines, respectively.[61] 159

An irrigation work causing a small inconvenience, however, but producing exceptional benefits should not be blocked; a well may encroach on someone else's land, as it occupies a small piece of land but yields a lot of water. 160

Should someone build an irrigation project in a field without ever notifying its owner, its yield is enjoyed by the owner or, in his absence, by the king. 161

When a man does not cultivate or get someone to cultivate a field even though it has been plowed, he should make the man compensate the harvest lost as a result of his failure to cultivate and get it cultivated by another person. 162

## ॥ अथ स्वामिपालविवादप्रकरणम् ॥

१६३ माषानष्टौ तु महिषी सस्यघातस्य कारिणी ।
दण्डनीया तदर्धं तु गौस्तदर्धमजाविकम् ॥

१६४ भक्षयित्वोपविष्टानां द्विगुणोऽवसतां दमः ।
सममेषां विवीतेऽपि खरोष्ट्रं महिषीसमम्[२६] ॥

१६५ यावत्सस्यं विनश्येत तावत्क्षेत्री फलं लभेत् ।
पालस्ताड्येत गोमी तु पूर्वोक्तं दण्डमर्हति ॥

१६६ पथिग्रामविवीतान्तक्षेत्रे दोषो न विद्यते ।
अकामतः कामकारे चोरवद्दण्डमर्हति ॥

१६७ महोक्षोत्सृष्टपशवः सूतिकागन्तुकी च गौ ।
पालो येषां च ते मोच्या दैवराजपरिप्लुताः[२७] ॥

१६८ यथार्पितान्पशून्गोपः सायं प्रत्यर्पयेत्तथा ।
प्रमादमृतनष्टांश्च प्रदाप्यः कृतवेतनः ॥

१६९ पालदोषविनाशे तु पाले दण्डो विधीयते ।
अर्धत्रयोदशपणः स्वामिने धनमेव च ॥

## TOPIC 22: DISPUTES BETWEEN OWNERS AND HERDSMEN

For a she-buffalo destroying a crop, the fine is eight *māṣas;* for a cow, half that amount; and for a goat or sheep, half the latter amount. 163

When they lie down after eating but do not abide there, the fine is doubled. The same fines apply when they do so also in a pasture. The fine for a donkey and a camel is the same as for a she-buffalo.[62] 164

The owner of the field should receive as much compensation as the amount of the crop that was destroyed. The herdsman should be beaten, while the owner of the cattle is assessed the fine given above. 165

There is no fault if it happens unintentionally in a field located at the edge of a road, village, or pastureland. If it is done intentionally, he ought to be punished like a thief. 166

Stud bulls, ritually released cattle, a cow that has just delivered, a stray cow, and ones whose herdsman has been hounded by fate or the king should be set free.[63] 167

A herdsman should return in the evening the animals in the same condition as they were handed over to him. If he receives wages, he should be made to pay compensation for any that die or are lost due to his negligence. 168

If they are lost due to the fault of the herdsman, however, a fine of thirteen and a half *paṇas* is prescribed, as also the payment of their value to the owner. 169

१७० ग्रामेच्छया गोप्रचारभूमी राजवशेन वा।
द्विजस्तृणैधपुष्पाणि सर्वतः स्ववदाहरेत्[२८] ॥
१७१ धनुःशतं परीणाहो ग्रामक्षेत्रान्तरं भवेत्।
द्वे शते कर्वटस्य स्यान्नगरस्य चतुःशतम्॥

॥ इति स्वामिपालविवादप्रकरणम्॥

## ॥ अथास्वामिविक्रयप्रकरणम्॥

१७२ स्वं लभेतान्यविक्रीतं क्रेतुर्दोषोऽप्रकाशिते।
हीनाद्रहो हीनमूल्ये वेलाहीने च तस्करः॥
१७३ नष्टापहृतमासाद्य हर्तारं ग्राहयेन्नरम्।
देशकालातिपत्तौ वा गृहीत्वा स्वयमर्पयेत्॥
१७४ विक्रेतुर्दर्शनाच्छुद्धिः स्वामी द्रव्यं नृपो दमम्।
क्रेता मूल्यमवाप्नोति तस्माद्यस्तत्र विक्रयी॥

Land for grazing cattle is established according to the wish of the village or the order of the king. A twice-born man may gather grass, firewood, and flowers from anywhere as if they were his own.[64] 170

An open patch of land one hundred "bows" in extent should be left between a village and cultivated fields; two hundred in the case of a town; and four hundred in the case of a city.[65] 171

## TOPIC 23: SALE WITHOUT OWNERSHIP

A person gets back his own property when it was sold by someone else. The guilt falls on the buyer when the purchase was not made in the open. If it was purchased from a lowly person, in secret, for a very low price, or at an unusual time, he is a thief. 172

When someone discovers an article of his that has been lost or stolen, he should have the man who took it arrested. Alternatively, if the place and time make that infeasible, he should arrest the man himself and hand him over. 173

That man is cleared by pointing out the seller. The owner gets his property, the king the fine, and the buyer the price he paid, from the man who sold it. 174

१७५ आगमेनोपभोगेन नष्टं भाव्यमतोऽन्यथा।
पञ्चबन्धो दमस्तत्र राज्ञस्तेनाप्यभाविते॥

१७६ हृतं प्रनष्टं यो द्रव्यं परहस्तादवाप्नुयात्।
अनिवेद्य नृपे दण्ड्यः स तु षण्णवतिं पणान्॥

१७७ शौल्किकैः स्थानपालैर्वा नष्टापहृतमाहृतम्।
अर्वाक्संवत्सरात्स्वामी लभेत परतो नृपः॥

१७८ पणानेकशफे दद्याच्चतुरः पञ्च मानुषे।
महिषोष्ट्रगवां द्वौ द्वौ पादं पादमजाविके॥

॥ इत्यस्वामिविक्रयप्रकरणम्॥

## ॥ अथ दत्ताप्रदानिकप्रकरणम्॥

१७९ स्वकुटुम्बाविरोधेन देयं दारसुतादृते।
नान्वये सति सर्वस्वं देयं यच्चान्यसंश्रितम्[२१]॥

१८० प्रतिग्रहः प्रकाशः स्यात्स्थावरस्य विशेषतः।
देयं प्रतिश्रुतं चैव दत्त्वा नापहरेत्पुनः॥

॥ इति दत्ताप्रदानिकप्रकरणम्॥

The claimant should prove his ownership of the lost property by means of legal title or possession; otherwise he is fined one-fifth of its value. If the other man also cannot prove his ownership, the property goes to the king. 175

When a man grabs a property of his that had been stolen or lost from the hand of someone else without informing the king, he should be fined ninety-six *paṇas*. 176

When a lost or stolen property has been seized by customs officials or police officers, the owner may claim it within one year; after that it goes to the king. 177

He should pay four *paṇas* for a single-hoofed animal; five for a human being; two each for a buffalo, camel, and cow; and a quarter *paṇa* each for a goat and sheep.[66] 178

## TOPIC 24: NON-DELIVERY OF GIFTS

Without detriment to his own family, he may give a gift with the exception of wife and sons. He may not give all his possessions if he has offspring, or what is jointly held with someone else.[67] 179

The acceptance of a gift should be made in public, especially that of immovable property; what has been promised must indeed be given; and after giving a gift one must not take it back. 180

## ॥ अथ क्रीतानुशयप्रकरणम् ॥

१८१ दशैकपञ्चसप्ताहमासत्र्यहार्धमासिकम् ।
बीजायोवाह्यरत्नस्त्रीदोह्यपुंसां परीक्षणम् ॥

१८२ अग्नौ सुवर्णमक्षीणं द्विपलं रजते शतम् ।
अष्टौ तु त्रपुसीसे च ताम्रे पञ्च दशायसि ॥

१८३ शते दशपला वृद्धिरौर्णे कार्पासिके तथा ।
मध्ये पञ्चपला हानिः सूक्ष्मे तु त्रिपला मता[३०] ॥

१८४ चार्मिके रोमबद्धे च त्रिंशद्भागः क्षयो मतः ।
न क्षयो न च वृद्धिः स्यात्कौशेये वाल्कले तथा ॥

१८५ देशं कालं च भोगं च ज्ञात्वा नष्टे बलाबलम् ।
द्रव्याणां कुशला ब्रूयुर्यत्तद्दाप्यमसंशयम् ॥

॥ इति क्रीतानुशयप्रकरणम् ॥

## TOPIC 25: CANCELLATION OF A PURCHASE

Seeds, iron, beasts of burden, gems, women, milch cattle, and men may be examined for ten days, one day, five days, seven days, one month, three days, and a fortnight, respectively. 181

When placed in fire, gold suffers no loss; the loss is two *palas* per hundred for silver, eight for tin and lead, five for copper, and ten for iron.[68] 182

The increase is ten *palas* per hundred for wool, as also for cotton; five *palas* less than that when they are medium thick; and three *palas* when they are fine.[69] 183

In the case of cloth made of skin or woven hair, one-thirtieth is considered the loss. In the case of cloth made of *kauśeya* silk or bark there is neither a loss nor an increase.[70] 184

Whatever experts of the products determine after examining the place, the time, and the use, as also the relative worth of the wasted product, the man should be forced to recompense that much without a doubt. 185

## ॥ अथाभ्युपेत्याशुश्रूषाप्रकरणम् ॥

१८६ बलाद्दासीकृतश्चोरैर्विक्रीतश्चापि मुच्यते ।
स्वामिप्राणप्रदो भाक्तस्तत्त्यागान्निष्क्रयादपि ॥

१८७ प्रव्रज्यावसितो राज्ञो दास आमरणान्तिकः ।
वर्णानामानुलोम्येन दास्यं न प्रतिलोमतः ॥

१८८ कृतशिल्पोऽपि निवसेत्कृतं कालं गुरोर्गृहे ।
अन्तेवासी गुरुप्राप्तभोजनस्तत्फलप्रदः ॥

॥ इत्यभ्युपेत्याशुश्रूषाप्रकरणम् ॥

## ॥ अथ संविद्व्यतिक्रमप्रकरणम् ॥

१८९ राजा कृत्वा पुरे स्थानं ब्राह्मणान्न्यस्य तत्र तु ।
त्रैविद्यं वृत्तिमद्ब्रूयात् स्वधर्मः पाल्यतामिति ॥

१९० निजधर्माविरोधेन यस्तु सामयिको भवेत् ।
सोऽपि यत्नेन संरक्ष्यो धर्मो राजकृतश्च यः ॥

## TOPIC 26: BREACH OF CONTRACT FOR SERVICE

Someone who has been made a slave by force and one who has been sold by thieves is to be freed, as also someone who saves the life of his owner. One who becomes a slave for the sake of food is freed by giving that up, as also by paying a ransom. 186

An apostate from renunciation becomes a slave of the king until his death. Slavery takes place in the direct order of social classes, not in the inverse order. 187

Even after he has mastered the craft, an apprentice must live in the teacher's house during the contracted period, receiving his meals from the teacher and giving him what he earns from his craft. 188

## TOPIC 27: BREACH OF CONTRACT

The king, however, after constructing a residence in his fortified city and locating Brahmans in it as a corporate body of scholars of the triple Veda provided with maintenance, should tell them: "Observe the dharma specific to you." 189

A dharma based on agreements that do not violate the dharma specific to oneself should also be observed assiduously, as also a dharma proclaimed by the king. 190

१९१ गणद्रव्यं हरेद्यस्तु संविदं लङ्घयेच्च यः।
सर्वस्वहरणं कृत्वा तं राष्ट्राद्विप्रवासयेत्॥

१९२ कर्तव्यं वचनं सर्वैः समूहहितवादिनः।
यस्तत्र विपरीतः स्यात्स दाप्यः प्रथमं दमम्॥

१९३ समूहकार्य आयातान्कृतकार्यान्विसर्जयेत्।
स दानमानसत्कारैः पूजयित्वा महीपतिः॥

१९४ समूहकार्यप्रहितो यल्लभेत तदर्पयेत्।
एकादशगुणं दाप्यो यद्यसौ नार्पयेत्स्वयम्॥

१९५ वेदज्ञाः शुचयोऽलुब्धा भवेयुः कार्यचिन्तकाः।
कर्तव्यं वचनं तेषां समूहहितवादिनाम्॥

१९६ श्रेणिनैगमपाषण्डिगणानामप्ययं विधिः।
भेदं चैषां नृपो रक्षेत्पूर्ववृत्तिं च पालयेत्॥

॥ इति संविद्व्यतिक्रमप्रकरणम्॥

When a man steals the property of an association or breaks a contract, the king should expel him from his kingdom after confiscating all his property. 191

All should follow the order of the person authorized to declare what is beneficial to an organization. A person who acts contrary to it should be made to pay the lowest fine.[71] 192

The king should dismiss those who have come for business relating to an organization once they have completed their business, after he has honored them with gifts, honors, and hospitality. 193

A man sent on business relating to an organization should hand over whatever he may receive. If he does not hand it over on his own, he should be made to pay eleven times that amount. 194

Those who look after such business should be people who know the Veda and are honest and without greed. One should carry out the order of those who are authorized to declare what is beneficial to the organization. 195

That is the rule also for guilds, traders' unions, religious orders, and associations. The king should safeguard their unique characteristics and uphold their traditional modes of life. 196

## ॥ अथ वेतनादानप्रकरणम् ॥

१९७ गृहीतवेतनः कर्म त्यजन्द्विगुणमावहेत् ।
अगृहीते समं कार्यं भृत्यैः पाल्य उपस्करः[३१] ॥

१९८ दाप्यस्तु दशमं भागं वाणिज्यपशुसस्यतः ।
अनिश्चित्य भृतिं यस्तु कारयेत्स महीभृता ॥

१९९ देशं कालं च योऽतीयात्कर्म कुर्याच्च योऽन्यथा ।
तत्र स्यात्स्वामिनश्छन्दोऽधिकं देयं कृतेऽधिके ॥

२०० यो यावत्कुरुते कर्म तावत्तस्य तु वेतनम् ।
उभयोरप्यशाठ्यं चेच्छाठ्ये कुर्याद्यथाकृतम्[३२] ॥

२०१ अराजदैविकान्नष्टं भाण्डं दाप्यस्तु वाहकः ।
प्रस्थानविघ्नकर्ता च प्रदाप्यो द्विगुणां भृतिम् ॥

## TOPIC 28: NON-PAYMENT OF WAGES

When a man abandons his work after receiving the wages, he should return twice that amount. If he has not received the wages, he should give an equal amount and have the work completed. Servants should take good care of household utensils.[72] 197

When someone gets work done without fixing the remuneration, however, the king should make him pay one-tenth of his earnings from trade, animal husbandry, or agriculture. 198

When a man does not abide by the stipulated place and time or does the work in a different manner, there the employer may act according to his wish. A greater amount should be paid when a greater amount of work has been done. 199

A man's wages, however, are in direct proportion to the amount of work he does, so long as there is no cheating by either of the two parties. If there is cheating, one should stick to what has been stipulated.[73] 200

When goods are destroyed except by an act of the king or fate, however, the carrier should be made to pay compensation, while an employer who impedes the start of a journey should be made to pay twice the man's wages. 201

२०२ प्रक्रान्ते सप्तमं भागं चतुर्थं पथि संत्यजेत्।
भृतिमर्धपथे सर्वां प्रदाप्यस्त्याजकोऽपि च॥

॥ इति वेतनादानप्रकरणम्॥

## ॥ अथ द्यूतसमाह्वयप्रकरणम्॥

२०३ गलत्सभिकवृद्धिस्तु सभिकः पञ्चकं शतम्।
गृह्णीयाद्धूर्तकितवादितराद्दशकं शतम्[३३]॥

२०४ स सम्यक्पालितो दद्याद्राज्ञे भागं यथाकृतम्।
जितमुद्ग्राहयेज्जेत्रे दद्यात्सत्यवचाः क्षमी॥

२०५ प्राप्ते नृपतिभागे तु प्रसिद्धे धूर्तमण्डले।
जितं ससभिके स्थाने दापयेदन्यथा न तु॥

२०६ द्रष्टारो व्यवहाराणां साक्षिणश्च त एव हि।
राज्ञा सचिह्ना निर्वास्याः कूटाक्षोपधिदेविनः॥

२०७ द्यूतमेकमुखं कार्यं तस्करज्ञानकारणात्।
एष एव विधिर्ज्ञेयः प्राणिद्यूते समाह्वये॥

॥ इति द्यूतसमाह्वयप्रकरणम्॥

If he dismisses a worker once the journey has started, he should be made to pay one-seventh of his wages; and if he does so while on the road, one-fourth; and if he dismisses the worker half way along the road, the full wages. 202

## TOPIC 29: GAMBLING AND BETTING

The master of the gambling hall should take 5 percent from the winning gambler and 10 percent from the other as profit for providing the gambling supplies.[74] 203

As he is provided with proper protection, he should give to the king the portion as stipulated. Being truthful and patient, he should have the winnings seized and give them to the winner.[75] 204

Once the king's portion has been set aside, however, he should have the winnings handed over when they have been won in a well-known circle of gamblers and in a hall with a gambling master; but not otherwise. 205

For, they themselves adjudicate disputes and act as witnesses. The king should brand those who gamble with false dice or fraudulently and send them into exile. 206

Gambling should be carried out in one location for the purpose of detecting thieves. This same rule, one should know, applies to betting on competitions among living beings. 207

## ॥ अथ वाक्पारुष्यप्रकरणम् ॥

२०८ सत्यासत्यान्यथास्तोत्रैर्हीनाङ्गेन्द्रियरोगिणाम् ।
क्षेपं करोति चेद्दण्ड्यः पणानर्धत्रयोदश ॥

२०९ अभिगन्तासि भगिनीं मातरं वा तवेति हि ।
शपन्तं दापयेद्राजा पञ्चविंशतिकं दमम्[३४] ॥

२१० अर्धोऽधमेषु द्विगुणः परस्त्रीषूत्तमेषु च ।
दण्डप्रणयनं कार्यं वर्णजात्युत्तराधरम् ॥

२११ प्रतिलोमापवादेषु चतुस्त्रिद्विगुणा दमाः ।
वर्णान्त्येष्वानुलोम्येन तस्मादेवार्धहानतः[३५] ॥

२१२ बाहुग्रीवानेत्रसक्थिविनाशे वाचिके दमः ।
शत्यस्तदर्धिकः पादनासाकर्णकरादिषु ॥

२१३ अशक्तस्तु वदन्नेवं दण्डनीयः पणान्दश ।
तथा शक्तः प्रतिभुवं दाप्यः क्षेमाय तस्य तु ॥

## TOPIC 30: VERBAL ASSAULT

If someone insults people who lack a limb or a sense organ or are sick, whether truthfully or untruthfully, or with phony praise, he should be fined thirteen and a half *paṇas*. 208

When a man abuses someone, saying: "You are a mother-fucker *or* a sister-fucker!" the king should make him pay a fine of twenty-five.[76] 209

The fine is halved when the abuse is directed at inferiors and doubled when directed at wives of others and at superiors. The imposition of punishment should be carried out according to a person's superiority or inferiority in terms of social class and caste. 210

When reviling is done in the inverse order of social class, the fines for people of the lowest social class are increased by four, three, and two times, respectively. When it is done in the direct order of social class, those same fines are reduced progressively by one half.[77] 211

For saying that one would destroy a man's arms, neck, eyes, or thighs, the fine is one hundred *paṇas;* half that amount if it is said with regard to the feet, nose, ears, and hands. 212

When a man says it without the ability to carry it out, he should be fined ten *paṇas,* while a man who is capable of carrying it out should be forced to provide, in addition, a surety to insure the other's safety. 213

२१४ पतनीयकृते क्षेपे दण्ड्यो मध्यमसाहम् ।
उपपातकयुक्ते तु दाप्यः प्रथमसाहसम् ॥

२१५ त्रैविद्यनृपदेवानां क्षेप उत्तमसाहसः ।
मध्यमो जातिपूगानां प्रथमो ग्रामदेशयोः ॥

॥ इति वाक्पारुष्यप्रकरणम् ॥

## ॥ अथ दण्डपारुष्यप्रकरणम् ॥

२१६ असाक्षिकहते चिह्नैर्युक्तिभिश्चागमेन च ।
द्रष्टव्यो व्यवहारस्तु कूटचिह्नकृताद्भयात्[३६] ॥

२१७ भस्मपङ्करजःस्पर्शे दण्डो दशपणः स्मृतः ।
अमेध्यपार्ष्णिनिष्ठ्यूतस्पर्शने द्विगुणस्ततः ॥

२१८ समेष्वेवं परस्त्रीषु द्विगुणस्तूत्तमेषु च ।
हीनेष्वर्धदमो मोहमदादिभिरदण्डनम् ॥

When someone reviles another with regard to a sin causing loss of caste, he is to be punished with the middle seizure-fine; with regard to a secondary sin causing loss of caste, however, he should be made to pay the lowest seizure-fine.[78] 214

For reviling a scholar of the triple Veda, the king, or a god, the punishment is the highest seizure-fine; for reviling a caste or association, the middle; and for reviling a village or region, the lowest. 215

## TOPIC 31: PHYSICAL ASSAULT

In the case of a physical attack to which there are no witnesses, however, he should try the lawsuit using marks, reasoning, and reports, for fear that someone may have made the marks by himself.[79] 216

For smearing someone with ash, mud, or dust, the punishment is said to be ten *paṇas;* it is double that for smearing someone with filth, the heel, or spit. 217

The above applies when it is done to equals; the fine is doubled in the case of wives of others and superiors and halved in the case of inferiors. When someone does it through delusion, intoxication, and the like, he is not to be punished. 218

२१९ विप्रपीडाकरं छेद्यमङ्गमब्राह्मणस्य तु ।
उद्गूर्णे प्रथमो दण्डः स्पर्शने तु तदर्धिकः ॥

२२० उद्गूर्णे हस्तपादे तु दशविंशतिकौ दमौ ।
परस्परं तु सर्वेषां शस्त्रे मध्यमसाहसः ॥

२२१ पादकेशांशुककरालुञ्चनेषु पणान्दश ।
पीडाकर्षाञ्चनावेष्टपादाध्यासे शतं दमः[३७] ॥

२२२ शोणितेन विना कुर्वन्दुःखं काष्ठादिभिर्नरः ।
द्वात्रिंशतं पणान्दाप्यो द्विगुणं दर्शनेऽसृजः ॥

२२३ करपाददन्तभङ्गे छेदने कर्णनासयोः ।
मध्यो दण्डो व्रणोद्भेदे मृतकल्पहते तथा ॥

२२४ चेष्टाभोजनवाग्रोधे नेत्रादिप्रतिभेदने ।
कन्धराबाहुसक्थ्नां च भङ्ग उत्तमसाहसः[३८] ॥

२२५ एकं घ्नतां बहूनां तु यथोक्ताद्द्विगुणा दमाः ।
कलहापहृतं देयं दण्डश्च द्विगुणस्ततः ॥

The limb with which a non-Brahman causes injury to a Brahman, however, should be cut off. For menacing, the punishment is the lowest fine,[80] but for grabbing, half the latter amount. 219

For menacing with hand or foot, however, the fines are ten and twenty *paṇas,* respectively; for menacing each other with a weapon, the middle seizure-fine in the case of all.[81] 220

For yanking someone's feet, hair, clothes, or hands, the fine is ten *paṇas;* and for squeezing, dragging, twisting, squashing, and stomping with the foot, one hundred.[82] 221

When a man causes pain using a stick and the like without drawing blood, he should be made to pay thirty-two *paṇas;* double that amount if blood is spotted. 222

For breaking a hand, foot, or tooth, and for cutting an ear or nose, the punishment is the middle fine, as also for opening up a wound and for beating a man almost to the point of death. 223

For causing an impediment to movement, eating, and speech, for damaging an eye and the like, and for breaking the neck, arm, or thigh, the punishment is the highest seizure-fine.[83] 224

For many people beating up a single man, however, the fines are double those given above. When a man steals something during a brawl, he should return it, and he is fined double its value. 225

२२६ दुःखमुत्पादयेद्यस्तु स समुत्थानजं व्ययम् ।
दाप्यो दण्डं च यो यस्मिन्कलहे समुदाहृतः ॥

२२७ तारिकः स्थलजं शुल्कं गृह्णन्दाप्यः पणान्दश ।
ब्राह्मणः प्रातिवेश्यानामेतदेवानिमन्त्रणे ॥

२२८ अभिघाते तथा भेदे छेदे कुड्यावपातने ।
पणान्दाप्यः पञ्च दश विंशतिं तद्द्वयं तथा ॥

२२९ दुःखोत्पादि गृहे द्रव्यं क्षिपन्प्राणहरं तथा ।
षोडशाद्ये पणान्दाप्यो द्वितीये मध्यमं दमम् ॥

२३० दुःखेऽथ शोणितोत्पादे शाखाङ्गच्छेदने तथा ।
दण्डः क्षुद्रपशूनां स्याद्द्विपणप्रभृति क्रमात् ॥

२३१ लिङ्गस्य छेदने मृत्यौ मध्यमो मूल्यमेव च ।
महापशूनामेतेषु स्थानेषु द्विगुणा दमाः ॥

२३२ प्ररोहशाखिकाशाखास्कन्धसर्वविदारणे ।
उपजीव्यद्रुमाणां तु विंशतिद्विगुणा दमाः[३९] ॥

When a man causes pain to someone, however, he should be made to pay the expenses for recovery and the fine prescribed for such an offense within the context of a brawl. 226

When a ferryman charges a toll fixed for land carriage, he should be made to pay ten *paṇas.* A Brahman who fails to invite his immediate neighbors should be made to pay the same amount.[84] 227

For battering a wall of a house, for damaging it, and for a breach that would cause it to fall, a man should be made to pay five, ten, and twenty *paṇas,* respectively, as also the expenses for its repair.[85] 228

When a man throws an object that can cause pain into a house, as also one that can endanger life, he should be made to pay sixteen *paṇas* for the former and the middle fine for the latter. 229

In the case of small farm animals, for causing pain, for drawing blood, and for cutting a part or a limb, the punishment is in increments beginning with two *paṇas;* for cutting off the genitals and for causing death, the middle fine and also payment of its value. For doing these same things to large farm animals, the fines are doubled.[86] 230–231

For hacking sprigs, small branches, stout branches, the trunk, and the entirety of a tree providing benefits, however, the fines begin with twenty, and are doubled progressively.[87] 232

२३३ चैत्यश्मशानसीमान्तपुण्यस्थाने नृपालये।
जातद्रुमाणां द्विगुणा दमा वृक्षे च विश्रुते[४०] ॥

२३४ गुल्मगुच्छक्षुपलताप्रतानौषधिवीरुधाम्।
पूर्वस्मृतादर्धदण्डः स्थानेषूक्तेषु कृन्तने ॥

॥ इति दण्डपारुष्यप्रकरणम् ॥

## ॥ अथ साहसप्रकरणम् ॥

२३५ सान्वयप्रसभद्रव्यहरणात्साहसं स्मृतम्।
तन्मूल्याद्द्विगुणो दण्डो निह्नवे तु चतुर्गुणः[४१] ॥

२३६ यः साहसं कारयति स दाप्यो द्विगुणं दमम्।
यस्त्वेवमुक्त्वाहं दाता कारयेत्स चतुर्गुणम् ॥

२३७ अर्घ्याक्रोशातिक्रमकृद्भ्रातृभार्याप्रहारदः।
संदिष्टस्याप्रदाता च समुद्रगृहभेदकृत्[४२] ॥

२३८ सामन्तकुलिकादीनामपकारस्य कारकः।
पञ्चाशत्पणिको दण्ड एषामिति विनिश्चयः ॥

The fines are doubled in the case of trees growing in sanctuaries, cemeterics, boundaries, holy places, and the royal palace, as well as in the case of a prominent tree.[88] 233

For cutting bushes, shrubs, plants, creepers, vines, herbs, and vegetation in the places stated above, the fines are half the amounts previously given. 234

## TOPIC 32: VIOLENCE AND FORCIBLE SEIZURE

Forcible seizure is said to consist of seizing a property by force in the presence of the victim.[89] The fine for it is twice the value of the property; if the man denies it, however, it is four times the value.[90] 235

A man who gets someone to commit forcible seizure should be made to pay double the above fine. When a man gets someone to do it by saying: "I will compensate you," he should be made to pay four times that fine. 236

A man who reviles or defies a venerable person, who strokes his brother's wife, who does not deliver something as directed, who breaks into a sealed house, who does harmful things to neighbors, kinsmen, and the like—the fine for these people is fifty *paṇas*. That is the firm conclusion.[91] 237–238

२३९ स्वच्छन्दविधवागामी विक्रुष्टेऽनभिधावकः।
अकारणे च विक्रोष्टा चण्डालश्चोत्तमान्स्पृशन्॥

२४० शूद्रप्रव्रजितानां च दैवे पित्र्ये च भोजकः।
अयुक्तं शपथं कुर्वन्नयोग्यो योग्यकर्मकृत्॥

२४१ वृषक्षुद्रपशूनां च पुंस्त्वस्य प्रतिघातकः।
साधारणस्यापलापी दासीगर्भविनाशकृत्॥

२४२ पितापुत्रस्वसृभ्रातृदम्पत्याचार्यशिष्यकाः।
एषामपतितान्योन्यत्यागी च शतदण्डभाक्॥

२४३ वसानस्त्रीन्पणान्दाप्यो रजकस्तु परांशुकम्।
विक्रयावक्रयाधानयाचितेषु पणान्दश॥

२४४ पितापुत्रविरोधादौ साक्षिणां द्विशतो दमः।
सान्तरश्च तयोर्यः स्यात्तस्याप्यष्टशतो दमः॥

२४५ तुलाशासनमानानां कूटकृन्नाणकस्य च।
एभिश्च व्यवहर्ता यः स दाप्यो दममुत्तमम्॥

२४६ अकूटं कूटकं ब्रूते कूटं यश्चाप्यकूटकम्।
स नाणकपरीक्षी तु दाप्यः प्रथमसाहसम्[४३]॥

Someone who has sex with a widow living on her own, who does not rush to render aid when somebody cries out for help, and who cries out for help for no reason; a Chandala who touches persons of the uppermost-class;[92] 239

someone who feeds Shudra recluses at a divine or ancestral rite, who administers an unauthorized oath, who performs official acts without being an appointed official;[93] 240

someone who destroys the virility of small farm animals used for stud, who conceals common property, and who destroys the fetus of a female slave; 241

among a father and son, a sister and brother, a husband and wife, a teacher and pupil, the one who abandons the other when the latter has not fallen from caste—these are subject to a fine of 100 *paṇas.* 242

A washerman, however, who wears someone else's clothes should be made to pay three *paṇas,* whereas for selling, renting, pledging, or lending them he should be made to pay ten *paṇas.* 243

The fine for witnesses to disputes such as that between a father and son is two hundred *paṇas.* For a person who comes between them, moreover, the fine is eight hundred *paṇas.*[94] 244

A man who makes fake weights, edicts, and measures, and also coins, as well as a man who deals in them, should be made to pay the highest fine. 245

An examiner of coins, however, who declares as fake a coin that is not fake, and as not fake a coin that is fake, should be made to pay the lowest seizure-fine.[95] 246

२४७ भिषङ्मिथ्याचरन्दाप्यस्तिर्यक्षु प्रथमं दमम् ।
मानुषे मध्यमं दाप्य उत्तमं राजमानुषे ॥

२४८ अबन्ध्यं यश्च बध्नाति बन्ध्यं यश्च प्रमुञ्चति ।
अप्राप्तव्यवहारं च स दाप्यो दममुत्तमम् ॥

२४९ मानेन तुलया वापि योंऽशमष्टमकं हरेत् ।
दण्डं स दाप्यो द्विशतं वृद्धौ हानौ च कल्पितम् ॥

२५० भेषजस्नेहलवणगन्धधान्यगुलादिषु ।
पण्येषु हीनं क्षिपतः पणान्दाप्यस्तु षोडश ॥

२५१ मृच्चर्ममणिसूत्रायःकाष्ठवल्कलवाससाम् ।
अजातेर्जातिकरणाद्विक्रयेऽष्टगुणो दमः ॥

२५२ समुद्गपरिवर्तं च सारभाण्डं च कृत्रिमम् ।
आधानं विक्रयं वापि नयतो दण्डकल्पना ॥

२५३ भिन्ने पणे तु पञ्चाशत्पणे तु शतमुच्यते ।
द्विपणे द्विशतो दण्डो मूल्यवृद्धौ तु वृद्धिमान् ॥

२५४ संभूय कुर्वतामर्घं साबाधं कारुशिल्पिनाम् ।
अर्घस्य हानौ वृद्धौ वा साहस्रो दण्ड उच्यते[४४] ॥

A physician engaging in malpractice should be made to pay the lowest fine in the case of animals; the middle in the case of humans; and the highest in the case of royalty. 247

A man who confines someone who should not be confined, who releases a man who ought to be confined, and who confines a minor should be made to pay the highest fine. 248

Someone who defrauds one-eighth portion by means of weights and measures should be made to pay a fine of two hundred *paṇas,* adjusted according to the increase or decrease.[96] 249

When a man adulterates merchandise such as medicine, oil, salt, perfume, grain, and sugar with inferior substances, he should be made to pay sixteen *paṇas.* 250

For selling clay, skins, gems, thread, iron, wood, bark, and clothes by passing off what is not genuine as genuine, the fine is eight times their value. 251

For someone presenting for pawn or sale an article whose container has been switched or a fake article as an article of high value, a fine should be devised as follows: 252

a fine of fifty *paṇas* for something valued less than one *paṇa;* one hundred *paṇas* for something valued one *paṇa;* two hundred *paṇas* for something valued two *paṇas*—the fine increases proportionate to the increase in value. 253

For artisans and craftsmen who collude to fix a price that causes hardship, whether the price is lower or higher, the fine is said to be one thousand *paṇas.*[97] 254

२५५ संभूय वणिजां पण्यमनर्घेणोपरुन्धताम् ।
विक्रीणतां वा विहितो दण्ड उत्तमसाहसः ॥

२५६ राजनि स्थाप्यते योऽर्घः प्रत्यहं तेन विक्रयः ।
क्रयो वा निस्रवस्तस्माद्वणिजां लाभतः स्मृतः ॥

२५७ स्वदेशपण्ये तु शतं वणिग्गृह्णीत पञ्चकम् ।
दशकं पारदेश्ये तु यः सद्यः क्रयविक्रयी ॥

२५८ पण्यस्योपरि संस्थाप्य व्ययं पण्यसमुद्भवम् ।
अर्घोऽनुग्रहकृत्कार्यः क्रेतुर्विक्रेतुरेव च ॥

॥ इति साहसप्रकरणम् ॥

## ॥ अथ विक्रीयासंप्रदानप्रकरणम् ॥

२५९ गृहीतमूल्यं यः पण्यं क्रेतुर्नैव प्रयच्छति ।
सोदयं तस्य दाप्योऽसौ दिग्लाभं वा दिशां गते ॥

२६० विक्रीतमपि विक्रेयं पूर्वक्रेतर्यगृह्णति ।
हानिश्चेत्क्रेतृदोषेण क्रेतुरेव हि सा भवेत्[४५] ॥

२६१ राजदैवोपघातेन पण्ये दोषमुपागते ।
हानिर्विक्रेतुरेवासौ याचितस्याप्रयच्छतः ॥

For traders who collude in withholding commodities or selling them at an inordinate price, the highest seizure-fine is prescribed as punishment. 255

Sale or purchase is done every day at the price fixed in front of the king. The proceeds from that, it is stated, go to the traders as profit. 256

In the case of local commodities, however, a trader should realize a profit of 5 percent, and in the case of foreign commodities, 10 percent, so long as he buys and sells them immediately. 257

Adding to a commodity expenditures resulting from that commodity, he should fix a price that is favorable to both the buyer and the seller. 258

## TOPIC 33: NOT DELIVERING THE GOODS AFTER SALE

When a man fails to deliver a piece of merchandise after receiving its price, he should be forced to give it along with any profit or, if he has gone to a foreign country, along with the foreign profit he has made.[98] 259

Even something that has already been sold may be sold again when the first buyer does not take delivery of it. When a loss is incurred due to the fault of the buyer, it falls squarely on the buyer himself.[99] 260

When the merchandise suffers damage due to an act of the king or fate, the loss falls solely on the seller if he has failed to deliver it after a request had been made. 261

२६२ अन्यहस्ते तु विक्रीतं दुष्टं वादुष्टवद्यदि।
विक्रीयते दमस्तत्र तन्मूल्याद्द्विगुणो भवेत्॥

२६३ क्षयं वृद्धिं च वणिजा पण्यानां तु विजानता।
क्रीत्वा नानुशयः कार्यः कुर्वन्षड्भागदण्डभाक्[४६]॥

॥ इति विक्रीयासंप्रदानप्रकरणम्॥

## ॥ अथ सम्भूयसमुत्थानप्रकरणम्॥

२६४ समवायेन वणिजां लाभार्थं कर्म कुर्वताम्।
लाभालाभौ यथाद्रव्यं यथा वा संविदाकृता॥

२६५ प्रतिषिद्धमनादिष्टं प्रमादाद्यच्च नाशितम्।
स तद्दद्याद्विप्लवाच्च रक्षिता दशमांशभाक्॥

२६६ अर्घप्रक्षेपणाच्छुल्कं विंशद्भागं नृपो हरेत्।
व्यासिद्धं राजयोग्यं च विक्रीतं राजगामि तत्॥

If something that had been already sold is sold again to another person, or something with faults is sold as if it were without faults, however, the fine for it is twice the original price. 262

A trader who knows the decrease and increase in value of merchandise, however, should not rescind a purchase he has made. Should he do so, he is to be fined one-sixth portion of the price.[100] 263

## TOPIC 34: PARTNERSHIPS

When, for the sake of profits, traders carry on their work under an agreement, any gain or loss is calculated according to either the proportion of the material each has contributed or the provisions of the contract they have entered into. 264

When something forbidden or unauthorized is carried out, or when something is destroyed through negligence, the man responsible should pay compensation, whereas when a person safeguards something from a disaster, he receives one-tenth portion of it. 265

The king should take as customs duty one-twentieth part of the price that was fixed by him. When an embargoed commodity or one befitting a king is sold, the entire price goes to the king. 266

२६७ मिथ्या वदन्परीमाणं शुल्कस्थानादपाक्रमन् ।
दाप्यस्त्वष्टगुणं यश्च स व्याजक्रयविक्रयी ॥

२६८ देशान्तरगते प्रेते द्रव्यं दायादबान्धवाः ।
ज्ञातयो वा हरेयुस्तदागतैस्तैर्विना नृपः ॥

२६९ जिह्मं त्यजेयुर्निर्लाभमशक्तोऽन्येन कारयेत् ।
अनेन विधिना ख्यातमृत्विक्कर्षककर्मिणाम् ॥

॥ इति सम्भूयसमुत्थानप्रकरणम् ॥

## ॥ अथ स्तेयप्रकरणम् ॥

२७० ग्राहकैर्गृह्यते चोरो लोप्त्रेणाथ पदेन वा ।
पूर्वकर्मापराधाद्वा तथैवाशुद्धवासकः ॥

२७१ अन्येऽपि शङ्कया ग्राह्या जातिनामादिनिह्नवैः ।
द्यूतस्त्रीपानसक्ताश्च शुष्कभिन्नमुखस्वराः ॥

२७२ परद्रव्यगृहाणां च पृच्छका गूढचारिणः ।
निराया व्ययवन्तश्च विनष्टद्रव्यविक्रयाः ॥

A person who discloses a false quantity or evades the place for collecting customs duty, however, should be made to pay eight times the amount, as also someone who buys or sells fraudulently. 267

Should a man die while traveling in a foreign country, his relatives who are heirs or his paternal relatives should take his property, and if they fail to turn up, the king. 268

They should eschew duplicity and anything adversely affecting profit. Anyone who is unable to do his work should get it done by someone else. This rule explains the conduct of officiating priests, farmers, and workmen. 269

## TOPIC 35: THEFT

Policemen arrest a thief on the basis of stolen goods or footprints, or on account of crimes he has previously committed, as also when he resides in a house of ill repute. 270

Others also may be arrested on suspicion when they conceal their caste, name, and the like and when they are addicted to gambling, women, and drink, as also those whose voice and facial complexion become parched and transformed, who inquire about other people's property and houses, who move about clandestinely, who spend without having a source of income, and who sell lost property.[101] 271–272

२७३ गृहीतः शङ्कया चौर्ये नात्मानं चेद्विशोधयेत्।
दापयित्वा हृतं द्रव्यं चोरदण्डेन दण्डयेत्॥

२७४ चोरं प्रदाप्यापहृतं घातयेद्विविधैर्वधैः।
सचिह्नं ब्राह्मणं कृत्वा स्वराष्ट्राद्विप्रवासयेत्॥

२७५ घातितापहृते दोषो ग्रामभर्तुरनिर्गते।
विवीतभर्तुस्तु पथि चोरोद्धर्तुरवीतके॥

२७६ स्वसीम्नि दद्याद्ग्रामस्तु पदं वा यत्र गच्छति।
पञ्चग्रामी बहिः क्रोशाद्दशग्राम्यपि वा तथा[४७]॥

२७७ बन्दिग्राहांस्तथा वाजिकुञ्जराणां च हारिणः।
प्रसह्यघातिनश्चैव शूलमारोपयेन्नरान्॥

२७८ उत्क्षेपकग्रन्थिभेदौ करसंदंशहीनकौ।
कार्यौ द्वितीयेऽपराधे करपादैकहीनकौ॥

२७९ क्षुद्रमध्यमहाद्रव्यहरणे सारतो दमः।
देशकालवयःशक्ति संचिन्त्यं दण्डकर्मणि॥

If a man arrested on suspicion of theft does not establish his innocence, he should be forced to return the stolen property and be subjected to the punishment for theft. 273

After forcing a thief to return what he has stolen, he should execute him using various kinds of corporal mutilations, whereas he should brand a Brahman and expel him from his kingdom. 274

When anything is killed or stolen, unless it has gone outside, the fault lies with the administrator of the village; when it happens along a road, with the administrator of pasture lands; and when it happens in an area beyond the pasture lands, with the officer responsible for suppressing thieves.[102] 275

Within its own boundary, however, the village should give, or where the footprints lead; outside the plowed area, the five-village unit or else the ten-village unit.[103] 276

He should impale on a stake housebreakers, robbers of horses and elephants, and those who commit violent murders. 277

He should make a cloth thief and a cutpurse lose his hand and his thumb and forefinger, respectively; at the second offense, they should be made to lose one hand and one foot.[104] 278

For stealing a small, middling, and great article, the fine is proportionate to its value. In imposing punishments one should take into consideration the place, time, age, and ability.[105] 279

२८० भक्तावकाशाग्न्युदकमन्त्रोपकरणव्ययान् ।
दत्त्वा चोरस्य हन्तुर्वा जानतो दण्ड उत्तमः ॥

२८१ शस्त्रावपाते गर्भस्य पातने चोत्तमो दमः ।
उत्तमो वाधमो वापि पुरुषस्त्रीप्रमापणे ॥

२८२ विषप्रदं स्त्रियं चैव पुरुषघ्नीमगर्भिणीम् ।
सेतुभेदकरं चाप्सु शिलां बध्द्वा प्रवेशयेत्[४८] ॥

२८३ विषाग्निदां पतिगुरुनिजापत्यप्रमापणीम् ।
विकर्णकरनासौष्ठीं कृत्वा गोभिः प्रमापयेत् ॥

२८४ अविज्ञातहतस्याशु कलहं सुतबान्धवाः ।
प्रष्टव्या योषितो वास्य परपुंसि रताः पृथक् ॥

२८५ स्त्रीवृत्तिद्रव्यकामो वा केन वायं गतः सह ।
मृत्युदेशसमासन्नं पृच्छेद्वापि जनं शनैः ॥

२८६ क्षेत्रवेश्मग्रामवनविवीतखलदाहकाः ।
राजपत्न्यभिगामी च दग्धव्यास्तु कटाग्निना ॥

॥ इति स्तेयप्रकरणम् ॥

For someone who knowingly provides food, shelter, fire, water, advice, tools, and spending money to a thief or murderer, the punishment is the highest fine. 280

For striking with a weapon and for causing a miscarriage, the punishment is the highest fine; and for killing a man or a woman, the highest or the lowest fine. 281

He should tie a rock and dump in water someone who administers poison, a woman who kills a man—unless she is pregnant—and someone who breaks a dike.[106] 282

In the case of a woman who is a poisoner or arsonist, or who slays her husband or elder, or her own offspring, he should first cut off her ears, hands, nose, and lips and then get cattle to slay her. 283

In the case of a man who has died suddenly under mysterious circumstances, he should interrogate these separately: his sons and relatives regarding any altercation they may have had with him; his wives who may be in love with another man; and someone who may covet his wife, livelihood, or property. He should also question gently people in the vicinity of the place where he was murdered: "With whom did this man go?"[107] 284–285

Those who set fire to a field, house, village, forest, pasture, or threshing ground, and a man who has sex with a wife of the king, should be burnt with a straw fire.[108] 286

## ॥ अथ स्त्रीसंग्रहणप्रकरणम् ॥

२८७ पुमान् संग्रहणे ग्राह्यः केशाकेशि परस्त्रियाः ।
सद्यैर्वा कामजैश्चिह्नैः प्रतिपत्तौ द्वयोस्तथा ॥

२८८ सजातावुत्तमो दण्ड आनुलोम्ये तु मध्यमः ।
प्रातिलोम्ये वधः पुंसां स्त्रीणां नासादिकृन्तनम्[४९] ॥

२८९ नीवीस्तनप्रावरणनाभिकेशावमर्शनम् ।
अदेशकालसंभाषां सहावस्थानमेव च[५०] ॥

२९० स्त्री निषिद्धा शतं दण्ड्या कुर्वती द्विशतं पुमान् ।
अनिषेधे तयोर्दण्डो यथा संग्रहणे तथा[५१] ॥

२९१ अलंकृतां हरन्कन्यामुत्तमं त्वन्यथाधमम् ।
दण्डं दद्यात्सवर्णस्तु प्रातिलोम्ये वधः स्मृतः ॥

२९२ सकामास्वनुलोमासु न दोषस्त्वन्यथाधमः ।
दूषणे तु करच्छेद उत्तमायां वधस्तथा ॥

## TOPIC 36: SEXUAL CRIMES AGAINST WOMEN

A man should be arrested for a sexual offense when he is caught in intimate contact with someone else's wife, when there are recent bodily marks from lovemaking, and when there is admission from both. 287

When they are of the same caste, the punishment is the highest fine;[109] when they are in the direct order of class, the middle fine; and when they are in the inverse order of class, the man is executed, while the woman's nose and so forth are cut off.[110] 288

Touching the waist band, blouse, navel, or hair; carrying on a conversation at an inappropriate place or time; and lingering together—when, after being forbidden, a woman does this she should be fined one hundred *paṇas,* and the man two hundred; when there was no prohibition, the punishment is the same as for a sexual offense.[111] 289–290

When a man seizes a virgin who is adorned, he should pay the highest fine; otherwise, the lowest—if he is of the same class. When it is done in the inverse order of class, however, execution is prescribed.[112] 291

In the case of willing virgins in the direct order of class, however, there is no offense; otherwise, the lowest fine is assessed. If she is deflowered, however, his hand is cut off; in the case of a woman of the highest class, he is executed. 292

२९३ शतं स्त्री दूषणे दाप्या द्वे तु मिथ्याभिशंसिता ।
पशून्गच्छञ्छतं दाप्यो हीनस्त्रीं गां च मध्यमम् ॥

२९४ अवरुद्धासु दासीषु भुजिष्यासु तथैव च ।
गम्यास्वपि पुमान्दाप्यः पञ्चाशत्पणिकं दमम् ॥

२९५ प्रसह्य दास्यभिगमे दण्डो दशपणः स्मृतः ।
बहूनां यद्यकामासौ द्विर्द्वादशपणः पृथक्[५२] ॥

२९६ अयोनौ गच्छतो योषां पुरुषं चाभिमेहतः ।
द्विर्द्वादशपणो दण्डस्तथा प्रव्रजितागमे ॥

२९७ अन्त्याभिगमने त्वङ्क्य कबन्धेन प्रवासयेत् ।
शूद्रस्तथान्त्य एव स्यादन्त्यस्यार्यागमे वधः ॥

॥ इति स्त्रीसंग्रहणप्रकरणम् ॥

For deflowering, a woman should be made to pay one hundred *paṇas,* whereas someone who makes a false accusation with regard to it should be made to pay two hundred. A man who has sex with farm animals should be made to pay one hundred, whereas a man who has sex with a low-caste woman or a cow should be made to pay the middle fine. 293

In the case of female slaves who have been secured, as also those who are for exclusive enjoyment, even if they are women with whom sexual relations are permitted, the man should be made to pay a fine of fifty *paṇas.*[113] 294

When a man engages in sexual relations by force with a female slave, the fine is said to be ten *paṇas,* whereas when many men have sex with her while she is unwilling, each should be fined twenty-four *paṇas.*[114] 295

For having sex with a woman in a place other than the vagina and for ejaculating in a man, a man is fined twenty-four *paṇas,* as also for having sex with a female recluse. 296

When a man has sex with a lowest-born woman, however, after branding him with a headless trunk, he should send him into exile, whereas a Shudra becomes reduced to the very condition of a lowest-born. When a lowest-born man has sex with an Arya woman, he should be executed.[115] 297

## ॥ अथ प्रकीर्णकप्रकरणम् ॥

२९८ न्यूनमभ्यधिकं वापि लिखेद्यो राजशासनम् ।
पारदारिकचोरौ वा मुञ्चतो दण्ड उत्तमः ॥

२९९ अभक्ष्यैर्दूषयन्विप्रं दण्ड्य उत्तमसाहसम् ।
क्षत्रियं मध्यमं वैश्यं प्रथमं शूद्रमर्धिकम् ॥

३०० कूटस्वर्णव्यवहारी विमांसस्य च विक्रयी ।
त्र्यङ्गहीनास्तु कर्तव्या दाप्याश्चोत्तमसाहसम् ॥

३०१ चतुष्पादकृते दोषो नापेहीति प्रभाषतः ।
काष्ठलोष्टेषुपाषाणबाहुयुद्धकृते तथा[५३] ॥

३०२ छिन्ननास्येन यानेन तथा भग्नयुगेन च ।
पश्चाच्चैवापसरता हिंसिते स्वाम्यदोषभाक् ॥

३०३ शक्तोऽप्यमोक्षयन्स्वामी शृङ्गिणो दंष्ट्रिणस्तथा ।
प्रथमं साहसं दाप्यो विक्रुष्टे द्विगुणं तथा ॥

३०४ जारं चोरेत्यभिवदन्दाप्यः पञ्चशतं दमम् ।
उपजीव्य धनं मुञ्चंस्तदेवाष्टगुणीकृतम्[५४] ॥

## TOPIC 37: MISCELLANEOUS

For a person who writes a royal edict with omissions or additions, or who frees an adulterer or thief, the punishment is the highest fine.[116] 298

A person who defiles a Brahman with forbidden food should be punished with the highest seizure-fine; a Kshatriya, with the middle; a Vaishya, with the lowest; and a Shudra, with half the lowest. 299

A person who trades in fake gold and a person who sells unfit meat should be deprived of three limbs and made to pay the highest seizure-fine.[117] 300

A person does not incur any blame when a quadruped causes injury after he has shouted: "Get out!"; likewise when an injury is caused during a fight with a piece of wood, a clod, an arrow, a stone, or hands.[118] 301

When an injury is caused by a vehicle with a draught animal whose nose-string strap has been severed or whose yoke has broken, or which slides backwards, the owner does not incur any blame. 302

He should impose the lowest seizure-fine on an owner when he does not rescue a man from a horned or tusked animal of his even when he is capable; double that if the man called for help. 303

When someone calls out a paramour as "Thief!" he should be made to pay a fine of five hundred *paṇas,* while when he releases the man by taking money, the fine is increased eightfold.[119] 304

३०५ राज्ञोऽनिष्टप्रवक्तारं तस्यैवाक्रोशकं तथा।
तन्मन्त्रस्य च भेत्तारं छित्त्वा जिह्वां प्रवासयेत्॥

३०६ मृताङ्गलग्नविक्रेतुर्गुरोस्ताडयितुस्तथा।
राजयानासनारोढुर्दण्डो मध्यमसाहसः[५५]॥

३०७ द्विनेत्रभेदिनो राजद्विष्टादेशकृतस्तथा।
विप्रत्वेन च शूद्रस्य जीवतोऽष्टशतो दमः॥

३०८ दुर्दृष्टं तु पुनर्दृष्ट्वा व्यवहारं नृपेण तु।
सभ्याः सजयिनो दण्ड्या विवादाद्द्विगुणं पृथक्॥

३०९ यो मन्येताजितोऽस्मीति न्यायेनापि पराजितः।
तमागतं पुनर्जित्वा दापयेद्द्विगुणं दमम्॥

३१० राज्ञान्यायेन यो दण्डो गृहीतो वरुणाय तम्।
निवेद्य दद्याद्विप्रेभ्यः स्वयं त्रिंशद्गुणीकृतम्॥

॥ इति प्रकीर्णकप्रकरणम्॥

॥ इति याज्ञवल्कीये धर्मशास्त्रे व्यवहाराख्यो
द्वितीयोऽध्यायः॥

He should cut off the tongue and send into exile a man who speaks ill of the king, reviles him, or divulges his secret counsel.[120] 305

For someone who sells anything attached to the body of a dead person, who beats up his elder, or who gets onto the king's vehicle or seat, the punishment is the middle seizure-fine.[121] 306

For someone who shatters both eyes of a person or gives instructions inimical to the king, and for a Shudra living as a Brahman, the fine is eight hundred *paṇas.* 307

After subjecting a lawsuit that has been wrongly tried to a new trial, however, the king should punish individually the assessors along with the victorious party with a fine that is twice the amount in dispute. 308

When a man thinks, "I am not defeated," although he has been clearly defeated according to proper procedure, and he returns and is defeated again, he should be made to pay a double fine. 309

When the king takes a fine illegitimately, he should dedicate it to Varuna and give it to Brahmans after he has himself increased it to thirty times the original amount. 310

# प्रायश्चित्ताध्यायः

## ॥ अथाशौचप्रकरणम् ॥

१ ऊनद्विवर्षं निखनेन्न कुर्यादुदकं ततः ।
आ श्मशानादनुव्रज्य इतरो ज्ञातिभिर्मृतः ॥

२ यमसूक्तं तथा गाथा जपद्भिर्लौकिकाग्निना ।
स दग्धव्य उपेतश्चेदाहिताग्न्यावृतार्थवत् ॥

३ सप्तमाद्दशमाद्वापि ज्ञातयोऽभ्यवयन्त्यपः ।
अप नः शोशुचदघमनेन पितृदिङ्मुखाः ॥

४ एवं मातामहाचार्यप्रत्तानां चोदकक्रिया ।
कामोदकं सखिप्रत्तास्वस्रीयश्वशुरर्त्विजाम्[1] ॥

५ सकृत्प्रसिञ्चन्त्युदकं नामगोत्रेण वाग्यताः ।
न ब्रह्मचारिणः कुर्युरुदकं पतिता न च ॥

# 3 *Expiation*

## TOPIC 38: IMPURITY

One should bury anyone who is less than two years old and not offer water after that. When anyone different from that dies, the paternal relatives should follow him until the cemetery. 1

Reciting the Yama-hymn and the Yama-verses, they should cremate him with ordinary fire, but if he has undergone Vedic initiation, according to the procedure for a man who has consecrated the Vedic fires, using as much of that procedure as is pertinent.[1] 2

Until the seventh or the tenth, the paternal relatives should get into water facing the south and reciting: "Blazing away the bad for us, blaze wealth here, o Agni,—blazing away the bad for us."[2] 3

Likewise, water offerings should be made also for maternal grandfathers, teachers, and unmarried daughters, and optional water offerings for a friend, married daughter, son of a daughter, father-in-law, and officiating priest.[3] 4

With restrained speech, they sprinkle water once reciting the name and lineage. Vedic students should not make a water offering, nor should people who have fallen from their caste. 5

६ पाषण्डमाश्रिताः स्तेना भर्तृघ्न्यः कामगास्तथा ।
सुराप्य आत्मत्यागिन्यो नाशौचोदकभाजनाः[२] ॥

७ कृतोदकान्समुत्तीर्णान्मृदुशाद्वलसंस्थितान् ।
स्नातानपवदेयुस्तानितिहासैः पुरातनैः ॥

८ मानुष्ये कदलीस्तम्भनिःसारे सारमार्गणम् ।
करोति यः स संमूढो जलबुद्बुदसंनिभे ॥

९ पञ्चधा संभृतः कायो यदि पञ्चत्वमागतः ।
कर्मभिः स्वशरीरोत्थैस्तत्र का परिदेवना ॥

१० गन्त्री वसुमती नाशमुदधिर्दैवतानि च ।
फेनप्रख्यः कथं नाशं मर्त्यलोको न यास्यति ॥

११ श्लेष्माश्रु बान्धवैर्मुक्तं प्रेतो भुङ्क्ते यतोऽवशः ।
अतो न रोदितव्यं स्यात्क्रियाः कार्याः च शक्तितः ॥

१२ इति संचिन्त्य गच्छेयुर्गृहान्बालपुरोगमाः ।
विदश्य निम्बपत्राणि नियता द्वारि वेश्मनः ॥

१३ आचम्याथाग्निमुदकं गोमयं गौरसर्षपान् ।
प्रविशेयुः समालभ्य कृत्वाश्मनि पदं शनैः ॥

People who have joined a heretical sect; thieves; and women who kill their husbands, are promiscuous, drink liquor, or commit suicide—for these there is no period of impurity and they do not receive water offerings.[4] 6

When they have made the water offerings and come out and, after bathing, are seated on soft grass, they should console them with ancient historical narratives.[5] 7

"That person is totally deluded who seeks substance in the human state that is as without substance as the trunk of a banana tree and resembles a water bubble. 8

If the body, composed of five elements, is reduced in death to those five elements as a result of actions rising from his own body, why lament for it? 9

The earth is bound to perish, as also the ocean and the gods. So, how will the mortal world, resembling foam, not perish? 10

The newly deceased person is forced to consume the mucus and tears shed by the relatives. Therefore, you must not cry; but you must perform the rites according to your ability." 11

After reflecting in this manner, they should go to their houses placing the children at the front. They should chew neem leaves at the door of their residence while maintaining self-control. 12

Then, after sipping some water and touching fire, water, cow-dung, and white sesame seeds, they should enter placing a foot slowly on a stone. 13

१४ क्रीतलब्धाशिनो भूमौ शयीरंस्ते पृथक्पृथक् ।
पिण्डयज्ञावृता देयं प्रेतायान्नं दिनत्रयम् ॥

१५ जलमेकाहमाकाशे स्थाप्यं क्षीरं च मृन्मये ।
वैतानिकाश्रयाः कार्याः क्रियाश्च श्रुतिदर्शनात्[३] ॥

१६ प्रवेशनादिकं कर्म प्रेतसंस्पर्शिनामपि ।
इच्छतां तत्क्षणाच्छुद्धिः परेषां स्नानसंयमात् ॥

१७ आचार्योपाध्यायपितॄन्निर्हृत्यापि व्रती व्रती ।
स कटान्नं च नाश्नीयान्न च तैः सह संवसेत्[४] ॥

१८ दशरात्रं त्रिरात्रं वा शावमाशौचमुच्यते ।
ऊनद्विवर्षमुभयोः सूतकं मातुरेव हि ॥

१९ ब्राह्मणस्य दशाहं तु भवति प्रेतसूतकम् ।
क्षत्रस्य द्वादशाहानि विशां पञ्चदशैव वा[५] ॥

२० त्रिंशद्दिनानि शूद्रस्य प्रेतसूतकमुच्यते ।
अन्तरा जन्ममरणे शेषाहोभिर्विशुध्यति[६] ॥

Eating what they have bought or received, for three days they should sleep separately on the floor and offer food to the newly deceased person according to the procedure of the ritual offering of rice-balls. 14

For one day water and milk placed in an earthen pot should be hung above ground, and rites with the use of Vedic fires should be carried out, because they are enjoined in Vedic scriptures.[6] 15

The rites beginning with entering the house may be carried out, if they want to, also by those who have come into contact with the newly deceased. Others become pure immediately after taking a bath and maintaining self-control.[7] 16

A votary remains a votary even if he has carried his deceased teacher, tutor, or father, but he should not eat the food of those associated with the bier or stay with them.[8] 17

The period of impurity resulting from a corpse is said to last ten nights or three nights. The period of impurity from the death of someone less than two years affects both parents, while the period of impurity from childbirth affects only the mother.[9] 18

For a Brahman, however, the period of impurity resulting from a death lasts ten days, for a Kshatriya twelve days, and for a Vaishya fifteen days.[10] 19

For a Shudra the period of impurity resulting from a death is said to last thirty days. When there is a birth or death in the midst of that period, a person is purified after the remaining number of days.[11] 20

२१ गर्भस्रावे मासतुल्या निशाः शुद्धेस्तु कारणम् ।
प्रोषिते कालशेषः स्यात्पूर्णे दत्त्वोदकं शुचिः ॥

२२ अहस्त्वदत्तकन्यासु बालेषु च विशोधनम् ।
गुर्वन्तेवास्यनूचानमातुलश्रोत्रियेषु च ॥

२३ अनौरसेषु पुत्रेषु भार्यास्वन्यगतासु च ।
निवासराजनि तथा तदहः शुद्धिकारणम् ॥

२४ गोनृपब्रह्महतानामन्वक्षं चात्मघातिनाम् ।
प्रायानाशकशस्त्राग्निविषाद्यैरिच्छतां स्वयम् ॥

२५ महीपतीनां नाशौचं हतानां विद्युता तथा ।
गोब्राह्मणार्थे संग्रामे यस्य चेच्छति भूमिपः ॥

२६ ब्राह्मणेनानुगन्तव्यो न शूद्रो हि मृतः क्वचित् ।
अनुगम्याम्भसि स्नात्वा स्पृष्ट्वाग्निं घृतभुक्शुचिः[७] ॥

At a miscarriage, however, purification is brought about by the passage of the same number of nights as the months of pregnancy. When a person has died while abroad, it is brought about after the passage of the time remaining from the period of impurity; if that period has already elapsed, one becomes pure after making a water offering.[12] 21

Purification takes place after one day, however, in the case of unmarried girls and children, as well as in the case of teachers, apprentices, instructors, maternal uncles, and Vedic scholars. 22

Purification takes place that very day in the case of the following: sons other than the natural,[13] wives cohabiting with other men, and the king of the region where one lives. 23

Purification is instantaneous for those killed by a cow, the king, or a Brahman, as well as for those who deliberately kill themselves by means of the great journey, fasting, weapon, fire, poison, and the like.[14] 24

There is no period of impurity in the case of kings and people killed by lightning, for the sake of cows and Brahmans, and in a war, and for someone whom the king so wishes.[15] 25

A Brahman should never follow a deceased Shudra. Should he follow, he becomes pure by bathing in water, touching fire, and consuming ghee.[16] 26

२७ ऋत्विजां दीक्षितानां च याज्ञे कर्मणि कुर्वताम्।
सत्रिव्रतिब्रह्मचारिदातृब्रह्मविदां तथा॥

२८ दाने विवाहे यज्ञे च संग्रामे देशविप्लवे।
आपद्यपि च कष्टायां सद्यःशौचं विधीयते॥

२९ पित्रोस्तु सूतकं मातुस्तदसृग्दर्शनाद्ध्रुवम्।
तदहर्न प्रदुष्येत पूर्वेषां जन्मकारणात्॥

३० उदक्याशौचिभिः स्नायात्संस्पृष्टस्तैरुपस्पृशेत्।
अब्लिङ्गाभिर्जपेच्चैव सावित्रीं मनसा सकृत्॥

३१ कालोऽग्निः कर्म मृद्वायुर्मनो ज्ञानं तपो जलम्।
पश्चात्तापो निराहारः सर्वेऽमी शुद्धिहेतवः॥

३२ अकार्यकारिणां दानं वेगो नद्यास्तु शुद्धिकृत्।
शोध्यस्य मृच्च तोयं च संन्यासो वै द्विजन्मनाम्॥

३३ तपो वेदविदां क्षान्तिर्विदुषां वर्ष्मणो जलम्।
जपः प्रच्छन्नपापानां मनसः सत्यमुच्यते॥

For officiating priests and consecrated persons as they are engaged in performing a sacrificial rite; for those engaged in a sacrificial session; for votaries,[17] Vedic students, donors, and those who know Brahma; during gift giving, marriage, and sacrifice; during a war, a calamity affecting the region, and a dire emergency—immediate purification is prescribed. 27–28

Impurity from childbirth, however, affects the parents; it affects the mother durably, because it is her blood that is seen. On that day a person does not become impure, because the ancestors have taken birth.[18] 29

When someone is touched by a menstruating woman or a person in a period of impurity, he should bathe; and when touched by those who have been so touched, he should touch water, while softly reciting the formula: "Waters, you are refreshing..."[19] and mentally recite the *sāvitrī* verse once. 30

Time, fire, ritual, earth, wind, mind, knowledge, ascetic toil, water, repentance, and fasting—all these are means of purification. 31

Gift giving purifies those who do forbidden things; the current, a river; earth and water, what requires cleaning; and renunciation, twice-born people. 32

Ascetic toil is said to purify those who know the Veda; forbearance, the wise; water, the body; soft recitation, those who have committed secret sins; and truth, the mind. 33

३४ भूतात्मनस्तपोविद्ये बुद्धेर्ज्ञानं विशोधनम् ।
क्षेत्रज्ञस्येश्वरज्ञानाद्विशुद्धिः परमा मता ॥

॥ इत्याशौचप्रकरणम् ॥

## ॥ अथापद्धर्मप्रकरणम् ॥

३५ क्षात्रेण कर्मणा जीवेद्विशां वाप्यापदि द्विजः ।
निस्तीर्यार्थं तमुत्सृज्य पाव्यात्मानं न्यसेत्पथि ॥

३६ फलोपलक्षौमसोममनुष्यापूपवीरुधः ।
तिलौदनरसक्षारान्दधि क्षीरं घृतं जलम् ॥

३७ शस्त्रासवं मधूच्छिष्टं मधु लाक्षाथ बर्हिषः ।
मृच्चर्मपुष्पकुतपकेशतक्रविषैरकान्[८] ॥

३८ कौशेयनीलीलवणमांसैकशफहेतवः ।
शाकार्द्रौषधिपिण्याकतूलगन्धांस्तथैव च[९] ॥

३९ वैश्यवृत्त्यापि संजीवन्विक्रीणीत न कर्हिचित् ।
धर्मार्थं विक्रयं नेयास्तिला धान्येन तत्समाः ॥

Ascetic toil and knowledge purify the elemental self; and knowledge, the intellect. Knowledge of the Lord is considered the highest purification of the knower of the field.[20] 34

## TOPIC 39: DHARMA IN TIMES OF ADVERSITY

During a time of adversity a Brahman may procure a livelihood through the profession of a Kshatriya or even a Vaishya. When that time has passed, he should discard that wealth, purify himself, and set himself on the right path. 35

Fruits, precious stones, linen, *soma,* humans, cakes, plants, sesame seeds, cooked rice, juices, sweeteners, curd, milk, ghee, water, 36

weapons, intoxicants, bees' wax, honey, lac, holy grass, soil, skins, flowers, goat's wool blankets, hair, butter milk, poison, fish,[21] 37

silk, indigo, salt, meat, single-hoofed animals, lethal substances, vegetables, fresh herbs, asafetida, cotton, and perfumes[22]— 38

even while living according to the profession of Vaishyas, he should never sell these. For a ritual purpose, he may barter sesame seeds for an equivalent amount of grain. 39

४० लवणं तनया लाक्षा पतनीयानि विक्रये ।
पयो दधि च मद्यं च हीनवर्णकराणि तु[१०] ॥

४१ आपद्गतः संप्रगृह्णन्भुञ्जानो वा यतस्ततः ।
न लिप्येतैनसा विप्रो ज्वलनार्कसमो हि सः ॥

४२ कृषिः शिल्पं भृतिर्विद्या कुसीदं शकटं गिरिः ।
सेवानूपो नृपो भैक्षमापत्तौ जीवनानि तु ॥

४३ बुभुक्षितस्त्र्यहं स्थित्वा धनमब्राह्मणाद्धरेत् ।
प्रतिगृह्य तदाख्येयमभियुक्तेन धर्मतः[११] ॥

४४ तस्य वृत्तं कुलं शीलं श्रुतमध्ययनं सुतान् ।
ज्ञात्वा राजा कुटुम्बात्स्वाद्धर्म्यां वृत्तिं प्रकल्पयेत्[१२] ॥

॥ इत्यापद्धर्मप्रकरणम् ॥

## ॥ अथ वानप्रस्थधर्मप्रकरणम् ॥

४५ सुतविन्यस्तपत्नीकस्तया वानुगतो वने ।
वानप्रस्थो ब्रह्मचारी साग्निः सौपासनः क्षमी[१३] ॥

Selling salt, a daughter, or lac causes a person to fall from his caste, while selling milk, curd, or liquor makes him a low-caste person.[23] 40

When he is in a time of adversity, a Brahman is not tainted with sin when he accepts gifts or eats from anywhere at all, for he is like a fire and the sun. 41

Agriculture, crafts, working for wages, learning, money lending, carting, mountain work, service, working in marshy land, working for the king, and begging for almsfood, however, are the means of livelihood in a time of adversity. 42

When he is hungry, he should endure for three days, and then he should steal provisions from someone who is not a Brahman. If he is caught and charged, he should confess it in keeping with dharma.[24] 43

After finding out his conduct, family, character, learning, education, and sons, the king should provide for him a righteous livelihood from his own household.[25] 44

## TOPIC 40: DHARMA OF FOREST HERMITS

Entrusting his wife to his sons or accompanied by her, a forest hermit should live in the forest along with his sacrificial fires and his household fire, observing chastity and remaining patient.[26] 45

४६ अफालकृष्टेनाग्नींश्च पितॄन्देवातिथींस्तथा ।
भृत्यांश्च तर्पयेच्छश्वच्छ्मश्रुलोमभृदात्मवान्[१४] ॥

४७ अह्नो मासस्य षण्णां वा तथा संवत्सरस्य वा ।
अर्थस्य निचयं कुर्यात्कृतमाश्वयुजे त्यजेत् ॥

४८ दान्तस्त्रिषवणस्नायी निवृत्तश्च प्रतिग्रहात् ।
स्वाध्यायवान्दानशीलः सर्वसत्त्वहिते रतः ॥

४९ दन्तोलूखलिकः कालपक्वाशी वाश्मकुट्टकः ।
श्रौतस्मार्तं फलस्नेहैः कर्म कुर्यात्क्रियास्तथा ॥

५० चान्द्रायणैर्नयेत्कालं कृच्छ्रैर्वा वर्तयेत्सदा ।
पक्षे गते वाप्यश्नीयान्मासे वाहनि वा गते ॥

५१ शुचिर्भूमौ स्वपेद्रात्रौ दिवसं प्रपदैर्नयेत् ।
स्थानासनविहारैर्वा योगाभ्यासेन वा पुनः ॥

५२ ग्रीष्मे पञ्चाग्निमध्यस्थो वर्षासु स्थण्डिलेशयः ।
आर्द्रवासाश्च हेमन्ते शक्त्या वापि तपश्चरेत् ॥

With food obtained from unplowed land, he should always satisfy the fires, ancestors, gods, guests, and dependents, keeping his beard and bodily hair uncut, and remaining self-possessed.[27] 46

He may accumulate resources sufficient for one day, one month, six months, or one year, and he should discard what he has accumulated in the month of Ashvayuja.[28] 47

He should be controlled, bathe at the three appointed times of the day,[29] stop accepting gifts, be devoted to Vedic recitation, cultivate the habit of giving gifts, and delight in what is beneficial to all creatures. 48

He may use his teeth as a mortar, eat what has been ripened by time, or use a grindstone. He should carry out the rites prescribed by the Veda and texts of recollection, as also other ritual activities, using oils extracted from fruits. 49

He should spend his time engaged in lunar fasts, or live his life always engaged in arduous penances. Alternatively, he should eat after the lapse of a fortnight, or after the lapse of a month or a day.[30] 50

Keeping himself pure, he should sleep on the ground at night and spend the day on tiptoes, or standing, sitting, or walking, or else engaged in yogic practice. 51

He should stand in the middle of five fires during the summer, sleep on bare ground during the rainy season, and remain with wet clothes during the winter; or else he should perform ascetic toil according to his ability.[31] 52

५३ यः कण्टकैर्वितुदति चन्दनैर्यश्च लिम्पति ।
अक्रुद्धोऽपरितुष्टश्च समस्तस्य च तस्य च ॥

५४ अग्नीन्वाप्यात्मसात्कृत्वा वृक्षावासी मिताशनः ।
वानप्रस्थगृहेष्वेव यात्रार्थं भैक्षमाचरेत् ॥

५५ ग्रामादाहृत्य वा ग्रासानष्टौ भुञ्जीत वाग्यतः ।
वाय्वशनः प्रागुदीचीं गच्छेद्वावर्ष्मसंक्षयात् ॥

॥ इति वानप्रस्थधर्मप्रकरणम् ॥

## ॥ अथ यतिधर्मप्रकरणम् ॥

५६ गृहाद्वनाद्वा कृत्वेष्टिं सर्ववेदसदक्षिणाम् ।
प्राजापत्यां तदन्ते तानग्नीनारोप्य चात्मनि ॥

५७ अधीतवेदो जपकृत्पुत्रवानन्नदोऽग्निमान् ।
शक्त्या च यज्ञकृन्मोक्षे मनः कुर्यात्तु नान्यथा ॥

Should someone prick him with thorns and someone else apply sandalwood paste, he does not get angry at the first or be delighted with the second; he remains the same toward the former and the latter. 53

Alternatively, after placing the fires in his self, residing under the foot of a tree, and eating little, he should beg for almsfood in just the houses of forest hermits to sustain his life. 54

Or else, he should silently eat eight mouthfuls of food that he has brought from a village. Or, subsisting on air, he should go toward the east or the north, until his body drops dead. 55

## TOPIC 41: DHARMA OF RENOUNCERS

From either home or forest—after making a sacrifice to Prajapati at which all his possessions are given as sacrificial gifts and at its conclusion depositing the fires in his self; 56

after studying the Veda, engaging in soft recitation, begetting sons, donating food, maintaining the sacred fires, and performing sacrifices according to his ability—he should set his mind on renunciation, not otherwise.[32] 57

५८ सर्वभूतहितः शान्तस्त्रिदण्डी सकमण्डलुः ।
एकारामः परिव्रज्य भिक्षार्थं ग्राममाश्रयेत् ॥

५९ अप्रमत्तश्चरेद्भैक्षं सायाह्नेऽनुपलक्षितः ।
रहिते भिक्षुकैर्ग्रामे यात्रामात्रमलोलुपः ॥

६० यतिपात्राणि मृद्वेणुदार्वलाबुमयानि च ।
सलिलं शुद्धिरेतेषां गोवालैश्चावघर्षणम् ॥

६१ संनिरुध्येन्द्रियग्रामं रागद्वेषौ प्रहाय च ।
भयं हित्वा च भूतानाममृतीभवति द्विजः ॥

६२ कर्तव्याशयशुद्धिस्तु भिक्षुकेण विशेषतः ।
ज्ञानोत्पत्तिनिमित्तत्वात्स्वातन्त्र्यकरणाय च ॥

६३ अवेक्ष्यो गर्भवासश्च कर्मजा गतयस्तथा ।
आधयो व्याधयश्चैव जरा रूपविपर्ययः[१५] ॥

६४ भवो जातिसहस्रेषु प्रियाप्रियविपर्ययः ।
ध्यानयोगेन संदृश्यः सूक्ष्म आत्मात्मनि स्थितः ॥

६५ नाश्रमः कारणं धर्मे क्रियमाणो भवेद्धि सः ।
अतो यदात्मनोऽपथ्यं परस्य न तदाचरेत् ॥

Doing what is beneficial to all creatures, serene, carrying a triple staff along with a water pot, and delighting in solitude, he should, after he has become a wandering ascetic, resort to a village in order to obtain almsfood. 58

Keeping vigilant and without being noticed, he should go on his begging round in the afternoon in a village without mendicants simply to sustain his life without being greedy. 59

The bowls of ascetics are made of clay, cane, wood, or gourd, and the cleansing of those bowls is done with water and by scrubbing with cow's hair. 60

By restraining all his organs, by forsaking love and hate, and by stopping being a source of fear to any creature, a twice-born becomes immortal. 61

Purification of the heart, however, should be carried out especially by a mendicant both because it brings about knowledge and in order to create independence. 62

One should ponder the residence in the womb; the states that are produced by action; mental anguishes; bodily diseases; old age; alteration of appearance;[33] 63

coming into being in thousands of births; and alternation between what is pleasing and not pleasing. Through the yoga of meditation, one should contemplate the subtle self abiding within the self. 64

An order of life does not cause dharma, for it comes about when it is put into practice. Therefore, one should not do to someone else what is disagreeable to oneself. 65

६६ सत्यमस्तेयमक्रोधो ह्रीः शौचं धीर्धृतिर्दमः।
संयतेन्द्रियता विद्या धर्मः सार्व उदाहृतः॥

६७ निश्चरन्ति यथा लोहपिण्डात्तप्तात्स्फुलिङ्गकाः।
सकाशादात्मनः सर्व आत्मानोऽपि तथैव हि॥

६८ तत्रात्मा हि स्वयं किंचित्कर्म किंचित्स्वभावतः।
करोति किंचिदभ्यासाद्धर्माधर्मभवात्मकम्[१६]॥

६९ निमित्तमक्षरं कर्ता बोद्धा ब्रह्म गुणी वशी।
अजः शरीरग्रहणात्स जात इति कीर्त्यते॥

७० सर्गादौ स यथाकाशं वायुं ज्योतिर्जलं महीम्।
सृजत्येकोत्तरगुणांस्तथादत्ते भवन्नपि[१७]॥

७१ आहुत्याप्यायते सूर्यस्तस्माद्वृष्टिरथौषधिः।
तदन्नं रसरूपेण शुक्रत्वमुपगच्छति॥

७२ स्त्रीपुंसयोः संप्रयोगे विशुद्धे शुक्रशोणिते।
पञ्चधातून्स्वयंषष्ठानादत्ते युगपत्प्रभुः॥

७३ इन्द्रियाणि मनः प्राणो ज्ञानमायुः सुखं धृतिः।
धारणाप्रेरणे दुःखमिच्छाहंकारमेव च॥

७४ प्रयत्नाकृतिरूपाणि स्वरद्वेषौ भवाभवौ।
तस्येदमात्मजं सर्वमनादेरादिमिच्छतः॥

Truthfulness, not stealing, not giving in to anger, modesty, purification, insight, resolve, self-control, restraint of the sense organs, and learning—this is said to be the entirety of dharma. 66

As sparks burst forth from a heated iron ball, so also do all the selves from the presence of the self.[34] 67

There the self performs some actions by itself, some actions by its very nature, and some actions through practice, actions that are in keeping with dharma, contrary to dharma, or part of the process of coming into being.[35] 68

He is the cause, the imperishable, the doer, the cognizer, Brahma, the ground of attributes, and the controller—he is unborn, yet is said to be born because of his taking on a body. 69

As at the beginning of the emitting process he emits ether, wind, fire, water, and earth, each succeeding one having one attribute more than each preceding, so he gathers them in as he comes into being.[36] 70

By sacrificial offerings the sun waxes; from the sun comes rain and then plants. From plants comes food, which in the form of sap is turned into semen.[37] 71

When a woman and man have intercourse and the semen and blood are pure, the lord gathers simultaneously the five elements with himself as the sixth. 72

Organs, mind, life breath, knowledge, lifespan, happiness, resolve, concentration, propelling, pain, desire, ego, effort, shape, color, voice, hate, coming into being, and ceasing to be—all these arise from the self of his, who, being without beginning, desires a beginning. 73–74

७५ प्रथमे मासि संक्लेदभूतो धातुविमूर्च्छितः।
मास्यर्बुदं द्वितीये तु तृतीयेऽङ्गेन्द्रियैर्युतः॥

७६ आकाशाल्लाघवं सौक्ष्म्यं शब्दं श्रोत्रं तथा बलम्।
वायोस्तु प्रेरणं चेष्टां व्यूहनं रौक्ष्यमेव च[१८]॥

७७ अग्नेस्तु दर्शनं पक्तिमौष्ण्यं रूपप्रकाशनम्।
रसेभ्यो रसनं शैत्यं स्नेहक्लेदनमार्दवम्[१९]॥

७८ भूमेर्गन्धं तथा घ्राणं गौरवं मूर्तिमेव च।
आत्मा गृह्णात्यतः सर्वं तृतीये स्पन्दते ततः॥

७९ दौहृदस्याप्रदानेन गर्भो दोषमवाप्नुयात्।
वैरूप्यं मरणं वापि तस्मात्कार्यं प्रियं स्त्रियाः॥

८० स्थैर्यं चतुर्थे त्वङ्गानां पञ्चमे शोणितोद्भवः।
षष्ठे बलस्य वर्णस्य नखरोम्णां च संभवः॥

८१ मनसा चेतसा युक्तो नाडीस्नायुसिराततः।
सप्तमे चाष्टमे चैव त्वचावान्स्मृतिमानपि[२०]॥

८२ पुनर्गर्भं पुनर्धात्रीमोजस्तस्य प्रधावति।
अष्टमे मास्यतो गर्भो जातः प्राणैर्विमुच्यते॥

८३ नवमे दशमे वापि प्रबलैः सूतिमारुतैः।
निःसार्यते बाण इव यन्त्रच्छिद्रेण सज्वरः॥

८४ तस्य षोढा शरीरं तत्षड्त्वचो धारयन्ति हि।
षडङ्गानि तथास्थ्नां च सषष्टिं वै शतत्रयम्॥

In the first month, it is a fluid mass coagulated from the elements; in the second month, it is an elongated lump; and in the third, it is endowed with the organs.[38] 75

Lightness, subtlety, sound, hearing, and strength from ether; propelling, action, arrangement, and roughness from wind;[39] 76

seeing, digestion, heat, color, and luster from fire; taste, cold, moistness, stickiness, and softness, from water;[40] 77

smell, sense of smell, heaviness, and physical form from earth—the self gathers all these, and, therefore, in the third month the fetus quickens. 78

By not satisfying the pregnancy craving, the fetus develops defects—deformity or even death. Therefore, one should provide whatever the woman likes. 79

In the fourth month, the limbs become firm; in the fifth, blood appears; in the sixth, strength, color, nails, and hair are produced. 80

In the seventh, it becomes endowed with mind and intellect and provided with pulse, sinews, and blood vessels. In the eighth, it comes to possess skin, as also memory.[41] 81

The life force gushes at one time to the fetus and at another time to the mother. A fetus born in the eighth month, therefore, becomes bereft of life breaths. 82

In the ninth or the tenth month, it is expelled painfully by forceful birth-winds through the hole in the body, like an arrow propelled by a machine. 83

That body of his has six parts, for it bears six skins, six limbs, and 360 bones.[42] 84

८५ स्थालैः सह चतुःषष्टिर्दन्ता वै विंशतिर्नखाः ।
पाणिपादशलाकाश्च तासां स्थानचतुष्टयम् ॥

८६ षष्ट्यङ्गुलीनां द्वे पाष्ण्योर्गुल्फेषु तु चतुष्टयम् ।
चत्वार्यरत्न्योरस्थीनि जङ्घयोस्तावदेव तु ॥

८७ द्वे द्वे जानुकपालोरुफलकांससमुद्भवे ।
अक्षः तालूषके श्रोणिफलके चैव निर्दिशेत् ॥

८८ भगास्थ्येकं तथा पृष्ठे चत्वारिंशच्च पञ्च च ।
ग्रीवा पञ्चदशास्थीनि जत्र्वेकं हि तथा हनुः ॥

८९ तन्मूले द्वे ललाटास्थि गण्डनासाघनास्थिका ।
पार्श्वकाः स्थालकैः सार्धमर्बुदैश्च द्विसप्ततिः[२१] ॥

९० द्वौ शङ्खकौ कपालानि चत्वारि शिरसस्तथा ।
उरः सप्तदशास्थीनि पुरुषस्यास्थिसंग्रहः ॥

९१ गन्धरूपरसस्पर्शशब्दास्तु विषयाः स्मृताः ।
नासिका लोचने जिह्वा त्वक् श्रोत्रं चेन्द्रियाणि तु ॥

९२ हस्तौ पायुरुपस्थं च मुखं पादौ च पञ्चमम् ।
कर्मेन्द्रियाणि जानीयान्मनश्चैवोभयात्मकम् ॥

९३ नाभिरोजो गुदं शुक्रं शोणितं शङ्खकौ तथा ।
मूर्धा च हृदयं कण्ठः प्राणस्यायतनानि तु ॥

९४ वपा वपावहननं नाभिः क्लोम यकृत्प्लिहा ।
क्षुद्रान्त्रं वृक्ककौ बस्तिः पुरीषाधानमेव च[२२] ॥

९५ आमाशयोऽथ हृदयं स्थूलान्त्रं गुद एव च ।
उदरं च गुदः कोष्ठ्यो विस्तारोऽयमुदाहृतः ॥

There are sixty-four teeth along with their receptacles; twenty nails and twenty terminal bones of the hands and feet, along with their four supports; 85

sixty bones of the fingers and toes; two of the heels; four of the ankles; four of the forearms; four of the shanks; 86

one should assign two each to the knees, knee caps, thighs, shoulder blades, shoulders, eyes, palate, and hip blades; 87

one pubic bone; forty-five of the back; fifteen neck bones; one in each collar bone; the chin; 88

two at the base of the chin; bone of the forehead; the solid bone of the cheeks and nostrils; rib bones on the sides along with their tubular sockets are seventy-two;[43] 89

two temporal bones; four cranial bones; seventeen bones of the chest—that is the totality of a man's bones.[44] 90

Smell, form, taste, touch, and sound are said to be the sense objects, while nose, eyes, tongue, skin, and ears are the sense organs. 91

Two hands, anus, genital, mouth, and, fifth, two feet should be known as the organs of action, while the mind has the nature of both. 92

Navel, life force, anus, semen, blood, two temporal bones, head, heart, and throat are the seats of the vital breaths.[45] 93

Omentum, omental binding, navel, lungs, liver, spleen, small intestine, kidneys, bladder, feces container, stomach, heart, large intestine, rectum, and anus—this is a detailed enumeration of the inner organs.[46] 94–95

९६ कनीनिके चाक्षिकूटे शष्कुली कर्णपुत्रकौ।
गण्डौ शङ्खौ भ्रुवौ दन्तावेष्टावोष्ठौ ककुन्दरौ॥

९७ वङ्क्षणौ वृषणौ वृक्कौ श्लेष्मसंघातके स्तनौ।
उपजिह्विका स्फिजौ बाहू जङ्घे चोरू सपिण्डिके॥

९८ तालूदरं बस्तिशीर्षं चिबुकं गलगण्डिका।
अवटुश्चैवमेतानि स्थानान्यत्र शरीरके॥

९९ अक्षिवर्त्मचतुष्कं च पद्धस्तहृदयानि च।
नव छिद्राणि तान्येव प्राणस्यायतनानि च॥

१०० सिराशतानि सप्तैव नव स्नायुशतानि च।
धमनीनां शते द्वे तु पञ्च पेशीशतानि च॥

१०१ एकोनत्रिंशतं लक्षास्तथा नव शतानि च।
षट्पञ्चाशच्च निर्दिष्टाः सिरा धमनिसंज्ञकाः॥

१०२ त्रयो लक्षास्तु विज्ञेयाः केशश्मश्रु मनीषिभिः।
अष्टोत्तरं मर्मशतं द्वे तु संधिशते तथा[२३]॥

१०३ रोम्णां कोट्यस्तु पञ्चाशत्तथा कोटिचतुष्टयम्।
सप्तषष्टिस्तथा लक्षाः सार्धाः स्वेदायनैः सह॥

१०४ वायवीयैर्विगण्यन्ते विभक्ताः परमाणवः।
यद्यप्यन्ये को नु वेदैषां भावानां चैव संस्थितिम्॥

१०५ रसस्य नव विज्ञेया जलस्याञ्जलयो दश।
सप्त चैव पुरीषस्य रक्तस्याष्टौ प्रकीर्तिताः॥

१०६ षट् श्लेष्मा पञ्च पित्तं तु चत्वारो मूत्रमेव च।
वसा त्रयो द्वौ तु मेदो मज्जैकार्धं च मस्तके॥

Pupils of the eyes, lacrimal caruncles, orifices of the ears, ear lobes, cheeks, temporal bones, eyebrows, upper and lower gums, lips, hollows of the buttocks, groins, testicles, kidneys, tonsils, breasts, uvula, buttocks, arms, calves and thighs along with their muscles, palate, abdomen, pelvis, chin, goiter, and nape—these are the areas of this body. 96–98

The four pathways of the eyes; feet, hands, and heart; and the nine openings—these same nine are the seats of vital breaths.[47] 99

There are seven hundred *sirā* veins, nine hundred sinews, two hundred *dhamanī* arteries, and five hundred muscles. 100

The *sirā* veins with the appellation *dhamanī* are stated to be 2,900,956. 101

Wise people point out that there are three hundred thousand hairs of the head and beard, 108 vital points, and two hundred joints.[48] 102

Bodily hairs are 540 million, plus 6,750,000, along with the sweat pores. 103

The minutest particles of the body are reckoned as separated by air elements. If there are others, who indeed would know the subsistence of these entities?[49] 104

Of sap, one should know, there are nine *añjalis,* and of water, ten. Of feces, there are declared to be seven; of blood, eight;[50] 105

of phlegm, six; of bile, five; of urine, four; of stomach fat, three; of fat, two; of marrow, one; and in the head, one-half; 106

१०७ श्लेष्मौजसस्तावदेव रेतसस्तावदेव तु ।
इत्येतदस्थिरं वर्ष्म यस्य मोक्षाय कृत्यसौ ॥

१०८ द्विसप्ततिसहस्राणि हृदयादभिनिःसृताः ।
हिता नाम हि ता नाड्यस्तासां मध्ये शशिप्रभम् ॥

१०९ मण्डलं तस्य मध्यस्थ आत्मा दीप इवाचलः ।
मध्ये यस्तं विदित्वा तु पुनराजायते न तु ॥

११० ज्ञेयमारण्यकमहं यदादित्यादवाप्तवान् ।
योगशास्त्रं च मत्प्रोक्तं ज्ञेयं योगमभीप्सता ॥

१११ अनन्यविषयं कृत्वा मनोबुद्धिस्मृतीन्द्रियम् ।
ध्येय आत्मा स्थितो योऽसौ हृदये दीपवत्प्रभुः ॥

११२ यथावधानेन पुमान्साम गायत्यविध्ययम् ।
सावधानस्तथाभ्यासात्परं ब्रह्माधिगच्छति[२४] ॥

११३ अपरान्तकमुल्लोप्यं मद्रकं प्रकरीं तथा ।
औवेणकं सरोबिन्दुमुत्तरं गीतिकानि तु ॥

११४ ऋग्गाथा पाणिका दक्षविहिता ब्रह्मगीतिका ।
गेयमेतत्तदभ्यासकरणाच्चोक्तसंज्ञकम्[२५] ॥

११५ वीणावादनतत्त्वज्ञः श्रुतिजातिविशारदः ।
तालज्ञश्चाप्रयासेन योगमार्गं निगच्छति[२६] ॥

११६ गीतिज्ञो यदि योगेन नाप्नोति परमं पदम् ।
रुद्रस्यानुचरो भूत्वा तेनैव सह मोदते ॥

and the same amount of phlegmatic vital fluid and of semen. A person who in this manner considers this body as impermanent is capable of achieving liberation. 107

Emerging from the heart are the seventy-two thousand veins called *hitā,* and in the middle of them is a disk having the luster of the moon. In the middle of it is the self like an unflittering lamp. By knowing him who is in the middle, however, a person is not born again. 108–109

Anyone who desires to master yoga should know the *Āraṇyaka* that I received from the sun, as well as the yoga treatise that I proclaimed.[51] 110

Having withdrawn his mind, intellect, memory, and organs from all other objects, he should contemplate that self, the lord who resides in the heart like a lamp. 111

As a man here sings a *sāman* chant without following a fixed rule by paying close attention, so a man, being quite attentive, attains the highest Brahma through constant practice.[52] 112

*Aparāntaka, ullopya, madraka, prakarī, auveṇaka, sarobindu,* and *uttara* are the songs.[53] 113

*Ṛggāthā, pāṇikā, dakṣavihitā,* and *brahmagītikā*—all these should be sung. By constantly practicing these having the stated names, a man who knows the essence of playing the vina, and a man who is proficient in the tones and notes, and a man who knows the beats enters the path of yoga without effort.[54] 114–115

If a knower of music does not attain the highest state through yoga, by becoming a servant of Rudra he will rejoice with him alone. 116

११७ अनादिरात्मा कथितस्तस्यादिश्च शरीरकम् ।
आत्मनश्च जगत्सर्वं जगतश्चात्मसंभवः ॥

११८ कथमेतद्विमुह्यामः सदेवासुरमानवम् ।
जगदुत्पन्नमात्मा च कथं न्वस्मिन्वदस्व नः ॥

११९ मोहजालमपास्येदं पुरुषो दृश्यते हि यः ।
सहस्रकरपन्नेत्रः सूर्यवर्चाः सहस्रशः ॥

१२० स आत्मा चैव यज्ञश्च विश्वरूपः प्रजापतिः ।
विराड्व सोमरूपेण यज्ञत्वमुपगच्छति[२७] ॥

१२१ यो द्रव्यदेवतात्यागसंभूतो रस उत्तमः ।
देवान्स संतर्प्य रसो यजमानं फलेन तु ॥

१२२ संयोज्य वायुना सोमं नीयते रश्मिभिस्ततः ।
ऋग्यजुःसामविहितं सौरं धामोपनीयते ॥

१२३ तन्मण्डलमसौ सूर्यः सृजत्यमृतमुत्तमम् ।
यज्जन्म सर्वभूतानामशनानशनात्मनाम् ॥

१२४ तस्मादन्नात्पुनर्यज्ञः पुनरन्नं पुनः क्रतुः ।
एवमेतदनाद्यन्तं चक्रं संपरिवर्तते ॥

१२५ अनादिरात्मा संभूतिर्विद्यते नान्तरात्मनः ।
समवायी तु पुरुषो मोहेच्छाद्वेषकर्मजः ॥

The self is proclaimed to be without beginning. His beginning is related to the body. And from the self arises the entire world, and from the world is the origin of the self. 117

"We are bewildered! How did this world with its gods, demons, and humans come into being? And how did the self come into being in this world? Tell us that." 118

After removing this net of delusion, the Purusha is seen with a thousand hands, feet, and eyes, and having one thousand times the luster of the sun. 119

That Purusha, indeed, is the self and the sacrifice; he is the omni-form Prajapati, and Viraj. In the form of *soma,* he takes on the nature of the sacrifice.[55] 120

The highest sap arisen from the sacrificial material, divinity, and offering—that sap, after it has satisfied the gods and united the sacrificer with the reward, is led by the wind to the moon, and from there by the sunrays to the abode of the sun consisting of the *ṛc, yajus,* and *sāman.*[56] 121–122

That sun emits the highest ambrosia that is within its orb, from which results the birth of all creatures, both those that eat and those that do not. 123

From that food arises once again the sacrifice; once again food; and once again the rite. In this manner, the wheel that is without beginning and end continues to roll on. 124

The self is without beginning; there is no coming into being of the inner self. The Purusha, however, takes on relationships caused by delusion, desire, hatred, and actions. 125

१२६ सहस्रात्मा मया यो व आदिदेव उदाहृतः ।
मुखबाहूरुपज्जातास्तस्य वर्णा यथाक्रमम् ॥

१२७ पृथिवी पादतस्तस्य शिरसो द्यौरजायत ।
नस्तः प्राणा दिशः श्रोत्रात् त्वचो वायुर्मुखाच्छिखी[२८] ॥

१२८ मनसश्चन्द्रमा जातश्चक्षुषश्च दिवाकरः ।
जघनादन्तरिक्षं च जगच्च सचराचरम् ॥

१२९ यद्येवं स कथं ब्रह्मन्पापयोनिषु जायते ।
ईश्वरः स कथं भावैरनिष्टैः संप्रयुज्यते ॥

१३० करणैरन्वितस्यापि पूर्वज्ञानं कथं च न ।
वेत्ति सर्वगतां कस्मात्सर्वगोऽपि न वेदनाम् ॥

१३१ अन्त्यपक्षिस्थावरतां मनोवाक्कायकर्मजैः ।
दोषैः प्रयाति जीवोऽयं भवन्जातिशतेषु च ॥

१३२ अनन्ता हि यथा भावाः शरीरेषु शरीरिणाम् ।
रूपाण्यपि तथैवेह सर्वयोनिषु देहिनाम् ॥

१३३ विपाकः कर्मणां प्रेत्य केषां चिदिह जायते ।
इह चामुत्र चैकेषां भावस्तत्र प्रयोजकः ॥

The primordial god with a thousand bodies that I have declared to you—from his mouth, arms, thighs, and feet were born the social classes in the proper order.[57] 126

The earth was born from his feet; heaven from his head; breaths from his nose; the directions from his ears; wind from his skin; and fire from his mouth.[58] 127

The moon was born from his mind; the sun from his eyes; and the mid-space, as well as the world along with mobile and immobile beings, from his loins. 128

"If he is like that, Oh Brahman, how can he take birth in evil wombs? How can he, being the Lord, be united with disagreeable mental states? 129

And, even though he is endowed with sense organs, how does he not have the knowledge of previous births? Even though he is present everywhere, how does he not know the thoughts present in all the beings?" 130

This embodied soul reaches the conditions of the lowest-born people, birds, and immobile beings because of sins caused by the actions of body, speech, and mind as it comes into being in hundreds of births. 131

For, as the mental states of embodied beings within their bodies are infinite, so also are the bodily forms here of embodied beings in all kinds of wombs. 132

After death, the effect of the actions of some people is produced in this world, whereas that of others is produced both in this world and in the next. In this regard, one's state of mind is the determining factor. 133

१३४ परद्रव्याण्यभिध्यायंस्तथानिष्टानि चिन्तयन् ।
वितथाभिनिवेशी च जायतेऽन्त्यासु योनिषु ॥

१३५ पुरुषोऽनृतवादी च पिशुनश्चैव मानवः ।
असंबन्धप्रलापी च मृगपक्षिषु जायते[२१] ॥

१३६ अदत्तादाननिरतः परदारोपसेवकः ।
हिंसकश्चाविधानेन स्थावरेषूपजायते ॥

१३७ आत्मज्ञः शौचवान्दान्तस्तपस्वी नियतेन्द्रियः ।
धर्मकृद्वेदविद्याति सात्त्विको देवयोनिषु ॥

१३८ असत्कार्यरतोऽधीर आरम्भी विषयी च यः ।
स राजसो मनुष्येषु मृतो जन्म प्रपद्यते ॥

१३९ निद्रालुः क्रूरकृल्लुब्धो नास्तिको याचकस्तथा ।
प्रमादवान्भिन्नवृत्तो भवेत्तिर्यक्षु तामसः ॥

१४० रजसा तमसा चैव समाविष्टो भ्रमन्निह ।
भावैरनिष्टैः संयुक्तः संसारं प्रतिपद्यते ॥

१४१ मलिनो हि यथादर्शो रूपालोकस्य न क्षमः ।
तथाविपक्वकरण आत्मा ज्ञानस्य न क्षमः ॥

By coveting the property of others, by thinking about undesirable things, and by adhering to false doctrines, a person is born in the wombs of the lowest-born people. 134

A person who tells lies and a man who commits slander, as also someone who engages in idle chatter are born among beasts and birds.[59] 135

A person who is intent on taking what is not given, violates the wives of others, or engages in unsanctioned killing is born among immobile beings.[60] 136

A person who knows the self, performs purifications, is self-controlled, engages in ascetic toil, keeps his senses restrained, carries out dharma, and knows the Veda—with goodness as his dominant attribute—goes to divine wombs. 137

A person who, taking delight in bad deeds, is inconstant, engages in activities, and is addicted to sense objects—with energy as his dominant attribute—after death takes birth among humans. 138

A person who is given to sleep, does cruel deeds, is greedy, is an infidel, solicits gifts, is careless, and leads a degenerate life—with darkness as his dominant attribute—comes into being among beasts. 139

Possessed by energy and darkness, meandering in this world, and linked to undesirable mental states, he enters upon the rebirth cycle. 140

For, as a dirty mirror is incapable of reflecting an image, so a self with immature organs is incapable of knowledge. 141

१४२ कटूर्वारौ यथापक्वे मधुरः सन्रसोऽपि न।
प्राप्यते ह्यात्मनि तथा नापक्वकरणे ज्ञता॥

१४३ सर्वाश्रयां निजे देहे देही विन्दति वेदनाम्।
योगी युक्तस्तु सर्वेषां यो नावाप्नोति वेदनाम्॥

१४४ आकाशमेकं हि यथा घटादिषु पृथग्भवेत्।
तथात्मैको ह्यनेकश्च जलाधारेष्विवांशुमान्॥

१४५ ब्रह्म खानिलतेजांसि जलं भूश्चेति धातवः।
इमे लोका एष चात्मा तस्माच्च सचराचरम्॥

१४६ मृद्दण्डचक्रसंयोगात्कुम्भकारो यथा घटम्।
करोति तृणमृत्काष्ठैर्गृहं वा गृहकारकः॥

१४७ हेममात्रमुपादाय रूपं वा हेमकारकः।
निजलालासमायोगात्कोशं वा कोशकारकः॥

१४८ कारणान्येवमादाय तासु तास्विह योनिषु।
सृजत्यात्मानमात्मैव संभूय करणानि च॥

१४९ महाभूतानि सत्यानि यथात्मापि तथैव हि।
कोऽन्यथैकेन नेत्रेण दृष्टमन्येन पश्यति॥

१५० वाचं वा को विजानाति पुनः संश्रुत्य संश्रुताम्।
अतीतार्थस्मृतिः कस्य को वा स्वप्नस्य कारकः॥

As in an immature snake cucumber, even though sweet, there is no sap, so knowledge is not found in a self with immature organs. 142

An embodied yogi with a concentrated mind knows in his own body the thoughts residing in all, but he does not appropriate their thoughts.[61] 143

As the single space becomes fragmented in pots and the like, so the self is truly both single and multiple, like the sun in lakes. 144

Brahma; space, wind, fire, water, and earth, which are the elements; these worlds; and this self—from that comes the universe of mobile and immobile beings.[62] 145

As a potter fashions a pot through a combination of clay, stick, and wheel; or as a house builder fashions a house with straw, mud, and lumber; 146

or as a goldsmith taking a chunk of gold fashions an artifact; or as a silkworm makes a cocoon by a combination of its own saliva— 147

so the self alone, taking in like manner the material causes and bringing together the organs, creates the self within various wombs in this world. 148

For, as the primary elements are real, so also is the self. If that were not so, who would see with one eye what has been seen with the other? 149

Or, who would recognize a voice that he has already heard when he hears it again? Who would possess the memory of a past event? Or, who would be the creator of a dream? 150

१५१ जातिरूपवयोवृत्तविद्यादिभिरहंकृतः।
सक्तः शब्दादिविषये कर्मणा मनसा गिरा॥

१५२ स संदिग्धमतिः कर्मफलमस्ति न वेति वा।
संप्लुतः सिद्धमात्मानमसिद्धोऽपि हि मन्यते॥

१५३ मम दारसुतामात्या अहमेषामिति स्थितः।
हिताहितेषु भावेषु विपरीतमतिः सदा॥

१५४ ज्ञेऽज्ञे च प्रकृतौ चैव विकारे चाविशेषवान्।
अनाशकाग्निप्रवेशजलप्रपतनोद्यमी[३०]॥

१५५ एवंवृत्तोऽविनीतात्मा वितथाभिनिवेशवान्।
कर्मणा द्वेषमोहाभ्यामिच्छया चैव बध्यते॥

१५६ आचार्योपासनं वेदशास्त्रस्यार्थविवेकिता।
तत्कर्मणामनुष्ठानं सङ्गः सद्भिर्गिरः शुभाः॥

१५७ स्त्र्यालोकालम्भविगमः सर्वभूतात्मदर्शनम्।
त्यागः परिग्रहाणां च जीर्णकाषायधारणम्॥

१५८ विषयेन्द्रियसंरोधस्तन्द्र्यालस्यविसर्जनम्।
शरीरपरिसंख्यानं प्रवृत्तिष्वघदर्शनम्॥

Proud of his birth, beauty, age, conduct, learning, and the like, and attached to the objects of sense such as sound through deed, mind, and speech[63]— 151

such a man with a doubting mind, vacillating: "Perhaps actions bear fruit. Perhaps, they do not," thinks that his self is perfected, even though he is not perfected. 152

Resolute in the thought: "Wife, sons, and members of the household belong to me, and I belong to them," his mind always confounded with regard to beneficial and detrimental conditions,[64] 153

unable to discriminate between the knower and the non-knower, and the original and the modified; bent on fasting to death, entering a fire, and plunging into water[65]— 154

a man in such a condition, his self unrestrained and adhering to error, is fettered by action, by hatred and delusion, and by desire. 155

Attending to the teacher, proper inquiry into the meaning of Vedic scriptures, performance of the activities prescribed therein, attachment to virtuous people, pleasant speech, 156

avoiding the sight of and contact with women, seeing the self in all beings, abandoning possessions, wearing old ochre clothes, 157

holding back the sense organs from sensory objects, abandoning lethargy and sloth, fully enumerating the body, seeing evil in worldly activities, 158

१५९ नीरजस्तमस्ता सत्त्वशुद्धिर्निस्पृहता शमः।
एतैरुपायैः संशुद्धः सत्त्वयोग्यमृती भवेत्[३१] ॥

१६० तत्त्वस्मृतेरुपस्थानात्सत्त्वयोगात्परिक्षयात्।
कर्मणां संनिकर्षाच्च सतां योगः प्रवर्तते ॥

१६१ शरीरसंक्षये यस्य मनः सत्त्वस्थमीश्वरम्।
अविप्लुतस्मृतिः सम्यक्स जातिस्मरतामियात् ॥

१६२ यथा हि भरतो वर्णैर्वर्तयत्यात्मनस्तनुम्।
नानारूपाणि कुर्वाणस्तथात्मा कर्मजस्तनुम् ॥

१६३ कालकर्मात्मबीजानां दोषैर्मातुस्तथैव च।
गर्भस्य वैकृतं दृष्टं नाङ्गहानं हि जन्मतः[३२] ॥

१६४ अहंकारेण मनसा गत्या कर्मफलेन च।
शरीरेण च नात्मायं मुक्तपूर्वः कदाचन ॥

१६५ दाता सत्यः क्षमी प्राज्ञः शुभकर्मा जितेन्द्रियः।
तपस्वी योगशीलश्च न रोगैः परिभूयते[३३] ॥

१६६ वर्त्याधारस्नेहयोगाद्यथा दीपस्य संस्थितिः।
विक्रियापि च दृष्टैवमकाले प्राणसंक्षयः ॥

freeing himself of the attributes of energy and darkness, purifying the mind, giving up longing, and becoming tranquil—purified by these means, the yogi absorbed in the attribute of goodness becomes immortal.[66] 159

Yoga prospers through attention to the recollection of the truth, union with the attribute of goodness, elimination of actions, and close association with virtuous people. 160

At the dissolution of the body, when a person's mind is fixed in the attribute of goodness and remains sovereign of itself, he becomes, with his recollection completely intact, capable of recalling previous births. 161

For, as an actor displays his body with makeup, so the self produced by action, while performing various kinds of actions, displays its body. 162

Deformity of a fetus is seen to arise from the defects of time, action, self, and semen, as well as those of the mother, for damage to limbs does not happen on account of birth.[67] 163

This self has never ever been freed from ego, mind, migration, result of action, and body. 164

A person who gives gifts; is truthful, patient, and intelligent; engages in wholesome activities; has restrained his sense organs; is given to ascetic toil; and is inclined to practice yoga, is not overwhelmed by sicknesses.[68] 165

As the persistence of a lamp and also its extinction are seen to be caused by the combination of wick, vessel, and oil, so also is the untimely termination of life. 166

१६७ अनन्ता रश्मयस्तस्य दीपवद्यः स्थितो हृदि।
सितासिताः कद्रुनीलाः कपिलापीतलोहिताः॥

१६८ ऊर्ध्वमेकः स्थितस्तेषां यो भित्त्वा सूर्यमण्डलम्।
ब्रह्मलोकमतिक्रम्य तेन याति परां गतिम्॥

१६९ यदस्यान्यद्रश्मिशतमूर्ध्वमेव व्यवस्थितम्।
तेन देवनिकायानां स धामानि प्रपद्यते[३४]॥

१७० येऽनेकरूपाश्चाधस्ताद्रश्मयोऽस्य मृदुप्रभाः।
इह कर्मोपभोगार्थास्तैश्च संचरतेऽवशः॥

१७१ वेदैः शास्त्रैः सविज्ञानैर्जन्मना मरणेन च।
आध्या गत्या तथागत्या सत्येन ह्यनृतेन च[३५]॥

१७२ श्रेयसा सुखदुःखाभ्यां कर्मभिश्च शुभाशुभैः।
निमित्तशकुनज्ञानैर्ग्रहसंयोगजैः फलैः॥

१७३ तारानक्षत्रसंचारैर्जलजैः स्वप्नजैरपि।
आकाशपवनज्योतिर्जलभूतिमिरैस्तथा[३६]॥

१७४ मन्वन्तरैर्युगप्राप्त्या मन्त्रौषधिबलैरपि।
वित्तात्मानं विद्यमानं कारणं जगतः तथा॥

१७५ अहंकारः स्मृतिर्मेधा द्वेषो बुद्धिः सुखं धृतिः।
इन्द्रियान्तरसंचार इच्छा धारणजीविते॥

The rays of him who abides in the heart like a lamp are without end; they are white and black, brown and blue, reddish brown, yellowish, and red. 167

One of them is located on the upper side. It breaks through the sun's orb and passes beyond the world of Brahma. By means of it he attains the highest state. 168

Another set of one hundred rays of his is located also on the upper side. With that he attains the abodes of the groups of gods.[69] 169

His rays of diverse appearances and with faint luster located on the lower side are for enjoying the fruits of his actions in this world. With them he helplessly goes around in the cycle of rebirth. 170

The Vedas and authoritative treatises along with deep insights; birth and death; mental anguish; motion and motionlessness; truth and falsehood;[70] 171

prosperity; happiness and suffering; good and evil deeds; knowledge of portents and omens; results rising from the conjunction of planets; 172

the movements of stars and asterisms; results from water; results from dreams; space, wind, fire, water, earth, and darkness;[71] 173

epochs of Manu; arrival of the world ages; the strengths of mantras and medicinal herbs—by means of these he comes to know the self that is the ever present cause of the world.[72] 174

Ego, memory, intelligence, hate, intellect, happiness, resolve, interaction among the sense organs, desire, concentration and life,[73] 175

१७६ स्वप्नेसर्गश्च भावानां प्रेरणं मनसोऽगतिः।
निमेषश्चेतना यत्न आदानं पाञ्चभौतिकम्[३७] ॥

१७७ यत एतानि चिह्नानि दृश्यन्ते परमात्मनः।
तस्मादस्ति परो देहाद्देही सर्वग ईश्वरः॥

१७८ बुद्धीन्द्रियाणि सार्थानि मनः कर्मेन्द्रियाणि च।
अहंकारश्च बुद्धिश्च पृथिव्यादीनि चैव ह॥

१७९ अव्यक्त आत्मा क्षेत्रज्ञः क्षेत्रस्यास्य निगद्यते।
ईश्वरः सर्वभूतानां सन्नसन्सदसच्च सः[३८] ॥

१८० बुद्धेरुत्पत्तिरव्यक्तात्ततोऽहंकारसंभवः।
तस्मात्खादीनि जायन्ते एकोत्तरगुणानि तु॥

१८१ शब्दः स्पर्शश्च रूपं च रसो गन्धश्च तद्गुणाः।
यो यस्मिन्नाश्रितस्तेषां स तत्रैव प्रलीयते[३९] ॥

१८२ यथात्मानं सृजत्यात्मा तथा वः कथितं मया।
विपाकस्त्रिप्रकाराणां कर्मणामीश्वरोऽपि सन्॥

१८३ सत्त्वं रजस्तमश्चैव गुणास्तस्यैव कीर्तिताः।
रजस्तमोभ्यामाविष्टश्चक्रवद्भ्राम्यते हि सः॥

१८४ अनादिमानादिमांश्च य एष पुरुषः परः।
लिङ्गेन्द्रियैरुपग्राह्यः सविकार उदाहृतः॥

creation of entities in dream, projections of the mind and its motionless state, blinking of the eyes, thinking, effort, and appropriation of the five elements[74]— 176

given that these signs of the supreme self are seen, there is, consequently, beyond the body the possessor of the body, who pervades all and is the lord. 177

Organs of perception along with their objects, mind, organs of action, ego, intellect, and the elements beginning with earth— 178

of this field, the self within the unmanifest principle is called the "knower of the field." He is the lord of all beings; he is both existing and non-existing, both the existent and the non-existent.[75] 179

From the unmanifest principle originates the intellect, and from it arises the ego. From the latter are born the elements beginning with space, each succeeding one having one attribute more than each preceding.[76] 180

Sound, touch, sight, taste, and smell are their attributes, and the one among these elements on which each of them is based, into that very one it dissolves.[77] 181

I have described to you the way the self creates the self, the result of the three kinds of actions, even though he remains the lord.[78] 182

Goodness, energy, and darkness are declared to be his attributes. When he is possessed by energy and darkness, he spins around like a wheel. 183

This highest Purusha, who is both without a beginning and with a beginning, when he is associated with modifications, is said to be graspable through signs and sense organs.[79] 184

१८५ पितृयानोऽजवीथ्याश्च यदगस्त्यस्य चान्तरम् ।
तेनाग्निहोत्रिणो यान्ति प्रजाकामा दिवं प्रति[४०] ॥

१८६ येऽपि दानपराः सम्यगष्टाभिश्च गुणैर्युताः ।
तेऽपि तेनैव गच्छन्ति सत्यव्रतपरायणाः ॥

१८७ अष्टाशीतिसहस्राणि मुनयो गृहमेधिनः ।
पुनरावर्तिनो बीजभूता धर्मप्रवर्तकाः ॥

१८८ सप्तर्षिनागवीथ्योस्तु देवलोकं समाश्रिताः ।
तावन्त एव मुनयः सर्वारम्भविवर्जिताः ॥

१८९ तपसा ब्रह्मचर्येण सङ्गत्यागेन मेधया ।
यातास्तत्रावतिष्ठन्ति यावदाभूतसंप्लवम् ॥

१९० यतो वेदाः पुराणं च विद्योपनिषदस्तथा ।
श्लोकाः सूत्राणि भाष्याणि यत्किंचिद्वाङ्मयं क्वचित् ॥

१९१ वेदानुवचनं यज्ञो ब्रह्मचर्यं तपो दमः ।
श्रद्धोपवाससातत्यमात्मनो ज्ञानहेतवः[४१] ॥

१९२ स ह्याश्रमैर्निदिध्यास्यः समस्तैरेवमेव तु ।
द्रष्टव्यस्त्वथ मन्तव्यः श्रोतव्यश्च द्विजातिभिः[४२] ॥

The path of the fathers lies between *ajavīthi* and *agastya*. By that path those who offer the daily fire sacrifice and desire offspring travel toward heaven.[80] 185

People properly intent on gift giving and endowed with the eight qualities also travel by the same path, devoted to the vow of truthfulness.[81] 186

The eighty-eight thousand householder sages are transformed into seed and destined to return again, becoming the promulgators of dharma.[82] 187

The very same number of sages who abstain from all activities, however, attain the world of gods along the path between the seven seers and the serpent's way.[83] 188

Having gone there by virtue of ascetic toil, chastity, abandonment of attachment, and intelligence, they remain there until the dissolution of the world. 189

From them are derived the Vedas, Puranas, knowledge systems, Upanishads, verses, aphorisms, commentaries, and anything composed of words.[84] 190

Recitation of the Veda, sacrifice, chastity, ascetic toil, self-control, and the constant engagement in faith and fasting are the causes that produce knowledge of the self.[85] 191

For it is he on whom all the orders of life should concentrate, and whom twice-born people should see, reflect on, and listen to.[86] 192

१९३ य एवमेनं विदन्ति ये चारण्यकमाश्रिताः।
उपासते द्विजाः सत्यं श्रद्धया परया युताः॥

१९४ क्रमात्ते संभवन्त्यर्चिरहः शुक्लं तथोत्तरम्।
अयनं देवलोकं च सवितारं सवैद्युतम्॥

१९५ ततस्तान्पुरुषोऽभ्येत्य मानसो ब्रह्मलौकिकान्।
करोति पुनरावृत्तिस्तेषामिह न विद्यते॥

१९६ यज्ञेन तपसा दानैर्ये हि स्वर्गजितो नराः।
धूमं निशां कृष्णपक्षं दक्षिणायनमेव च॥

१९७ पितृलोकं चन्द्रमसं नभो वायुं जलं महीम्।
क्रमात्ते संभवन्तीह पुनरेव व्रजन्ति च॥

१९८ एतद्यो न विजानाति मार्गद्वितयमात्मनः।
दन्दशूकः पतङ्गो वा भवेत्कीटोऽथ वा कृमिः[४३]॥

१९९ ऊरुस्थोत्तानचरणः सव्ये न्यस्येतरं करम्।
उत्तानं किंचिदुन्नम्य मुखं विष्टभ्य चोरसा॥

२०० निमीलिताक्षः सत्त्वस्थो दन्तैर्दन्तानसंस्पृशन्।
तालुस्थाचलजिह्वश्च संवृतास्यः सुनिश्चलः॥

२०१ संनिरुध्येन्द्रियग्रामं नातिनीचोच्छ्रितासनः।
द्विगुणं त्रिगुणं वापि प्राणायाममुपक्रमेत्॥

Those who know him thus, and those twice-born persons who resort to the wilderness, when they, endowed with supreme faith, venerate truth, they enter in due order the flame, the day, the bright fortnight, the period when the sun moves north, the world of gods, and the sun along with lightning.[87] 193–194

Thence a person consisting of mind approaches them and makes them dwellers in the world of Brahma. For them there is no return to this world. 195

Those men who do win heaven by means of sacrifice, ascetic toil, and giving gifts, enter in due order the smoke, the night, the dark fortnight, the period when the sun moves south, the world of the fathers, the moon, the sky, the wind, the water, and the earth, and they proceed once again to this world. 196–197

The person who does not know these two paths of the self becomes a snake, a fly, an insect, or a worm.[88] 198

Placing his feet facing upward on his thighs, putting his right hand facing upward on his left, lifting up his face somewhat, keeping himself erect with his chest, keeping his eyes closed, abiding in the attribute of goodness, keeping the upper teeth and lower teeth from touching each other, keeping his tongue motionless against the palate, keeping his mouth closed, keeping himself motionless, keeping all his organs under restraint, and sitting on a seat that is neither too low nor too high, he should control his breath two or three times.[89] 199–201

२०२ ततो ध्येयः स्थितो योऽसौ हृदये दीपवत्प्रभुः ।
धारयेत्तत्र चात्मानं धारणां धारयन्बुधः ॥

२०३ अन्तर्धानं स्मृतिः कान्तिर्दृष्टिः श्रोत्रज्ञता तथा ।
निजं शरीरमुत्सृज्य परकायप्रवेशनम् ॥

२०४ अर्थानां छन्दतः सृष्टिर्योगसिद्धेस्तु लक्षणम् ।
सिद्धे योगे त्यजन्देहममृतत्वाय कल्पते ॥

२०५ अथ वाप्यभ्यसन्वेदं न्यस्तकर्मा सुते वसन् ।
अयाचिताशी मितभुक्परां सिद्धिमवाप्नुयात्[४४] ॥

२०६ न्यायार्जितधनस्तत्त्वज्ञाननिष्ठोऽतिथिप्रियः ।
श्राद्धकृत्सत्यवादी च गृहस्थोऽपि विमुच्यते ॥

॥ इति यतिधर्मप्रकरणम् ॥

Then, he should contemplate that lord who abides in his heart like a lamp. And the wise man should concentrate on the self abiding there, as he performs mental concentration. 202

Becoming invisible, memory, beauty, sight, hearing, knowledge, leaving one's own body and entering another's body, and the creation of things at will—these, however, are the characteristics of yogic accomplishment. Once yogic accomplishment has been achieved, abandoning the body, he becomes fit for immortality.[90] 203–204

Alternatively, he will obtain the highest accomplishment when he recites the Veda and gives up ritual activity while living with his son, eating what he obtains unasked and eating little.[91] 205

Even a householder is liberated when he acquires wealth by lawful means, is firmly established in the knowledge of the truth, loves guests, performs ancestral offerings, and speaks the truth. 206

## ॥ अथ प्रायश्चित्तप्रकरणम् ॥

२०७ महापातकजान्घोरान्नरकान्प्राप्य गर्हितान् ।
कर्मक्षयात्प्रजायन्ते महापातकिनस्त्विह[४५] ॥

२०८ श्वसूकरमृगोष्ट्राणां ब्रह्महा याति योनिषु ।
खरपुल्कसवेनानां सुरापो नात्र संशयः ॥

२०९ कृमिकीटपतङ्गत्वं स्वर्णहारी समाप्नुयात् ।
तृणगुल्मलतात्वं च क्रमशो गुरुतल्पगः ॥

२१० ब्रह्महा क्षयरोगी स्यात्सुरापः श्यावदन्तकः ।
हेमहारी तु कुनखी दुश्चर्मा गुरुतल्पगः ॥

२११ यो येन संपिबत्येषां स तल्लिङ्गोऽभिजायते ।
अन्नहर्तामयावी स्यान्मूको वागपहारकः[४६] ॥

२१२ धान्यमिश्र्यतिरिक्ताङ्गः पिशुनः पूतिनासिकः ।
तैलहृत्तैलपायी स्यात्पूतिवक्त्रस्तु सूचकः ॥

२१३ परस्य योषितं हृत्वा ब्रह्मस्वमपहृत्य च ।
अरण्ये निर्जले देशे जायते ब्रह्मराक्षसः ॥

# TOPIC 42: EXPIATION

After reaching frightful and contemptible hells resulting from grievous sins causing loss of caste, however, upon the exhaustion of their karma, people guilty of grievous sins causing loss of caste are born in this world.[92] 207

A murder of a Brahman enters the womb of a dog, a pig, a deer, and a camel; someone who drinks liquor, that of a donkey, a Pulkasa, and a Vena;[93] 208

someone who steals gold becomes a worm, an insect, and a fly; and someone who has sex with his elder's wife becomes grass, a bush, and a vine—in that order. 209

A murderer of a Brahman gets consumption; someone who drinks liquor, black teeth; someone who steals gold, rotten nails; and someone who has sex with his elder's wife, skin disease. 210

When someone drinks water with any one of them, he is born with the same marks as the latter. Someone who steals food becomes dyspeptic, and someone who steals speech becomes dumb.[94] 211

Someone who adulterates grains gets an excess limb; and a slanderer, a smelly nose. Someone who steals oil becomes a cockroach, and an informant gets a smelly mouth. 212

By abducting someone else's wife and by stealing the property of a Brahman, a man is born as a Brahman fiend living in a waterless region of the wilderness. 213

२१४ हीनजातौ प्रजायन्ते रत्नानामपहारकाः ।
पत्रशाकं शिखी हृत्वा गन्धांश्छुच्छुन्दरी शुभान् ॥

२१५ मूषिको धान्यहारी स्याद्यानमुष्ट्रः फलं कपिः ।
अजः पशुं पयः काको गृहकार उपस्करम्[४७] ॥

२१६ मधु दंशः पलं गृध्रो गां गोधाग्निं बकस्तथा ।
श्वित्री वस्त्रं श्वा रसं तु चीरी लवणमेव च ॥

२१७ प्रदर्शनार्थमेतत्तु मयोक्तं स्तेयकर्मणि ।
द्रव्यप्रकारा हि यथा तथैव प्राणिजातयः ॥

२१८ यथाकर्म निषेव्यैवं तिर्यक्त्वं कालपर्ययात् ।
जायन्ते लक्षणभ्रष्टा दरिद्राः पुरुषाधमाः ॥

२१९ ततो निष्कल्मषीभूताः कुले महति भोगिनः ।
जायन्ते लक्षणोपेता धनधान्यसमन्विताः[४८] ॥

२२० विहितस्याननुष्ठानान्निन्दितस्य च सेवनात् ।
अनिग्रहाच्चेन्द्रियाणां नरः पतनमृच्छति ॥

२२१ तस्मात्तेनेह कर्तव्यं प्रायश्चित्तं विशुद्धये ।
एवमस्यान्तरात्मा च लोकश्चैव प्रसीदति ॥

Those who steal gems are born in a low caste. By stealing leafy vegetables one becomes a peacock; and by stealing fragrant perfumes, a muskrat. 214

Someone who steals grain becomes a rat. By stealing a cart, one becomes a camel; by stealing fruit, a monkey; by stealing a farm animal, a goat; by stealing milk, a crow; by stealing a household utensil, a mason-wasp;[95] 215

by stealing honey, a gnat; by stealing meat, a vulture; by stealing a cow, a monitor lizard; by stealing fire, a *baka* heron; by stealing a garment, a person with leukoderma; by stealing sweets, a dog; and by stealing salt, a cricket. 216

I have told you this simply as an illustration, however, with reference to theft. For, the species of living beings correspond to the kinds of articles. 217

Having gone through in this manner the animal condition corresponding to their actions, in the course of time they are born as the lowest of human beings, in dire poverty and devoid of auspicious marks. 218

Thereafter, having become freed from taint, they are born in a great family enjoying luxuries, endowed with auspicious marks and possessing wealth and grain.[96] 219

By not performing what is prescribed, by indulging in despicable deeds, and by not restraining his organs, a man falls. 220

Therefore, he should perform expiations in this world to purify himself. In this way, both his inner self and the world become pacified. 221

२२२ प्रायश्चित्तैरपैत्येनो यदज्ञानकृतं भवेत्।
कामतो व्यवहार्यस्तु वचनादिह जायते॥

२२३ प्रायश्चित्तमकुर्वाणाः पापेषु निरता नराः।
अपश्चात्तापिनः कष्टान्नरकान्यान्ति दारुणान्॥

२२४ तामिस्रं लोहशङ्कुश्च महानिरयशल्मली।
रौरवं कुड्मलं पूतिमृत्तिकं कालसूत्रकम्॥

२२५ संघातं लोहितोदं च सविषं संप्रतापनम्।
महानरककाकोलं संजीवननदीपथम्[४९]॥

२२६ अवीचिमन्धतामिस्रं कुम्भीपाकं तथैव च।
असिपत्रवनं चैव तपनं चैकविंशकम्॥

२२७ महापातकजैर्घोरैरुपपातकजैस्तथा।
अन्विता यान्त्यचरितप्रायश्चित्ता नराधमाः॥

२२८ ब्रह्महा मद्यपः स्तेनस्तथैव गुरुतल्पगः।
एते महापातकिनो यश्चैतैः संपिबेत्समाम्[५०]॥

२२९ गुरूणामत्यधिक्षेपो वेदनिन्दा सुहृद्वधः।
ब्रह्महत्यासमं ह्येतदधीतस्य च नाशनम्॥

२३० निषिद्धभक्षणं जैह्म्यमुत्कर्षे च वचोऽनृतम्।
रजस्वलामुखास्वादः सुरापानसमानि तु॥

Expiations wipe out a sin that has been committed unknowingly. When it is committed deliberately, however, the obligation to have social intercourse with such a person arises in this world because of the explicit statement to that effect.[97] 222

Men who do not perform expiations, take delight in sinful acts, and do not show any remorse, go to harsh and frightful hells. 223

*Tāmisra, lohaśaṅku, mahāniraya, śalmalī, raurava, kuḍmala, pūtimṛttika, kālasūtraka, saṃghāta, lohitoda, saviṣa, saṃpratāpana, mahānaraka, kākola, saṃjīvana, nadīpatha, avīci, andhatāmisra, kumbhīpāka, asipatravana,* and *tapana,* the twenty-first[98]— 224–226

to these go the vilest of men who are tainted with the frightful evils caused by grievous and secondary sins causing loss of caste, and who have not performed expiations. 227

A murderer of a Brahman, someone who drinks liquor, a thief, and someone who has sex with an elder's wife— these are people guilty of a grievous sin causing loss of caste; as also someone who drinks water with them for a year.[99] 228

Treating one's elders with utter contempt, reviling the Veda, and killing a friend are equal to the murder of a Brahman, as also letting what one has learnt go into oblivion. 229

Eating what is forbidden, cheating, a lie concerning one's superiority, and kissing the mouth of a menstruating woman are equal to drinking liquor. 230

२३१ अश्वरत्नमनुष्यस्त्रीभूधेनुहरणं तथा ।
निक्षेपस्य च सर्वं हि सुवर्णस्तेयसंमितम् ॥

२३२ सखिभार्याकुमारीषु स्वयोनिष्वन्त्यजासु च ।
सगोत्रासु सुतस्त्रीषु गुरुतल्पसमं विदुः ॥

२३३ पितृष्वसां मातुलानीं स्नुषां मातृष्वसामपि ।
मातुः सपत्नीं भगिनीमाचार्यतनयां तथा ॥

२३४ आचार्यपत्नीं स्वसुतां गच्छंस्तु गुरुतल्पगः ।
छित्त्वा लिङ्गं वधस्तस्य सकामायाश्च योषितः ॥

२३५ गोवधो व्रात्यता स्तैन्यमृणानां चानपक्रिया ।
अनाहिताग्निितापण्यविक्रयः परिविन्दनम् ॥

२३६ भृतादध्ययनादानं भृतकाध्यापनं तथा ।
पारदार्यं पारिवित्त्यं वार्धुष्यं लवणक्रिया ॥

२३७ स्त्रीशूद्रविड्क्षत्रवधो निन्दितार्थोपजीवनम् ।
नास्तिक्यं व्रतलोपश्च सुतानां चैव विक्रयः ॥

२३८ धान्यरूप्यपशुस्तेयमयाज्यानां च याजनम् ।
पितृमातृसुहृत्त्यागस्तटाकारामविक्रयः[५१] ॥

Stealing a horse, a gem, a man, a woman, land, or a cow, as also a deposit—all that is equal to the theft of gold. 231

Having sex with the wives of friends, young girls, uterine relatives, lowest-born women, women belonging to his own lineage, and wives of his sons is considered equal to having sex with an elder's wife. 232

Father's sister, maternal uncle's wife, daughter-in-law, mother's sister, mother's co-wife, sister, teacher's daughter, teacher's wife, and one's own daughter—when he has sex with any of these he is guilty of having sex with an elder's wife. Such a man, after cutting off his genitals, should be executed, as also the woman if she was willing. 233–234

Killing a cow; being in the state of a *vrātya;* theft; not paying one's debts; not establishing the three Vedic fires; selling what is forbidden to be sold; a younger brother marrying before his older brother;[100] 235

receiving instruction from a paid teacher; giving instruction as a paid teacher; adultery; remaining unmarried while one's younger brother is married; usury; dealing in salt; 236

killing a woman, Shudra, Vaishya, or Kshatriya; subsisting on forbidden wealth; being an infidel; breaking a vow; selling children; 237

stealing grain, silver, or farm animals; officiating at a sacrifice of persons at whose sacrifice one is forbidden to officiate; abandoning one's father, mother, or friend; selling a reservoir or park;[101] 238

२३९ कन्याया दूषणं चैव परिविन्दकयाजनम् ।
कन्याप्रदानं तस्यैव कौटिल्यं ब्रह्मलोपनम्[५२] ॥

२४० आत्मार्थे च क्रियारम्भो मद्यपस्त्रीनिषेवणम् ।
स्वाध्यायाग्निसुतत्यागो बान्धवत्याग एव च ॥

२४१ इन्धनार्थं द्रुमच्छेदः स्त्रीहिंस्रौषधिजीवनम् ।
हिंस्रयन्त्रविधानं च व्यसनान्यात्मविक्रयः[५३] ॥

२४२ असच्छास्त्राधिगमनमाकरेष्वधिकारिता ।
भार्याविक्रयणं चैषामेकैकमुपपातकम् ॥

२४३ शिरःकपालध्वजवान्भैक्षाशी कर्म वेदयन् ।
ब्रह्महा द्वादश समा मितभुक्शुद्धिमाप्नुयात् ॥

२४४ लोमभ्यः स्वाहेति हि वा लोमप्रभृति वै तनुम् ।
मज्जान्तां जुहुयाद्वापि मन्त्रैरेभिर्यथाक्रमम् ॥

२४५ ब्राह्मणस्य परित्राणाद्गवां द्वादशकस्य वा ।
तथाश्वमेधावभृथस्नानाद्वा शुद्धिमाप्नुयात् ॥

२४६ दीर्घतीव्रामयग्रस्तं ब्राह्मणं गामथापि वा ।
दृष्ट्वा पथि निरातङ्कं कृत्वा वा ब्रह्महा शुचिः ॥

violating a virgin; officiating at a sacrifice of a man who has married before his elder brother; giving a virgin in marriage to such a person; crookedness; neglecting the Veda;[102] 239

undertaking activities for one's own sake; having sex with a woman who drinks liquor; abandoning Vedic recitation, sacred fire, or a son; abandoning a relative; 240

cutting a tree for firewood; using his wife or harmful medicines to make a living; constructing harmful equipment; engaging in vices; selling oneself;[103] 241

studying fallacious treatises; having a supervisory role in mines; and selling a wife—each of these is a secondary sin causing loss of caste. 242

Bearing a banner with a head, carrying a skull bowl, and eating what he has begged while announcing his deed, a murderer of a Brahman, subsisting on a little food, obtains purification in twelve years.[104] 243

Alternatively, he should offer his body in a fire beginning with his hair and ending with his marrow, reciting these mantras in the proper order: "To the hairs, *svāhā!*"[105] 244

Or, by rescuing a Brahman or twelve cows, or by participating in the bath that concludes a horse sacrifice, he obtains purification. 245

Or, by curing a Brahman or a cow whom he sees on the road afflicted with a long and accute sickness, a murderer of a Brahman becomes purified. 246

२४७ आनीय विप्रसर्वस्वं हृतं घातित एव वा ।
तन्निमित्तं क्षतः शस्त्रैर्जीवन्नपि विशुध्यति ॥

२४८ अरण्ये नियतो जप्त्वा त्रिष्कृत्वो वेदसंहिताम् ।
शुध्येत वा मिताशीत्वा प्रतिस्रोतः सरस्वतीम्[५४] ॥

२४९ संग्रामे वा हतो लक्षभूतः शुद्धिमवाप्नुयात् ।
मृतकल्पः प्रहारार्तो जीवन्नपि विशुध्यति ॥

२५० पात्रे धनं वा पर्याप्तं दत्त्वा शुद्धिं निगच्छति ।
आदातुश्च विशुद्ध्यर्थमिष्टिर्वैश्वानरी स्मृता ॥

२५१ यागस्थक्षत्रविड्घाते चरेद्ब्रह्महणो व्रतम् ।
गर्भहा च यथावर्णं तथात्रेयीनिषूदकः ॥

२५२ चरेद्व्रतमहत्वापि घातार्थं चेत्समागतः ।
द्विगुणं सवनस्थे तु ब्राह्मणे व्रतमाचरेत् ॥

२५३ सुराम्बुघृतगोमूत्रपयसामग्निसंनिभम् ।
सुरापोऽन्यतमं पीत्वा मरणाच्छुद्धिमृच्छति ॥

By recoving the entire property of a Brahman that has been robbed or by being killed or wounded with weapons in that attempt, he is purified even while alive. 247

By reciting softly three times a Collection of the Veda in the wilderness while remaining self-controlled, or by eating little as he goes upstream along the Sarasvati River, he becomes purified.[106] 248

Or, he obtains purification by being killed in a battle where he makes himself a target, or, nearly dead and suffering from his wounds, he becomes purified even while alive. 249

Or, by giving copious wealth to a deserving recipient he attains purity. The Vaishvanara offering is prescribed for the purification of that receiver. 250

For killing a Kshatriya or a Vaishya while engaged in a sacrifice, one should perform the observance for a murderer of a Brahman. Someone who kills a fetus should perform the observance according to the social class to which it belongs, as also someone who kills a woman soon after her menstrual period.[107] 251

A man should perform this observance if he has come with the intention of killing, even though he may not have actually killed. In the case of a Brahman engaged in a sacrifice, however, he should perform double the observance. 252

Liquor, water, ghee, cow's urine, and milk—by drinking any one of these boiling hot, a man who has drunk liquor obtains purification through death. 253

२५४ वालवासा जटी वापि चरेद्ब्रह्महणव्रतम्।
पिण्याकं वा कणान्वापि भक्षयीत समां निशि[५५]॥

२५५ अज्ञानात्तु सुरां पीत्वा रेतो विण्मूत्रमेव वा।
पुनःसंस्कारमर्हन्ति त्रयो वर्णा न संशयः[५६]॥

२५६ पतिलोकं न सा याति ब्राह्मणी या सुरां पिबेत्।
इहैव सा शुनी गृध्री सूकरी वोपजायते॥

२५७ ब्राह्मणस्वर्णहारी तु राज्ञे मुसलमर्पयेत्।
स्वकर्म ख्यापयंस्तेन हतो मुक्तोऽपि वा शुचिः॥

२५८ अनाख्याय नृपे शुद्ध्यै सुरापव्रतमाचरेत्।
आत्मतुल्यं सुवर्णं वा दद्याद्वा विप्रतुष्टिकृत्॥

२५९ तप्तेऽयःशयने सार्धमायस्या योषिता स्वपेत्।
गृहीत्वोत्कृत्य वृषणौ नैर्ऋत्यां चोत्सृजेत्तनुम्॥

२६० प्राजापत्यं चरेत्कृच्छ्रं समां वा गुरुतल्पगः।
चान्द्रायणं वा त्रीन्मासानभ्यसन्वेदसंहिताम्॥

२६१ एभिस्तु संपिबेद्यो वै वत्सरात्सोऽपि तत्समः।
कन्यां समुद्वहेदेषां सोपवासामकिंचनाम्[५७]॥

Or else, wearing a hair garment and matted hair, he should perform the observance for killing a Brahman, or he should eat oil-cake or broken grain at night for one year.[108] 254

After consuming liquor, semen, feces, or urine unknowingly, people of the three social classes should undoubtedly undergo Vedic initiation once again.[109] 255

A Brahman woman who drinks liquor does not go to the world of her husband. She is reborn in this very world as a female dog, female vulture, or sow. 256

A man who has stolen a Brahman's gold, however, should present a pestle to the king, proclaiming his deed. Whether he is killed or released by him, he is purified. 257

To become purified without proclaiming it to the king, he should perform the observance for a man who has drunk liquor. Or, he should give gold of the same weight as himself or as much as would gratify a Brahman. 258

A man who has sex with his elder's wife should sleep with a woman made of iron on a heated iron bed; cutting off his testicles and holding them, he should give up his body in the southeastern direction; or he should perform the *prājāpatya* penance for one year or the lunar fast for three months while reciting a Collection of the Veda.[110] 259–260

A man who drinks water with these people, however, becomes equal to them in one year. One may marry a virgin girl of theirs after she has observed a fast and without bringing any property at all with her.[111] 261

२६२ चान्द्रायणं चरेत्सर्वानपकृष्टान्निहत्य तु।
शूद्रोऽधिकारहीनोऽपि कालेनानेन शुध्यति॥

२६३ मिथ्याभिशंसिनो दोषो द्विः समो भूतवादिनः।
मिथ्याभिशस्तपापं च समादत्ते मृषा वदन्॥

२६४ पञ्चगव्यं पिबन्गोघ्नो मासमासीत संयतः।
गोष्ठेशयो गोऽनुगामी गोप्रदानेन शुध्यति॥

२६५ कृच्छ्रं चैवातिकृच्छ्रं च चरेद्वापि समाहितः।
दद्यात्त्रिरात्रं वोपोष्य ऋषभैकादशास्तु गाः॥

२६६ उपपातकशुद्धिः स्यादेवं चान्द्रायणेन वा।
पयसा वापि मासेन पराकेणापि वा पुनः॥

२६७ ऋषभैकसहस्रा गा दद्यात्क्षत्रवधे पुमान्।
ब्रह्महत्याव्रतं वापि वत्सरत्रितयं चरेत्॥

२६८ वैश्यहाब्दं चरेदेतद्दद्याद्वैकशतं गवाम्।
षण्मासाच्छूद्रहा वापि दद्याद्वा धेनवो दश॥

A man should perform the lunar penance, however, after killing any person inferior to himself. A Shudra, even though he is without competence, is purified after this length of time.[112] 262

A person who makes a false accusation incurs double the guilt, while a person who makes an accusation that is factual incurs an equal guilt. A man speaking falsely, furthermore, takes upon himself the sin of the person who is falsely accused.[113] 263

A killer of a cow should remain self-controlled for one month drinking the five products of the cow, sleeping in a cowshed and following a cow. He is purified by gifting a cow.[114] 264

Or, remaining self-possessed, he should perform an arduous penance and an extreme arduous penance. Or, after fasting for three nights, he should gift ten cows and a bull.[115] 265

Purification of a secondary sin causing loss of caste is done in the same manner, or by means of a lunar fast, or by subsisting on milk for a month, or else by means of a *parāka* penance.[116] 266

For killing a Kshatriya, a man should give one thousand cows along with a bull, or he should perform for three years the observance for the murder of a Brahman. 267

A man who kills a Vaishya should perform this for one year or give 101 cows, while a man who kills a Shudra should do it for six months or give ten milch cows. 268

२६९ दुर्वृत्तब्राह्मणक्षत्रविट्छूद्रस्त्रीप्रमापणे।
दृतिं धनुर्बस्तमविं क्रमाद्दद्याद्विशुद्धये॥

२७० अप्रदुष्टां स्त्रियं हत्वा शूद्रहत्याव्रतं चरेत्।
अस्थन्वतां सहस्रं च तथानस्थिमतामनः॥

२७१ मार्जारगोधानकुलमण्डूकश्वपतत्रिणः।
हत्वा त्र्यहं पिबेत्क्षीरं कृच्छ्रं वा पादिकं चरेत्॥

२७२ गजे नीला वृषाः पञ्च शुके वत्सो द्विहायनः।
खराजमेषेषु वृषो देयः क्रौञ्चे त्रिहायनः॥

२७३ हत्वा श्येनकपिक्रव्याज्जलस्थलशिखण्डिनः।
भासं च हत्वा दद्याद्गामक्रव्यादेषु वत्सिकाम्[५८]॥

२७४ उरगेष्वायसो दण्डः पण्डके त्रपुमाषकः।
कोले घृतघटो देय उष्ट्रे गुञ्जा हयेऽशुकम्[५९]॥

२७५ तित्तिरौ तु तिलद्रोणं गजादीनामशक्नुवन्।
दानं दातुं चरेत्कृच्छ्रमेकैकस्य विशुद्धये॥

For killing an immoral wife of a Brahman, Kshatriya, Vaishya, and Shudra, a man should give a leather water bag, a bow, a goat, and a sheep, respectively, in order to purify himself. 269

For killing a woman who is not corrupt, a man should perform the observance for killing a Shudra, as also for killing one thousand creatures with bones or a cart full of boneless creatures. 270

After killing a cat, monitor lizard, mongoose, frog, dog, or bird, a man should drink milk for three days or perform one quarter of an arduous penance. 271

For killing an elephant, a man should give five black bulls; for killing a parrot, a two-year-old calf; for killing a donkey, goat, or ram, a bull; and for killing a *krauñca* crane, a three-year-old calf.[117] 272

After killing a vulture, monkey, carnivorous animal, water or land bird, or peacock, as also a *bhāsa* vulture, a man should give a cow; for killing a non-carnivorous animal, a heifer.[118] 273

For killing a snake, a man should give an iron staff; for killing a castrated animal, a *māṣaka* of tin; for killing a pig, a pot of ghee; for killing a camel, a *guñjā;* for killing a horse, a garment;[119] 274

for killing a *tittira* partridge, a *droṇa* of oil. If a man is unable to make the gift prescribed for killing an elephant and so forth, he should perform an arduous penance in order to obtain purification for each one of them.[120] 275

२७६ किंचित्सास्थिवधे देयं प्राणायामस्त्वनस्थिके ।
वृक्षगुल्मलतावीरुच्छेदने जप्यमृक्शतम्[६०] ॥

२७७ पुंश्चलीवानरखरैर्दष्टश्चैव श्ववायसैः ।
प्राणायामाञ्जले कृत्वा घृतं प्राश्य विशुध्यति[६१] ॥

२७८ फलपुष्पान्नरसजसत्त्वघाते घृताशनः ।
स्यादोषधिवृथाछेदे क्षीराशी गोऽनुगो दिनम् ॥

२७९ यन्मेऽद्य रेत इत्याभ्यां स्कन्नं रेतोऽभिमन्त्र्य वा ।
स्तनान्तरं भ्रुवोर्वापि तेनानामिकया स्पृशेत् ॥

२८० मयि तेज इति छायां स्वां दृष्ट्वाम्बुगतां जपेत् ।
गायत्रीमशुचौ दृष्टे चापलेऽथानृतेऽपि च ॥

२८१ अवकीर्णी भवेद्गत्वा ब्रह्मचारी तु योषितम् ।
गर्दभं पशुमालभ्य नैर्ऋतं स विशुध्यति ॥

A little something should be given for killing a creature with bones, while one should perform the control of breath in the case of a boneless creature. For cutting down a tree, shrub, vine, or plant, a man should recite one hundred *ṛc* verses.[121] 276

A person bitten by a prostitute, monkey, or donkey, or by dogs or birds, is purified when, after he has controlled his breath in water, he has consumed some ghee.[122] 277

For killing creatures born in fruits, flowers, food, or sweets, a man should subsist on ghee; and for cutting plants for no reason, he should subsist on milk and follow a cow for one day. 278

When he has spilled semen, after reciting these two mantras over it: "I retrieve this semen that fell on earth today, into water or plants though it may have seeped. May I regain my virility, my ardor, my passion; let the fire and the fire-mounds each return to its place,"[123] he should rub that semen between his breasts or between his eyebrows using his ring finger. 279

After seeing his reflection in water, he should softly recite: "May vigor, virility, fame, wealth, and merit remain in me."[124] When he sees something impure, he should softly recite the *gāyatrī* verse, as also when he acts recklessly or tells a lie. 280

A Vedic student breaks his vow of chastity when he approaches a woman. He is purified by sacrificing a donkey dedicated to Nirriti.[125] 281

२८२ भैक्षाग्निकार्ये त्यक्त्वा तु सप्तरात्रमनातुरः।
कामावकीर्ण इत्याभ्यां हुत्वाज्येनाहुतिद्वयम् ॥

२८३ उपस्थानं ततः कुर्यात्सं मा सिंचेत्यनेन तु।
मधुमांसाशने कार्यः कृच्छ्रः शेषव्रतानि च ॥

२८४ कृच्छ्रत्रयं गुरुः कुर्यान्म्रियेत प्रहितो यदि।
प्रतिकूलं गुरोः कृत्वा तं प्रसाद्य विशुध्यति[६२] ॥

२८५ औषधान्नप्रदानाद्यैर्भिषग्योगाद्युपक्रमैः।
क्रियमाणोपकारे तु मृते विप्रे न पातकम्।
विपाके गोवृषादीनां भैषज्याग्निक्रियासु च[६३] ॥

२८६ महापापोपपापाभ्यां योऽभिशंसेन्मृषा परम्।
अब्भक्षो मासमासीत स जापी नियतेन्द्रियः॥

२८७ अभिशस्तो मृषा कृच्छ्रं चरेदाग्नेयमेव वा।
निर्वपेत पुरोडाशं वायव्यं पशुमेव वा ॥

When he neglects begging for almsfood or performing the fire ritual for seven nights without being sick, he should make two offerings of ghee in the fire with these two formulas: "Oh Lust! I have spilled semen! I have spilled semen, Oh Lust! To Lust, *svāhā!*" and "Oh Lust, I have been squeezed out! I have been squeezed out, Oh Lust! To Lust, *svāhā!*"[126] 282

Then he should perform the fire worship, saying, "May the Maruts pour upon me, may Indra and Brihaspati; and may this fire pour upon me long life and strength. May they make me live long."[127] When he has consumed honey or meat, he should perform an arduous penance and complete the rest of his observances. 283

The teacher should perform three arduous penances if a pupil he has sent on an errand dies. When a pupil does something offensive to his teacher, he is purified by propitiating him.[128] 284

Should a Brahman die while he is being assisted through such means as administering medicine and food, and by remedies such as medical procedures, it does not result in a sin causing loss of caste; so also in the case of a mishap to cows, bulls, and the like in the course of medical treatment or branding.[129] 285

Should someone falsely accuse another person of a grievous or secondary sin causing loss of caste, he should remain for one month subsisting on water, engaged in soft recitation and controlling his organs. 286

The person who is falsely accused should perform an arduous penance or offer a sacrificial cake dedicated to Fire or an animal dedicated to Wind. 287

२८८ अनियुक्तो भ्रातृजायां गच्छंश्चान्द्रायणं चरेत् ।
त्रिरात्रान्ते घृतं प्राश्य गत्वोदक्यां विशुध्यति ॥

२८९ गोष्ठे वसन्ब्रह्मचारी मासमेकं पयोव्रतः ।
गायत्रीजापनिरतो मुच्यतेऽसत्प्रतिग्रहात्[६४] ॥

२९० त्रीन्कृच्छ्रानाचरेद्व्रात्ययाजकोऽभिचरन्नपि ।
वेदप्लावी यवाश्यब्दं त्यक्त्वा च शरणागतम् ॥

२९१ प्राणायामांश्चरेत्स्नात्वा खरयानोष्ट्रयानगः ।
नग्नः स्नात्वा च सुप्त्वा च गत्वा चैव दिवा स्त्रियम्[६५] ॥

२९२ गुरुं त्वंकृत्य हुंकृत्य विप्रं निर्जित्य वादतः ।
हत्वावबध्य वा क्षिप्रं प्रसाद्योपवसेद्दिनम्[६६] ॥

२९३ विप्रदण्डोद्यमे कृच्छ्रस्त्वतिकृच्छ्रो निपातने ।
कृच्छ्रातिकृच्छ्रोऽसृक्पाते कृच्छ्रोऽभ्यन्तरशोणिते ॥

२९४ देशं कालं वयः शक्तिं पापं चावेक्ष्य यत्नतः ।
प्रायश्चित्तं प्रकल्प्यं स्याद्यत्र चोक्ता न निष्कृतिः ॥

A man who has sex with his brother's wife without being appointed should perform the lunar fast. A man who has sex with a menstruating woman is purified by consuming some ghee at the end of the third night.[130] 288

When a man accepts a gift from an unrighteous person, he is purified by remaining in a cowshed for one month while observing chastity, keeping the vow of subsisting on milk, and being devoted to the soft recitation of the *gāyatrī* verse.[131] 289

A man who officiates at the sacrifice of a *vrātya,* as also someone who performs sorcery, should perform three arduous penances. A man who ruins the Veda should subsist on barley for one year, as also a man who abandons someone who has come to him for refuge.[132] 290

A man who travels by a donkey or camel cart should bathe and perform breath controls, so also someone who bathes or sleeps naked and who has sex with a woman during the day.[133] 291

When someone addresses an elder as "you" or says "*huṃ*" to him, defeats a Brahman in an argument, or strikes or ties him up, he should quickly propitiate him and fast for one day.[134] 292

For raising a stick at a Brahman, one should perform an arduous penance; for striking with it, an extreme arduous penance; for drawing blood, an arduous plus extreme arduous penance; and when there is internal bleeding, an arduous penance. 293

Where no penance has been prescribed, an expiation should be devised taking into account carefully the place, the time, the age, the ability, and the sin. 294

२९५ दासीघटमपां पूर्णं निनयेरन्स्वबान्धवाः ।
पतितस्य बहिष्कुर्युः सर्वकार्येषु चैव तम्[६७] ॥

२९६ चरितव्रत आयाते निनयेरन्नवं घटम् ।
जुगुप्सेयुर्न चाप्येनं संपिबेयुश्च सर्वशः[६८] ॥

२९७ एष एव विधिः स्त्रीणां पतितानां प्रकीर्तितः ।
वासो गृहान्तिके देय अन्नं वासः सरक्षणम् ॥

२९८ नीचाभिगमनं गर्भपातनं भर्तृहिंसनम् ।
विशेषपतनीयानि स्त्रीणामेतान्यपि ध्रुवम् ॥

२९९ शरणागतबालस्त्रीहिंसकान्संपिबेन्न तु ।
चीर्णव्रतानपि सतः कृतघ्नसहितानिमान्[६९] ॥

३०० घटेऽपवर्जिते ज्ञातिमध्यस्थः प्रथमं गवाम् ।
प्रदद्याद्यवसं गोभिः सत्कृतस्य सहक्रिया[७०] ॥

३०१ विख्यातदोषः कुर्वीत पर्षदानुमतं व्रतम् ।
अनभिख्यातदोषस्तु रहस्यं व्रतमाचरेत् ॥

३०२ त्रिरात्रोपोषितो जप्त्वा ब्रह्महा त्वघमर्षणम् ।
अन्तर्जले विशुध्येत दत्त्वा गां च पयस्विनीम् ॥

The relatives of a man who has fallen from his caste should overturn a pot of a slave woman filled with water, and they should exclude him from all their activities.[135] 295

When he returns after performing the observance, they should overturn a new pot. And they should not spurn him, but at all times drink water with him.[136] 296

The very same rule has been declared with respect to women who have fallen from their caste. They should be provided lodging near the house, as also food and clothes along with protection. 297

Sex with a low-caste man, causing an abortion, and doing harm to her husband—in the case of women these undoubtedly are the special causes for fall from caste. 298

One should not drink water, however, with those who cause harm to people who have come for refuge and to children and women, or with ungrateful people, even though they may have completed their observances.[137] 299

Once the pot has been overturned, standing in the midst of his relatives, he should first give fodder to cows. Should he be treated respectfully by the cows, one may associate with him.[138] 300

A man whose sin is publicly known should perform the observance approved by the legal assembly.[139] A man whose sin is not publicly known, however, should perform a secret observance. 301

A murderer of a Brahman, however, is purified by fasting for three nights, softly reciting the *aghamarṣaṇa* hymn while remaining in water, and then giving a cow that yields milk.[140] 302

३०३ लोमभ्यः स्वाहेति हि वा दिवसं मारुताशनः।
जले सुप्त्वाभिजुहुयाच्चत्वारिंशद्घृताहुतीः[७१]॥

३०४ त्रिरात्रोपोषितो हुत्वा कूष्माण्डीभिर्घृतं शुचिः।
सुरापः स्वर्णहारी तु रुद्रजापी जले स्थितः॥

३०५ सहस्रशीर्षाजापी तु शुध्यते गुरुतल्पगः।
गौर्देया कर्मणश्चान्ते पृथगेभिः पयस्विनी॥

३०६ प्राणायामशतं कुर्यात्सर्वपापापनुत्तये।
उपपातकजातानामनिर्दिष्टस्य चैव हि॥

३०७ ओङ्काराभिषुतं सोमसलिलं पावनं पिबेत्।
कृतोपवसनं रेतोविण्मूत्रप्राशने द्विजः॥

३०८ निशायां वा दिवा वापि यदज्ञानकृतं त्वघम्।
त्रिष्कालसंध्याकरणात्तत्सर्वं विप्रणश्यति॥

३०९ शुक्रियारण्यकजपो गायत्र्याश्च सहस्रशः।
सर्वपापहरः प्रोक्तो रुद्रैकादशिनी तथा[७२]॥

३१० यत्र यत्र च संकीर्णमात्मानं मन्यते द्विजः।
तत्र तत्र तिलैर्होमः सावित्र्या जप एव वा॥

Or, having remained lying down in water for one day while subsisting on wind and reciting: "To hairs, *svāhā!*," he should make forty offerings of ghee into the fire.[141] 303

A man who drinks liquor is purified by fasting for three nights and making an offering of ghee in the fire reciting the *kūṣmāṇḍī* verses, whereas a man who steals gold is purified by softly reciting the *rudra* verses while standing in water. 304

A man who has had sex with an elder's wife is purified by softly reciting the *sahasraśīrṣa* hymn. At the end of their rites, these people should each give a cow that yields milk.[142] 305

For erasing every kind of sin, a man should control his breath one hundred times, as also for transgressions resulting from secondary sins causing loss of caste and for those for which a penance has not been prescribed. 306

For consuming semen, feces, or urine, a twice-born person should observe a fast and drink the purifying *soma* water pressed while reciting the syllable OṂ. 307

Whatever sin committed unknowingly at night or during the day, all that is destroyed by performing the twilight worship at the three junctures of the day.[143] 308

The silent recitation of *śukriya* and *āraṇyaka* and of the *gāyatrī* verse a thousand times is said to wipe out all sins; as also the eleven *rudra* verses.[144] 309

On whatever occasion a twice-born person considers himself polluted, on every such occasion he should perform a fire offering with sesame seeds or just softly recite the *sāvitrī* verse. 310

३११ वेदाभ्यासरतं क्षान्तं पञ्चयज्ञक्रियारतम् ।
न स्पृशन्तीह पापानि महापातकजान्यपि ॥

३१२ वायुभक्षो दिवा तिष्ठन्रात्रिं नीत्वाप्सु सूर्यदृक् ।
जप्त्वा सहस्रं गायत्र्याः शुध्येद्ब्रह्मवधादृते ॥

३१३ ब्रह्मचर्यं दया क्षान्तिर्ध्यानं सत्यमकल्कता ।
अहिंसास्तेयमद्रोहो दमश्चैते यमाः स्मृताः[७३] ॥

३१४ स्नानमौनोपवासेज्यास्वाध्यायोपस्थनिग्रहाः ।
नियमा गुरुशुश्रूषा शौचाक्रोधप्रदातृताः[७४] ॥

३१५ पञ्चगव्यं तु गोक्षीरं दधि मूत्रं शकृद्घृतम् ।
पीत्वा परेद्युपवसेत्कृच्छ्रं सान्तपनं चरन्[७५] ॥

३१६ पृथक् सान्तपनद्रव्यैः षडहः सोपवासकः ।
सप्ताहेन तु कृच्छ्रोऽयं महासान्तपनः स्मृतः ॥

३१७ पर्णोदुम्बरराजीवबिल्वपत्रकुशोदकैः ।
प्रत्येकं प्रत्यहाभ्यस्तैः पर्णकृच्छ्र उदाहृतः ॥

Sins, even those arising from grievous sins causing loss of caste, do not touch in this world a person who is intent on reciting the Veda, is patient, and finds delight in rites connected with the five great sacrifices.[145] 311

A man is purified, except in the case of killing a Brahman, when he keeps standing during the day while subsisting on wind, spends the night in water, and, when he sees the sun, softly recites the *gāyatrī* verse one thousand times. 312

Chastity, compassion, patience, meditation, truthfulness, not being crooked, non-injury, not stealing, not hating, and self-control—these are declared to be the central restraints.[146] 313

Bathing, silence, fasting, sacrificial offering, Vedic recitation, control of the sexual organ, service to elders, purification, refraining from anger, and giving gifts are the secondary restraints.[147] 314

While performing the *sāntapana* penance, one should drink the five products of the cow—cow's milk, curd, urine, dung, and ghee—and fast the following day.[148] 315

When a person subsists on each of the substances of the *sāntapana* for six days and fasts on the seventh day, that arduous penance is declared to be the great *sāntapana*. 316

Decoctions of the leaves of *parṇa, udumbara, rājīva, bilva,* and *kuśa* grass—taking each of these each day is called leaf-penance.[149] 317

३१८ तप्तक्षीरघृताम्बूनामेकैकं प्रत्यहं पिबेत् ।
एकरात्रोपवासश्च तप्तकृच्छ्र उदाहृतः ॥

३१९ एकभक्तेन नक्तेन तथैवायाचितेन च ।
उपवासेन चैकेन पादकृच्छ्रः प्रकीर्तितः ॥

३२० यथाकथंचित्त्रिगुणः प्राजापत्योऽयमुच्यते ।
अयमेवातिकृच्छ्रः स्यात्पाणिपूरान्नभोजिनः ॥

३२१ कृच्छ्रातिकृच्छ्रः पयसा दिवसानेकविंशतिम् ।
द्वादशाहोपवासेन पराकः परिकीर्तितः ॥

३२२ पिण्याकाचामतक्राम्बुसक्तूनां प्रतिवासरम् ।
एकैकमुपवासश्च कृच्छ्रः सौम्योऽयमुच्यते ॥

३२३ एषां त्रिरात्रमभ्यासादेकैकस्य यथाक्रमम् ।
तुलापुरुष इत्येष ज्ञेयः पञ्चदशाहिकः ॥

३२४ तिथिवृद्ध्याचरेत्पिण्डाञ्छुक्ले शिख्यण्डसंमितान् ।
एकैकं ह्रासयेत्पिण्डान्कृष्णे चान्द्रायणं चरन् ॥

३२५ यथाकथंचित्पिण्डानां चत्वारिंशच्छतद्वयम् ।
मासेनैवोपभुञ्जीत चान्द्रायणमथापरम् ॥

३२६ कुर्यात्त्रिषवणस्नायी कृच्छ्रं चान्द्रायणं तथा ।
पवित्राणि जपेत्पिण्डं गायत्र्या चाभिमन्त्रयेत् ॥

One should drink each day one of these: hot milk, hot ghee, and hot water, and fast for one night. This is called the hot-penance. 318

Eating once a day, eating only at night, eating what is received unasked, and fasting once—this has been declared to be a quarter-penance. 319

When this is in any way whatsoever increased threefold, it is called *prājāpatya*. The same is also the extreme arduous penance for a person who eats only the amount of food that fills his hand. 320

When one subsists on milk for twenty-one days, it is the arduous plus extreme arduous penance. When one fasts for twelve days, it is declared to be *parāka*. 321

Oil-cake, rice scum, whey, water, and barley—subsisting on one of these each day followed by a fast is called the gentle arduous penance. 322

When each of these items is taken in due order for three nights, it should be known as *tulāpuruṣa* lasting fifteen days. 323

While performing the lunar fast, one increases by one the rice balls, each the size of a peahen egg, with the increase of each lunar day during the bright fortnight and decreases by one the rice balls during the dark fortnight.[150] 324

When one eats 240 rice balls in any manner whatsoever during a full month, it is another kind of lunar fast. 325

While performing an arduous penance, as also a lunar fast, one should bathe at the three appointed times each day, softly recite the purificatory verses, and consecrate the balls of rice with the *gāyatrī* verse.[151] 326

३२७ अनादिष्टेषु पापेषु शुद्धिश्चान्द्रायणेन तु ।
धर्मार्थं यश्चरेदेतच्चन्द्रस्यैति सलोकताम् ॥

३२८ कृच्छ्रकृद्धर्मकामस्तु महतीं श्रियमश्नुते ।
यथागुरु क्रतुफलं प्राप्नोति च न संशयः[७६] ॥

॥ इति प्रायश्चित्तप्रकरणम् ॥

३२९ श्रुत्वैतानृषयो धर्मान्याज्ञवल्क्येन भाषितान् ।
इदमूचुर्महात्मानो योगीन्द्रममितौजसम्[७७] ॥

३३० य इदं धारयिष्यन्ति धर्मशास्त्रमतन्द्रिताः ।
इह लोके यशः प्राप्य ते यास्यन्ति त्रिविष्टपम् ॥

३३१ विद्यार्थी चाप्नुयाद्विद्यां धनकामो धनानि च ।
आयुष्कामस्तथैवायुः श्रीकामो महतीं श्रियम् ॥

३३२ श्लोकत्रयमपि ह्यस्माद्यः श्राद्धे श्रावयिष्यति ।
पितॄणां तत्र तृप्तिः स्यादानन्त्याय न संशयः ॥

With regard to sins for which no penance has been prescribed, however, purification is obtained by means of the lunar fast. A person who performs it for the sake of dharma will obtain residence in the same world as the moon. 327

A man who desires merit and performs an arduous penance attains immense prosperity; and, according to the degree of its severity, he also obtains the fruit of a sacrifice without a doubt.[152] 328

## CONCLUSION

After listening to these dharmas declared by Yajnavalkya, the most noble seers said this to the chief of yogis of immeasurable might:[153] 329

"When people retain this treatise on dharma tirelessly in their memory, having achieved fame in this world, they will go to the highest heaven. 330

One who seeks learning will obtain learning; one who desires wealth will obtain wealth; one who desires long life will obtain a long life; and one who desires prosperity will obtain immense prosperity. 331

When someone makes people listen to even three verses from this at an ancestral offering, there his forefathers will obtain gratification that lasts forever—there is no doubt. 332

३३३ ब्राह्मणः पात्रतां याति क्षत्रियो विजयी भवेत् ।
वैश्यश्च धान्यधनवानस्य शास्त्रस्य धारणात् ॥

३३४ य इदं श्रावयेद्विप्रान्द्विजः पर्वसु संयतः ।
अश्वमेधफलं तस्य तद्भवाननुमन्यताम्[७८] ॥

३३५ श्रुत्वैतद्याज्ञवल्क्यस्तु प्रीतात्मा मुनिभाषितम् ।
एवमस्त्विति होवाच नमस्कृत्वा स्वयंभुवे ॥

॥ इति याज्ञवल्कीये धर्मशास्त्रे प्रायश्चित्ताख्यस्तृतीयोऽध्यायः ॥

By retaining this treatise in his memory, a Brahman becomes fit to receive gifts, a Kshatriya becomes victorious, and a Vaishya comes to possess grain and wealth. 333

When a twice-born person, maintaining self-restraint, makes Brahmans listen to this at the days of the moon's change, he obtains the reward of a horse sacrifice. Let your honor assent to this."[154] 334

When he heard this discourse of the sages, Yajnavalkya was delighted and, after paying homage to the Self-existent One, said: "Let it be so!" 335

# ABBREVIATIONS

| | |
|---|---|
| *AitB* | *Aitareya Brāhmaṇa* |
| Apar | Aparārka |
| *ĀpDh* | *Āpastambadharmasūtra* |
| *BāU* | *Bṛhadāraṇyaka Upaniṣad* |
| *BDh* | *Baudhāyanadharmasūtra* |
| *ChU* | *Chāndogya Upaniṣad* |
| *DhKo* | *Dharmakośa* |
| *GDh* | *Gautamadharmasūtra* |
| *HirGṛ* | *Hiraṇyakeśigṛhyasūtra* |
| *KAŚ* | Kauṭilya, *Arthaśāstra* |
| *KātSm* | *Kātyāyanasmṛti* |
| *KS* | *Kāṭhaka Saṃhitā* |
| M | Malayalam manuscripts of *YDh* |
| *MānGṛ* | *Mānavagṛhyasūtra* |
| *MDh* | *Mānavadharmaśāstra* |
| Ms(s). | Manuscript(s) |
| *NSm* | *Nāradasmṛti* |
| *PārGṛ* | *Pāraskaragṛhyasūtra* |
| *ṚV* | *Ṛg Veda* |
| *ŚB* | *Śatapatha Brāhmaṇa* |
| *TĀ* | *Taittirīya Āraṇyaka* |
| *TB* | *Taittirīya Brāhmaṇa* |
| *TS* | *Taittirīya Saṃhitā* |
| v/vv | verse(s) |
| *VaDh* | *Vasiṣṭhadharmasūtra* |
| *ViDh* | *Viṣṇudharmaśāstra* |
| Vijna | Vijnaneshvara |
| Vishva | Vishvarupa |
| *VS* | *Vājasaneyi Saṃhitā* |
| Vulg | Vulgate version of the *YDh* |
| *YDh* | *Yājñavalkyadharmaśāstra* |

# NOTES TO THE TEXT

## १ आचाराध्यायः

१ Verses 4–5 of the Vulg read: मन्वत्रिविष्णुहारीतयाज्ञवल्क्योशनोऽङ्गिराः । यमापस्तम्बसंवर्ताः कात्यायनबृहस्पती ॥ पराशरव्यासशङ्खलिखिता दक्षगौतमौ । शातातपो वसिष्ठश्च धर्मशास्त्रप्रयोजकाः ॥

२ कुल्यो ] कल्यो Vulg. अध्याप्याः साधुशक्ताप्तस्वार्थदा धर्मतस्त्विमे] अध्याप्या धर्मतः साधुशक्ताप्तज्ञानवित्तदाः Vulg

३ मातामहो ] पितामहो Vulg. स्वकुलयो ] सकुल्यो Vulg.

४ सर्वभक्षत्वं ] सर्वमेध्यत्वं Vulg. The reading of the edition is supported by *BDh* 2.4.5.

५ After verse 75, the Vulg adds: आज्ञासंपादिनीं दक्षां वीरसूं प्रियवादिनीम् । त्यजन्दाप्यस्तृतीयांशमद्रव्यो भरणं स्त्रियाः ॥

६ परगृहं ] परगृहे Vulg. The term *paragṛha* appears to have the technical meaning of visiting other people's houses, while *yāna* refers to recreational excursions. See *MDh* 9.13 where excursion (*aṭaṇa*) and staying in other people's houses (*anyagehavāsa*) are given as separate entries. See also *KAŚ* 3.4.6; 4.13.3.

७ सर्वधर्मविगर्हितः ] सर्वधर्मबहिष्कृतः Vulg.

८ सेवनं ] आसनं and अन्वासनं Vulg.

९ धर्ममर्थं च कामं च ] धर्मार्थकामान्स्वे काले Vulg. The Vulg also transposes the first and second lines of this verse.

१० शूद्रभिक्षिता ] शूद्रभिक्षितात् Vulg. The former is the *lectio difficilior.* Vishva explains: *śūdrabhikṣukasya*, showing that the compound (nom. sing. of *bhikṣitṛ*) refers to the sacrificer who begs from a Shudra (corresponding to adadad of *pāda-c*) and not to the sacrificial material begged from a Shudra.

११ नार्चयेत् ] वर्जयेत् Vulg.

१२ विषान्यप्सु ] रेतांस्यप्सु Vulg.

१३ द्विजः ] बहिः Vulg.

१४ सूकरैः ] मूषकैः Vulg.

१५ परस्य च ] परस्त्रियाः Vulg.

१६ अस्वत्तं ] अस्वर्ग्यं Vulg. The reading adopted is the *lectio difficilior,* which is found in Vishva, who clearly saw the grammatical difficulty of the reading *asvatta* and attempted to explain it: *asvattam asugatam asupariniścitam ity arthaḥ*. He takes the root √*ad* here, of which *atta* is taken as the past participle, to have the meaning of going:

*anekārthatvād dhātūnām ader gatyarthatvam.*

१७ ज्ञाति ] जामि Vulg.

१८ अमात्य ] अपत्य Vulg. The reading *amātya* is the *lectio difficilior.* It has the older meaning of a member of the household, a meaning found also in *YDh* 2.153.

१९ सुधाजीव ] सुराजीव Vulg.

२० पर्याचान्तं ] पर्यायान्नं Vulg. The reading of the edition is confirmed by *MDh* 4.212.

२१ लोहितावृश्चनानि च ] लोहितान्व्रश्चनांस्तथा Vulg. The term *āvraścana* is a very old form found in the *TS* 3.1.5.1. The reference appears to be to growths such as mushrooms sprouting on tree stumps.

२२ मत्स्यांश्चाकामतो ] मत्स्यांश्च कामतो Vulg. The reading adopted is supported by *MDh* 5.20.

२३ चैव वाससाम् ] धान्यवाससाम् Vulg.

२४ सौत्रिकम् ] कौशिकम् Vulg.

२५ नृखजा ] नरजा Vulg. The reading *kha* for a bodily orifice is confirmed by the parallel in *MDh* 5.132: ऊर्ध्वं नाभेर्यानि खानि. See also *YDh* 1.20.

२६ चिन्तकाः ] वित्तमाः Vulg.

२७ After this verse, the Vulg adds: यावद्वत्सस्य पादौ द्वौ मुखं योन्यां च दृश्यते। तावद्गौः पृथिवी ज्ञेया यावद्गर्भं न मुञ्चति॥ This is probably a comment intended to explain the expression *ubhayatomukhī.*

२८ भूमिपश्वन्न ] भूदीपांश्चान्न Vulg.

२९ वृक्षजलं ] वृक्षं प्रियं Vulg.

३० क्रूरः ] क्लीबः Vulg.

३१ सुतत्यागी ] गुरुत्यागी Vulg.

३२ After this verse, the Vulg adds: तथाच्छादनदानं च करशौचार्थमम्बु च॥

३३ After pāda-b, the Vulg adds: अपहता इति तिलान्विकीर्य च समन्ततः॥

३४ In the Vulg pādas c-d read: विश्वेदेवाश्च प्रीयन्तां विप्रैश्चोक्त इदं जपेत्॥

३५ In the Vulg pādas c-d read: ब्रह्मचारी भवेत्तां तु रजनीं ब्राह्मणैः सह॥

३६ शेषं त्वर्घ्यादि पूर्ववत् ] शेषं पूर्ववदाचरेत् Vulg.

३७ अपत्यं मुख्यतां सुतान् ] समृद्धिं मुख्यतां शुभम् Vulg.

३८ प्रज्ञां ] प्रजां Vulg.

३९ गर्भमेव च ] गर्भमङ्गना Vulg.

४० साद्येनोच्छादितस्य ] साज्येनोत्सादितस्य Vulg. The reading of the edition is supported by *MānGṛ* 2.14.27.

४१ After this verse, the Vulg adds: दध्यन्नं पायसं चैव गुडपिष्टं समोदकम्। एतान्सर्वान्समाहृत्य भूमौ कृत्वा ततः शिरः॥

४२ श्रियं पुण्यान् ] धनं देहि Vulg.

४३ तिलकस्वामिनस्तथा ] तिलकं स्वामिनस्तथा Vulg. The correctness of the adopted reading is demonstrated by the fourth prefatory verse of Vacaspati's *Bhāmatī* commentary on the *Brahmasūtras:* मार्तण्डतिलकस्वामिमहागणपतीन् वयम् । विश्ववन्द्यान् नमस्याम: सर्वसिद्धिविधायिन: ॥

४४ दध्ना चैव समन्विता: ] दध्ना क्षीरेण वा युता: Vulg.

४५ अक्षुद्रपरिषत्तथा ] अक्षुद्रोऽपरुषस्तथा Vulg. धार्मिको दृढभक्तिश्च ] धार्मिकोऽव्यसनश्चैव Vulg. The readings for this verse adopted in the edition are supported by the parallel passages in *KAŚ* 6.1.13; 1.9.1. See also *KAŚ* 1.5.17; 1.15.60; *MDh* 7.105.

४६ चिन्तयेत्कार्यं ] चिन्तयेद्राज्यं Vulg.

४७ अलब्धं लब्धुमीहेत conj. Vulg reads: अलब्धमीहेद्धर्मेण and Vishva and M. read: धर्मेण लब्धुमीहेत. The parallel passage in *MDh* 7.99 reads: *alabdhaṃ caiva lipseta,* and in *KAŚ* 1.4.3: *alabdhalābhārthā* (as characteristic of *daṇḍanīti*). We also have the proverbial saying cited in the *Pañcatantra* (1.2): *alabdhaṃ arthaṃ lipseta.* It is clear from the various readings that the first word should be *alabdha*. The *KAŚ* expression *lābhārtha* has been rendered by the desiderative of √*labh* (*lipseta*) in the *MDh* and *Pañcatantra,* and by *labdhum īheta* in Vishva. One can envisage a possible scenario for this textual confusion. It appears that at some point interpreters of the *YDh* wanted to specify that the king should seek to obtain riches righteously. Thus, there may have been a gloss *"dharmeṇa"* (marginal or written above line?), which caused the reading: *alabdham* (*dharmeṇa*) *labdhum īheta.* But this created the metrical problem of too many syllables, and it appears that the traditions of Vishva and Vulg resolved the problem differently, the former by eliminating the initial *alabdham* and the latter by eliminating *labdhum* and changing the verb from the Ātmanepada to the Parasmaipada: *īhed*. But this form is never encountered in the Dharmaśāstras, where *īheta* is the preferred form: *MDh* 3.126, 205; 4.15; 9.207. I have given a conjectural reading in the edition, based on the readings of Vishva, Vulg, *MDh*, and *KAŚ*. नित्यं ] नीत्या Vulg.

४८ आगामिक्षुद्र ] आगामिभद्र Vulg.

४९ बुद्धा ] बुद्ध्या Vulg.

५० यस्मान्न्यायेन ] यस्मात्प्रजानां Vulg.

५१ संमानयेन्नित्यं ] संमानयेद्राजा Vulg.

५२ यदासम्यग्गुणोपेतं ] यदा सस्यगुणोपेतं Vulg.

५३ The Vulg has a very different reading of this verse: केचिद्दैवात् स्वभावाद्वा कालात् पुरुषकारत: । संयोगे केचिदिच्छन्ति फलं कुशलबुद्धय: ॥ It appears that the interpreter responsible for this reading basically misunderstood the Sanskrit *kecit* ("some"), taking it to refer to the opinions of various people rather than how various human enterprises (*arthāḥ*) become successful or not.

५४ न स नेतुमततः शक्यो ] स नेतुं न्यायतोऽशक्यो Vulg.

५५ सहस्रशतदक्षिणैः ] समाप्तवरदक्षिणैः Vulg.

२ व्यवहाराध्यायः

१ कुलीनाः ] धर्मज्ञाः Vulg.

२ द्वेषाद् ] लोभाद् Vulg.

३ स्मृतेर्विरोधे ] स्मृत्योर्विरोधे Vulg. The reading of the edition agrees with the parallel in *KAŚ* 3.1.45, where we have the technical use of *nyāya* to refer to the command or edict of the king.

४ सर्वेष्वेव विवादेषु ] सर्वेष्वर्थविवादेषु Vulg.

५ This verse is omitted in the Vulg.

६ नृपोऽर्थाधिकृताः ] नृपेणाधिकृताः Vulg.

७ The Vulgate gives this verse as 1.361 in its enumeration (after 1.356 in the enumeration of my edition).

८ The text of Vijna transposes the verses 40 and 41.

९ The Vulg places this verse after verse 52.

१० दण्ड्योऽन्यथा ] स्तेनोऽन्यथा Vulg.

११ भाजनस्थमनाख्याय ] वासनस्थमनाख्याय Vulg. For the container (*bhājana*) in which valuables are placed, see *KAŚ* 2.7.33.

१२ भ्रेषश्चेन् ] दोषश्चेन् Vishva and M. For भ्रेष, see *KAŚ* 3.12.23, 29; 4.1.6.

१३ पञ्चयज्ञक्रियारताः ] श्रौतस्मार्तक्रियापराः Vulg.

१४ चौर्यपारुष्य ] दण्डपारुष्य Vishva and M.

१५ The Vulg places verses 75 and 76 after 79.

१६ Vijna reads ते समाः eliminating the *avagraha.*

१७ This verse is omitted in the Vulg.

१८ प्रविष्टमधमर्णिकात् ] दत्त्वा दत्त्वर्णिको धनम् Vulg.

१९ The Vulg places this verse after 103.

२० वृद्धार्त ] वृद्धान्ध Vulg. वाशूद्रस्य ] वा शूद्रस्य Vijna.

२१ The Vulg places this verse after 122.

२२ अंशं समाप्नुयात् ] अंशं समं हरेत् Vulg.

२३ अन्योदर्यस्य ] अन्योदर्यस्तु Vulg. सोदर्यो ] संसृष्टो Vulg.

२४ पति ] सुत Vishva and M. Here I have adopted the Vulg reading with some hesitation, because the only other place where the four occur, *KātSm* 902, also has *pati.* All other sources (*MDh* 9.194;

*NSm* 13.8; *KātSm* 894) list only three: *pitṛmātṛbhrātṛ*.

२५ क्षेत्रस्य हरणे तथा । सीमातिक्रमणे तथा Vulg. सीमातिक्रमणे ] क्षेत्रस्य हरणे Vulg

२६ द्विगुणोऽवसतां दमः ] यथोक्ताद्विगुणो दम: Vulg.

२७ In Vijna and many Vulg sources, the verse reads: महोक्षोत्सृष्टपशव: सूतिकागन्तुकादय: । पालो येषां न ते मोच्या दैवराजपरिप्लुता: ॥

२८ स्ववदाहरेत् ] सर्वदा हरेत् Vijna and many Vulg sources.

२९ देयं यच्चान्यसंश्रितम् ] यच्चान्यस्मै प्रतिश्रुतम् Vulg.

३० हानि: ] वृद्धि: Vulg. The former means loss, which is not the case here. As Vishva says, the term *hāni* here means "less", that is, less than the amount stated earlier, i.e., ten *palas* (see the use of *hānataḥ* with the same meaning in verse 211). Either reading produces the same result: middling textile loses five *palas*.

३१ कार्यं ] दाप्य: Vulg.

३२ अशाठ्यं चेच्छाठ्ये ] असाध्यं चेत्साध्ये Vulg.

३३ गलत्सभिकवृद्धिस्तु ] ग्लहे शतिकवृद्धेस्तु Vulg.

३४ अभिगन्तासि ] अभिगन्तास्मि Vulg. One factor to prefer the former reading is that vv. 208–209 deal with insults about the other person's disabilities or character, while the section on harming the other person begins at v. 212.

३५ चतुस्त्रिद्विगुणा ] द्विगुणत्रिगुणा Vulg. वर्णान्त्येष्वानुलोम्येन ] वर्णानामानुलोम्येन Vulg.

३६ After this verse Vishva and M add this verse: यत्र नोक्तो दम: सर्वै: प्रमादेन महात्मभि: । तत्र कार्यं परिज्ञाय कर्तव्यं दण्डधारणम् ॥ This verse is possibly from an earlier commentary used by Vishva, who apparently thought that it was part of the root text. This verse is given in support of his contention that verse 216 is a general provision applying to all *vyavahārapadas*. In *DhKo* I: 1792 this verse is found in several sources and ascribed to Ushanas. If my hypothesis is correct, then we have the first evidence for a pre-Vishva commentary on the *YDh*. The use of *mahātmabhiḥ* to refer to authors of dharma treatises is another indication that this verse has a commentarial origin.

३७ पीडाकर्षाञ्चनावेष्टपादाध्यासे ] conj.; पीडाकर्षाञ्जनावेष्ट्य पादाध्यासे Vishva M; पीडाकर्षांशुकावेष्टपादाध्यासे Vulg. I think both textual traditions have misunderstood the original reading, which was probably based on *KAŚ* 3.19.6: पीडनावेष्टनाञ्चनप्रकर्षनाध्यासनेषु पूर्व: साहसदण्ड: ("For pressing, squashing, twisting, dragging, and pinning down, the punishment is the lowest seizure-fine"). The two manuscript traditions of *YDh* have misunderstood *añcana*, one rendering it as *añjana* (or *āñjanā*) and the other as *aṃśuka*. The *KAŚ* clear refers to different kinds of actions that cause bodily pain or harm to another person. In this context, *añcana* means "twisting" and *āveṣṭa* means "squashing or throttling." I have emended the text conjecturally following the reading of *KAŚ*.

३८ उत्तमसाहसः ] मध्यमसाहसः Vulg. The reading of the parallel passage at *KAŚ* 3.19.14 has *madhyamasāhasa,* but its parallel to the previous verse 223 (*KAŚ* 3.19.13) has the penalty of *pūrvasāhasa;* so there is a gradation. In the *YDh,* the previous penalty is raised to *madhyamasāhasa,* and correspondingly the penalty here is also raised to *uttamasāhasa.*

३९ प्ररोहशाखिकाशाखास्कन्धसर्वविदारणे ] प्ररोहिशाखिनां शाखास्कन्धसर्वविदारणे Vulg. The reading of the edition is supported by the parallel passage in *KAŚ* 3.19.28.

४० नृपालये ] सुरालये Vulg.

४१ सान्वयप्रसभद्रव्यहरणात् conj. ] सामान्यप्रसभद्रव्यहरणात् Vishva M; सामान्यद्रव्यप्रसभहरणात् Vulg. We have two different readings of the long compound of the first line in both the Vulg and Vishva. Both, I think, have misunderstood the original passage of *KAŚ* 3.17.1 on which this verse is based. The Vulg modified Vishva's version, making *sāmānya* qualify *dravya.* Yet, the definition of *sāhasa* as taking by force common property is rather peculiar and differs from the definitions given by Manu and Kautilya. The *KAŚ* reads: *sāhasam anvayavat prasabhakarma.* This is the basis for the verse of *MDh* 8.332: *syāt sāhasaṃ tv anvayavat prasabhaṃ karma yat kṛtam.* It is the technical term *anvayavat,* in the alternate form *sānvaya,* that caused problems to later readers of the *YDh,* who failed to understand and sought to emend that expression. The first word of the compound in the original version was probably *sānvaya,* a synonym of *anvayavat* found already in the *MDh* 8.198: *avahāryo bhavec caiṣa sānvayaḥ ṣaṭśataṃ damam.* Taking this term to be an error, some scribe or commentator prior to Vishva changed it to *sāmānya,* giving rise to all later readings. The reading of the edition is thus a conjecture based on the above reasoning.

४२ प्रहारदः ] प्रहारकः Vulg. Both Vijna and Apar take the term to mean strike or beat. However, an act of violence against the wife of a brother is incongruous here. The parallel passage in the *KAŚ* (3.20.15) refers to some kind of sexual impropriety with her. The reading adopted by the edition, *-prahāradaḥ,* opens the possibility of "giving" or "gifting" something to her. One meaning of *prahāra* is pearl necklace (see *hāra* in *KAŚ* 2.11.9, 17, 20). But I think *prahāra* here is a rendering of the *KAŚ* expression *hastena laṅghayataḥ* ("violating with the hand") and probably stands for some kind of stroking or caressing.

४३ प्रथमसाहसम् ] उत्तमसाहसम् Vulg. The reading of the edition accords with the parallel in *KAŚ* 4.1.44, which prescribes a fine of only 12 *paṇas.*

४४ साहस्रो दण्ड उच्यते ] जानतो दम उत्तमः Vulg.

४५ This verse is omitted by Vishv. and M. I think, however, that it may have been an oversight, because in Vishva's commentary on the previous verse (as printed in the edition) he seems to presuppose this one also. It also nicely parallels the statement in the very next verse. Perhaps he commented on both together, as he often does, and scribes dropped the second verse.

४६ तु विजानता ] अविजानता Vulg.

४७ कृष्टाद् ] क्रोशाद् Vulg.

४८ विषप्रदं conj. ] विषप्रदां Vishva; विप्रदुष्टां Vulg. Both the Vulg and Vishva appear to have misunderstood this passage dependent on *KAŚ* 4.11.17–18. Their readings are in the feminine qualifying *striyaṃ;* but see the woman poisoner mentioned in the very next verse. This is mistaken, as the *KAŚ* clearly shows that the giver of poison is a man or, given that the masculine is often used generically, simply any person, while the killing of the husband refers specifically to a woman. सेतुभेदकरं conj. ] सेतुभेदकरीं Vishva, M., Vulg. The reading of textual traditions is in the feminine, when it should refer to a man or simply to any person. I have conjecturally emended the manuscript readings.

४९ स्त्रीणां नासादिकृन्तनम् ] नार्याः कर्णादिकर्तनम् Vulg. The Vulg places this verse after verse 290.

५० नाभि ] सक्थि Vulg. सहावस्थानमेव ] सहैकस्थानमेव Vulg.

५१ The Vulg reading of this verse is: स्त्री निषेधे शतं दद्याद्द्विशतं तु दमं पुमान् । प्रतिषेधे तयोर्दण्डो यथा संग्रहणे तथा ॥

५२ After this verse many sources of the Vulgate add a verse: गृहीतवेतना वेश्या नेच्छन्ती द्विगुणं वहेत् । अगृहीते समं दाप्यः पुमानप्येवमेव च ॥

५३ युद्ध ] युग्य Vulg.

५४ जारं ] चोरं Vishva, M. The Vulg reading, which I follow, is supported by the parallel at *KAŚ* 4.12.34.

५५ मध्यमसाहसः ] उत्तमसाहसः Vulg.

## ३ प्रायश्चित्ताध्याय:

१ प्रत्तानां ] प्रेतानां Vulg.
२ पाषण्डमाश्रिता: ] पाषण्ड्यनाश्रिता: Vulg.
३ वैतानिकाश्रया: ] वैतानोपासना: Vulg.
४ The Vulg places vv. 16–17 before verse 14.
५ Pādas a-b are omitted in the Vulg. From this verse onward the sequence of verses in the critical edition and the Vulg diverge. For the sequence, see Concordance of Verses.
६ प्रेतसूतकमुच्यते ] तदर्धं न्यायवर्तिन: Vulg. In the Vulg, pādas c-d and 21ab are placed after verse 29.
७ न शूद्रो हि मृत: क्वचित् ] न शूद्रो न द्विज: क्वचित् Vulg.
८ विषैकरान् ] विषक्षिती: Vulg.
९ हेतव: ] सीसकान् Vulg.
१० लवणं तनया लाक्षा ] लाक्षालवणमांसानि Vulg.
११ धनम् ] धान्यम् Vulg.
१२ सुतान् ] तप: Vulg. कुटुम्बात्स्वाद् ] कुटुम्बं च Vulg.
१३ वने ] वनम् Vulg. क्षमी ] व्रजेत् Vulg.
१४ In pādas c-d, the Vulg reads: तर्पयेच्छ्मश्रुजटालोमभृदात्मवान् ।
१५ व्याधयश्चैव ] व्याधय: क्लेशा: Vulg.
१६ धर्माधर्मभवात्मकम् ] धर्माधर्मोभयात्मकम् Vulg. The reading of the edition is the *lectio difficilior.*
१७ तथादत्ते भवन्नपि ] तथादत्तेऽभवन्नपि Viśva.
१८ प्रेरणं ] स्पर्शनं Vulg. The *Caraka Saṃhitā* (*śarīrasthāna*, 4.12) lists both *sparśana* and *preraṇa*.
१९ अग्नेस्तु ] पित्तात्तु Vulg.
२० त्वचावान्स्मृतिमानपि ] त्वङ्मांसस्मृतिमानपि Vulg.
२१ ललाटास्थि गण्डनासाघनास्थिका ] ललाटाक्षिगण्डे नासा घनास्थिका Vulg.
२२ वपावहननं ] वसावहननं Vulg.
२३ मनीषिभि: ] शरीरिणां Vulg. अष्टोत्तरं ] सप्तोत्तरं Vulg.
२४ Pādas a-b in the Vulg reads: यथाविधानेन पठन्सामगायमविच्युतम् ।
२५ चोक्तसंज्ञकम् ] मोक्षसंज्ञितम् Vulg.
२६ योगमार्गं ] मोक्षमार्गं Vulg.
२७ विराड्व सोमरूपेण ] विराज: सोऽन्नरूपेण Vulg.
२८ त्वचो ] स्पर्शाद् Vulg.
२९ पिशुनश्चैव मानव: ] पिशुन: परुषस्तथा Vulg.
३० ज्ञेऽज्ञे च ] ज्ञेयज्ञे, ज्ञेये च variously in Vulg. The Vulg sources have confused readings created by the inability to understand the compound *jñejñe* (in manuscripts, which normally do not mark the loss of 'a' with an *avagraha*).

३१ नीरजस्तमस्ता conj. ] नीरजस्तमसा Vulg, नीरजस्तमसः Vishva, नीरजस्तमता Apar. It is probable that this was originally an abstract compound, paralleling *nispṛhatā*. Vijna's commentary supports such a compound: *rajastamovidhuratā*, as does the reading of Aparарka (*-tamatā*), which is probably an erroneous rendering of *-tamastā*.

३२ नाङ्गहानं हि जन्मतः ] अङ्गहीनादि जन्मनः Vulg.

३३ This verse is omitted in most Vulg sources.

३४ Pādas c-d in the Vulg reads: तेन देवशरीराणि सधामानि प्रपद्यते ॥

३५ The issue in pāda-b is whether the word is जन्मनामरणेन (i.e., *āmaraṇena* through Sandhi) or simply जन्मना मरणेन. I have opted for the latter as it corresponds to the other positives and negatives in this verse.

३६ जलजैः ] जागरैः Vulg. I take the two terms *jalajaiḥ* and *svapnajaiḥ* as connected to *phalaiḥ*, which is the last word of the previous sentence.

३७ स्वप्नेसर्गश्च ] स्वर्गः स्वप्नश्च Vulg.

३८ अव्यक्त (= अव्यक्ते ) ] अव्यक्तम् Vulg. सर्वभूतानां ] सर्वभूतस्थः Vulg.

३९ यो यस्मिन्नाश्रितस्तेषां ] यो यस्मान्निःसृतश्चैषां Vulg.

४० प्रजाकामा ] स्वर्गकामा Vulg.

४१ श्रद्धोपवाससातत्यमात्मनो ] श्रद्धोपवासः स्वातन्त्र्यमात्मनो Vulg.

४२ निदिध्यास्यः ] विजिज्ञास्यः Vulg.

४३ आत्मनः ] आत्मवान् Vulg.

४४ सुते ] वने Vulg.

४५ गर्हितान् ] दारुणान् Vulg.

४६ संपिबत्येषां ] संवसत्येषां Vulg. As Vishva explains, it appears that the original term used was the unusual *saṃpibati* ("drink together") as a shorthand for commensality and other forms of social and ritual interactions (Vishva uses the term *saṃsarga*). The Vulgate editors appear to have changed the reading to the easier *saṃvasati*. See also 3.228, 261, 296, 299.

४७ अजः पशुं ] जलं प्लवः Vulg.

४८ लक्षणोपेता ] विद्ययोपेता Vulg.

४९ नदीपथम् ] महापथम् Vulg.

५० संपिबेत् ] संवसेत् Vulg. See note 46.

५१ रूप्य ] कुप्य Vulg. सुहृत् ] सुत Vulg. But see verse 240 where the abandonment of a son is listed.

५२ ब्रह्मलोपनम् ] व्रतलोपनम् Vulg. But see *vratalopa* in verse 237.

५३ स्त्रीहिंस्रौषधिजीवनम् ] स्त्रीहिंसौषधजीवनम् Vulg. After verse 241, the Vulg adds this verse: शूद्रप्रेष्यं हीनसख्यं हीनयोनिनिषेवणम् । तथैवानाश्रमे

वासः परान्नपरिपुष्टता ॥

५४ मिताशीत्वा ] The readings of Vulg sources differ widely here because of the inability to properly understand the Sandhi in *mitāśītvā*. Vishva explains the Sandhi of *mitāśītvā: mitāśī itvā gatvety arthaḥ*. Vijna reads: मिताशित्वात्, while Apar reads: मिताशी वा. Yet, Vijna in his commentary appears to recognize the form *itvā* with the gloss: *itvā gatvā*. The Vulg transposes verses 248 and 249.

५५ भक्षयीत समां निशि ] भक्षयेत् त्रिसमा निशि some Vulg sources.

५६ न संशयः ] द्विजातयः Vulg.

५७ संपिबेद् ] संवसेद् Vulg. See note 46.

५८ हत्वा श्येन ] हंसश्येन Vulg.

५९ त्रपुमाषकः ] त्रपुसीसकम् Vulg.

६० Many Vulg sources, including Vijna, place 278ab before 276 ab.

६१ दष्टश्चैव श्ववायसैः ] दष्टः श्वोष्ट्रादिवायसैः Vulg, दष्टश्वोष्ट्रादिवायसैः Apa. The Vulg places 278cd before 277ab.

६२ The Vulg transposes pādas a-b and c-d.

६३ Pādas ab and ef are omitted in the Vulg.

६४ The Vulg transposes verses 289 and 290.

६५ सुप्त्वा ] भुक्त्वा Vulg.

६६ हत्वावबध्य वा ] बद्ध्वा वा वाससा Vulg.

६७ दासीघटमपां पूर्णं निनयेरन् ] दासीकुम्भं बहिर्ग्रामान्निनयेरन् Vulg.

६८ संपिबेयुश्च ] संवसेयुश्च Vulg. See note 46.

६९ संपिबेन्न ] संवसेन्न Vulg. See note 46.

७० सहक्रिया ] सत्क्रिया Vulg.

७१ जले सुप्त्वाभिजुहुयाच् ] जले स्थित्वाभिजुहुयाच् Vulg.

७२ सहस्रशः ] विशेषतः Vulg.

७३ ध्यानं ] दानं Vulg. अहिंसास्तेयमद्रोहो दमश्चैते ] अहिंसास्तेयमाधुर्यदमाश्चैते Vulg, अहिंसास्तेयमाधुर्ये दमश्चैते Vijna.

७४ शौचाक्रोधप्रदातृताः ] शौचाक्रोधाप्रमादता Vulg.

७५ In the Vulg the first line reads: गोमूत्रं गोमयं क्षीरं दधि सर्पिः कुशोदकम्। Vishva notes the absence of *kuśa* and says that the term is understood here. Thus, the six substances noted in verse 316 make sense.

७६ न संशयः ] सुसमाहितः Vulg.

७७ महात्मानो ] महात्मानं Vulg.

७८ विप्रान् ] विद्वान् Vulg.

# NOTES TO THE TRANSLATION

*1 Proper Conduct*

1 Note the very first word "*yogīśvara,*" signaling the centrality of yoga and the search for liberation in the text. Yajnavalkya is identified later (3.110) with the author of a treatise on yoga (*yogaśāstra*). The meaning of "the rest" is not clear (see *MDh* 1.2). Commentators refer to persons of mixed class through intermarriage and to people living in states other than the four recognized orders of life.

2 For the first time in the *dharmaśāstras,* we have a reference to geography: the conversation takes place in Mithila in eastern India, the center of Gupta power. The blackbuck is an antelope (*Antilope cervicapra*) whose natural range is the north central part of India. The *MDh* (2.23) recognized this as one of the sacred regions associated with the proper observance of dharma.

3 Commentators give different enumerations of the fourteen. Vishvarupa takes logic and hermeneutics as a single category and *purāṇa* as containing both *purāṇa* and *itihāsa* (epic): *purāṇa* = 2 (*purāṇa* + *itihāsa*), logic and hermeneutics (*nyāya* + *mīmāṃsā*) = 1 (single category), legal treatises = 1, supplement (*vedāṅga*) = 6, Vedas = 4. Both Vijnaneshvara and Apararka have the following enumeration: *purāṇa* =1, logic = 1, hermeneutics = 1, legal treatises = 1, supplements = 6, Vedas = 4. The six Vedic supplements are: phonetics, ritual, grammar, etymology, metrics, and astronomy.

4 This list gives twenty authors. The Vulg provides a different list: "Manu, Atri, Vishnu, Harita, Yajnavalkya, Ushanas, Angiras, Yama, Apastamba, Samvarta, Katyayana, Brihaspati, Parashara, Vyasa, Shankha, Likhita, Daksha, Gautama, Shatatapa, and Vasishtha are the composers of legal treatises."

5 The neuter abstract noun *traividyam* here may simply refer to a single individual who knows all three Vedas (see *MDh* 12.111 *traividyaḥ,* and 12.113) or two or three individuals, each knowing a single Veda, as in *MDh* 12.112). For a detailed treatment of the epistemology of dharma, see Olivelle 2016a; for "what is pleasing to oneself" as a source of dharma, see Davis 2007.

6 The use of the masculine pronoun *teṣām* here is intended to show that Vedic mantras are used only for males. For females, these

childhood rites are performed without mantras: see *YDh* 1.13.

7 "Season" (*ṛtu*) refers to the fertile season of a woman soon after her monthly period: see *YDh* 1.78.

8 The great calls (*mahāvyāhṛti*), according to Vishvarupa, are the sacred words: *bhūr bhuvaḥ svaḥ* (earth, mid-space, heaven) preceded by the sacred syllable OṂ. See *MDh* 2.76–81.

9 Various parts of the palm are called *tīrtha,* thus homologized with fords of rivers considered sacred. It is through these *tīrthas* that water flows into the mouth.

10 The upper orifices are eyes, ears, nostrils, and mouth.

11 The purification with water reaching the heart, throat, and palate refers to Brahmans, Kshatriyas, and Vaishyas, respectively.

12 The formulas addressed to water (called *abdaivata* or *abliṅga*) are: "Waters, you are refreshing. Further us to strength, to see great joy. The auspicious flavor that is yours, accord to us here, like eager mothers. To him may we come with satisfaction, to whose dwelling you quicken us, O waters, and propagate us" (*TS* 4.1.5.1). The *gāyatrī* or *sāvitrī* is the verse: "That excellent glory of Savitri, the god, we meditate, that he may stimulate our thoughts" (*ṚV* 3.62.10).

13 The *śiras* formula is: "oṃ the Waters, the Light, the Taste, the Immortal, Brahman! Earth, Mid-space, Heaven, oṃ!" See *Mahānārāyaṇa Upaniṣad* 342. For the calls, see above, note 8.

14 See above, n. 12.

15 Instead of "from a good family" the Vulg reads "healthy." In the second half of the verse also, in place of "or part of his family, or who give him money" the Vulg reads "or persons who give knowledge or money."

16 The request for food as the student stands in front of a house is made with the following formula: "Lady, give almsfood" (*bhavati bhikṣāṃ dehi*), indicating that it was the woman of the house who usually gave the food to religious mendicants. The placement of the address "Lady" (*bhavati*) indicates the social class of the student.

17 The rite of sipping water (*apośāna*) before a meal is accompanied by the ritual formula: "You are the underlayer of the immortal" (*amṛtopastaraṇam asi*). After the meal one sips water saying: "You are the cover of the immortal" (*amṛtāpidhānam asi*). See 1.105 for this rite.

18 The term *vrātya* is used in the legal literature to refer to individuals

who have not undergone Vedic initiation at the proper time. The *vrātyastoma* is a special rite for those who have failed to be initiated at the proper time in order to recover their ritual status. See Heesterman 1962.

19 *Muñja* is a species of rush belonging to the sugar-cane family used for girdles; *Sanseviera roxburghiana*.

20 Verses 40–48 parallel the passage in the *ŚB* 11.5.6.4–8.

21 For a list of texts that a person studies, see *ChU* 7.1.2, and my note to it (Olivelle 1998: 563). Regarding "sciences" (*vidyā*), that list gives several specific ones: science of gods, science of the ritual, science of spirits, science of government, science of heavenly bodies, and science of serpents. See also *ŚB* 13.4.3.9–10.

22 The meaning here is that when the student recites the Vedic passages dealing with a particular sacrifice, he obtains the fruit of having actually performed the sacrifice.

23 The term *sādhayan,* which I have translated "subduing," is somewhat ambiguous. It can mean to subdue with austerities (so Vijnaneshvara) or to bring to an end, that is, to die (so Vishvarupa), which is more plausible.

24 After Vedic initiation, the pupil can either study the entire Veda or simply carry out the obligatory observances, such as begging for food.

25 See ch. 1, n. 33.

26 The prospective wife must be no more closely related to his mother than five generations removed, and to his father than seven generations. For relationship through lineage, see ch. 1, n. 33.

27 For the possibility of Brahmans and other twice-born men taken Shudra wives according to the principle of hypergamy, see *MDh* 9.149–157. Yajnavalkya rejects this traditional view. The doctrine of a man being born again through his wife as his son is articulated in several Vedic texts: *TB* 1.5.5.6; *AitB* 7.13.1.

28 The meaning is that a Brahman man can marry a wife who is a Brahman, Kshatriya, or Vaishya, according to the principle of hypergamy. A Kshatriya or Vaishya man, likewise, can marry a woman of his own or lower class.

29 Such a son purifies ten generations before and ten generations after, with the man himself as the twenty-first. This same paradigm applies to the following verses as well.

30 The term "primary" (*ādya*) here means that it is prior to the

previously given seers' marriage.

31 The Vulg reads "father's father" in place of "mother's father." A brother from her own family (*bhrātā svakulyaḥ*) excludes those who are often referred to as brothers but are not from the same family, such as first cousins. The Vulg has the readings *sakulyaḥ* instead, meaning a person belonging to the broader family group, and thus does not modify the term *bhrātā* (brother) but is a separate category of people competent to give a girl in marriage. The expression "in sound shape" (*prakṛtistha*) refers to both physical and mental stability and health.

32 The blemish here refers to virginity: see *MDh* 8.224–235. The meaning and semantic history of *sāhasa* (seizure fine) as a particular kind of fine with lowest, middle, and highest amounts are not altogether clear. It has been assumed that the standard crime whose punishment became a currency for other kinds of crime was *sāhasa,* the forcible seizure of property or violent robbery, defined at KAŚ 3.17.1 as: "Forcible seizure is a violent act in the presence of the victim." In the *MDh* (8.138) the three levels of fines for forcible seizure are: lowest 250 *paṇas,* middle 500 *paṇas,* and highest 1,000 *paṇas.* The KAŚ (3.17.8–10), on the other hand, gives them as 48 to 96, 200 to 500, and 500 to 1,000. For the amounts in the *YDh,* see 1.361. Sometimes the term *sāhasa* is left out, but the expressions "highest fine," etc. refers to the same scheme.

33 The issue here is a woman whose husband has died without begetting a son. In such a case, early legal authorities permit the so-called "levirate" where a son is produced for the deceased husband by his brother or close relative. Lineage (*gotra*) refers to a family line that is connected to a single ancient teacher as a common ancestor. The definition of this relationship is quite vague and often confused in the literature (Kane 1962–1975, II: 479–501). The relationship based on common ancestry (*sapiṇḍa*) refers to a group of close relatives, but there is controversy in the tradition with regard to both its meaning and the extent of the group covered. In general, the relationship extends to six generations before and after the father and five generations before and after the mother (Kane 1962–1975, II: 452–478).

34 In this agricultural metaphor, the wife is considered the field in which the husband plants the seed. The issue is whether the child so produced belongs to the owner of the field (husband) or the

owner of the seed (the biological father). Arguments are given for both positions, but here the owner of the field (the deceased husband) is viewed as the person to whom the son belongs. For an extended argument, see *MDh* 9.32–53.

35 The Vulg reads "total purity" or "purity in all situations" in place of "capacity to eat anything." See *VaDh* 28.5 for the Vedic verse that provides the basis for this view.

36 The reference is to the wife becoming pregnant by another man. When she kills her husband, she is abandoned by the extended family of the husband. There are five grievous sins causing loss of caste: killing a Brahman, drinking liquor, stealing gold, having sex with an elder's wife, and associating with a person guilty of such a sin. See *MDh* 11.55; *YDh* 3.207–211.

37 The triple set (*trivarga*) refers to the three goals of life: righteous living (*dharma*), material success (*artha*), and pleasure (*kāma*). See ch. 1, verse 114.

38 Uma is another name for Parvati, the wife of Shiva. After this verse the Vulg adds another verse: "When a man abandons a wife who carries out his orders, is skillful, begets strong sons, and speaks affably, he should be made to give one-third portion; if he is without property, he should maintain the woman." The one-third portion refers to the man's property.

39 See ch. 1, n. 36.

40 "World, eternity, and heaven" are viewed as referring to this world, the mid-space or atmosphere, and heaven. This verse is derived from *MDh* 9.137.

41 A woman's "season" is the period after her menstrual period when she was considered fertile. The belief was that when conception takes place on an even night after the start of her season, a male child is born, while girls are conceived on odd nights (see *MDh* 3.48). The days of the moon's change consist of the new moon, the eighth day after the new moon, the full moon, and the fourteenth day after the full moon: see *MDh* 4.128.

42 According to the understanding of the commentators Vijnaneshvara and Apararka, who take *kṣamā* (here translated as sick) as making the wife weak through fasting and the like, the translation would be: "Approaching his weak wife in this manner, he should avoid the constellations of *maghā* and *mūla.*" *Mūla* is the nineteenth constellation, Scorpionis.

43 See verse 71 regarding the wishes granted to women. In the original Vedic text (*TS* 2.5.1.5), one of the wishes granted by Indra is to enjoy sex at any time: "let us obtain offspring from menses, and enjoy intercourse at will up to birth" (Tr. Keith).

44 According to the Vulg reading, the translation would be: "laughing, and going to other people's houses."

45 The Vulg reads "excluded from all dharmas" (see ch. 1, v. 38), in place of "banned from all dharmas."

46 The second half of this verse is terse and cryptic, and commentators too appear to be providing educated guesses. Apararka provides the clearest explanation. If, for example, a Brahman follows the occupation of a Kshatriya ("occupational activities are inverted"), then sons and grandsons born to him, who also follow such an occupation, reach the same status as a Kshatriya within five or seven generations. Their descent and ascent along the caste ladder follows the same process spelt out earlier in the first half of the verse.

47 The three sacred fires are the householder's fire (*gārhapatya*), the southern fire (*dakṣiṇāgni*), and the offertorial fire (*āhavanīya*). They are required for Vedic sacrifices. The rites that are given in texts on domestic rites (*gṛhyasūtra*) and texts of recollection (*smṛti*) and called *smārta* are offered in a fire often called *aupāsana*, which is kindled either at marriage or when a separate household is established.

48 Vijnaneshvara identifies the ritual formulas addressed to the sun as *ud u tyaṃ jātavedasam*, that is, *ṚV* 1.50, which begins: "Up do the beacons convey this god Jātavedas, the Sun, for all to see." See *BDh* 2.8.12 for other ritual formulas for the worship of the sun.

49 The term *atharvans* refers to the texts contained in the *Atharva Veda*, and *itihāsas* refer generally to the Sanskrit epics, *Mahābhārata* and *Rāmāyaṇa*. The expression *vidyām ādhyātmakīm* is unclear, but the commentators take it as a reference to the Upanishads that deal with the highest self.

50 Sipping water before eating provides a base for the food and makes it non-naked, and sipping after eating provides the food with a cover and makes it immortal. See also above, n. 17.

51 "One faithful to his vows" (*suvrata*) is generally interpreted as a Vedic student (*brahmacārin*). The *MDh* 3.94 also, within the same context, mentions the Vedic student along with the mendicant.

52 The Vulg has the readings "seat" or "orderly seating" in place of "attendance," i.e., some kind of service.

53 "Honey-mixture" (*madhuparka*) is a drink given to important guests. It is made by mixing honey into curd, milk, or water. See *ĀpDh* 2.8.5–8.

54 It is common courtesy to accompany a guest as he leaves. How far the host follows the guest depends on several factors. The *ĀpDh* (2.9.1–4) says: "If a guest has come in a carriage, he should follow him as far as the carriage; others he should follow until they give him leave to return. If a guest forgets to do so, he may turn back at the village boundary."

55 The Vulg reads "He should not neglect dharma, success, and pleasure, each at its proper time, as far as he is able." The time sacred to Brahma is defined as the last watch (about three hours) of the night.

56 The issue here is whether this verse is directed at Shudras. That appears to be the view of all the commentators. A Shudra performs the five great sacrifices (see v. 101) simply by uttering *namaḥ* ("Homage!") and not with Vedic mantras.

57 The *vaiśvānara* is a sacrifice to the "fire present in all men" generally cooked in twelve potsherds. The second line of this verse is terse and ambiguous, resulting in multiple interpretations. I follow Vishvarupa and Apararka in understanding it as referring to a "voluntary rite" (*kāmyakarma*), where one is not allowed to perform it with an inferior format, such as omitting parts of the rite that may require expensive material. Vijnaneshvara, however, takes the lines to have two separate rules. The first forbids the use of an inferior format when a person has sufficient material or wealth (*sati dravye*), such as not performing the *soma* sacrifice but the *vaiśvānara* oblation even if he has the means to perform the former. The second forbids the use of an inferior format in the case of a voluntary rite. He thus takes *na kurvīta sati dravya* twice, once with *hīnakalpam* and again with *phalapradam.*

58 The Vulg reads "A man who performs a sacrifice with what is begged from a Shudra is born...."

59 The Vulg reads "He should shun" in place of "He should not honor." On the way of herons, called the "heron-vow," *MDh* 4.196 says, "A twice-born who goes around with downcast eyes but is cruel, given to furthering his own ends, crooked, and being falsely

sanctimonious, is a man who is observing the 'heron-vow.'"

60 The meaning of "earth" (*mṛd*) is unclear. Vijnaneshvara takes it to mean earth that has been drawn out from a sacred bathing place, perhaps for the purposes of purification. The sense is that when these items are encountered on the road, he should honor them by circumambulating.

61 *Pāraskaragṛhyasūtra* 2.7.7.

62 The Vulg reads "semen" in place of "poison."

63 Brahmans who are bath-graduates are expected to devote a period of time every year to the intense study of the Veda. This sacred period begins and ends on particularly auspicious days (for this period and for the suspension of Vedic recitation, see Olivelle 2006). The phrase "when plants sprout" refers to the time when rice and other grains begin to sprout, taken by Vijnaneshvara to be the month Shravana (July–August). *Śravaṇa* is the twenty-third lunar constellation, Aquillae; *hasta* is the thirteenth lunar constellation, Corvi.

64 According to the Vulg reading, the translation would be: "on the eighth day, he should perform the rite of terminating the Vedic study outside the village and according to rule." Pausha corresponds to December–January. The eighth day (*aṣṭakā*) refers to the eighth day after the full moon. According to the *PārGṛ* (2.12.1), the termination of Vedic study is done on the middle *aṣṭakā*. There are three *aṣṭakā* days on the eighth days of the three dark fortnights following the full moon of Agrahayana (November–December).

65 The Vulg reads "mouse" in place of "pig." The reference is to these animals coming between the reciters. The raising and lowering of the flag of Indra (*śakra*) refers to the beginning and conclusion of a festival in his honor.

66 The Vulg reads "of another person's wife" in place of "of another person." Neither of these terms occurs in parallel passages of other *dharmaśāstras* (see *MDh* 4.130, 132). If *parasya* is taken as syntactically connected to blood, etc. listed in the second line, then the translation would be "on blood . . . bath-powder of another person."

67 The term *ucchiṣṭa* ("sullied with remnants") refers to a person who is impure after eating or answering a call of nature because he has remnants of food, feces, or urine sticking to him.

68 The Vulg reads *asvargyam* ("not conducive to heaven") in place of the very difficult form *asvattam*, which, following Vishva, I have translated as "does not lead to a good outcome."

69 The Vulg reads "sister" in place of "paternal relative," and "child" in place of "member of household."

70 See ch. 1, n. 18.

71 The term *śvavṛtti*, which I, following Vijna, have taken to mean hunters and fowlers who use dogs, is interpreted by Vishva and Apar to mean servants who do mean tasks, such as washing the feet of other people.

72 The Vulg reads "those who make a living through liquor" in place of "those who make a living by whitewashing."

73 The Vulg reading *paryāyānnam* is interpreted by Vijna to mean Shudra food given by a Brahman or Brahman food given by a Shudra. Apar says that it is food given sequentially, such as: on Sunday to this person and on Monday to this other person.

74 The meaning of "someone who has presented himself" is unclear. See *MDh* 4.253 for a similar list. There the commentators interpret this expression to mean a Shudra who has fallen on hard times and has voluntarily become someone's slave or merely a servant or worker.

75 The Vulg reads "red juices flowing from incisions" in place of "red sap of trees; growths on tree stumps." The reference appears to be to growths such as mushrooms growing on tree stumps. The parallel at *MDh* 5.6 (*vraścanaprabhava*) probably also refers to these growths rather than "juices flowing from incisions on trees," which was my previous interpretation based on commentators (Olivelle 2005: 138). The *śigru* is the tree *Moringa oleifera* or *pterygosperma*, commonly called "drumstick" tree (Murunga), whose long pods are widely used as a vegetable.

76 On the classification of bird (e.g., feed by pecking and scratching with feet) and animals (e.g., single-hoofed, five-nailed), see Olivelle 2002a, 2002b. *Dātyūha* is a name given to a variety of birds, including the hawk cuckoo and several water birds, such as the black ibis, white-breasted waterhen, and the purple moorhen: see Dave 2005: 294. *Ṭiṭṭibha* is a kind of plover; lapwing: see Dave 2005: 357–363. *Sārasa* is a species of crane. *Ardea sibirica. Haṃsa* is the ruddy goose, the most celebrated species of Indian goose. The term is often applied to other large geese and swans.

77 The *koyaṣṭhi* is the red or yellow-wattled lapwing. Dave (2005: 358) identifies these birds also as "the smaller crested Herons and Bitterns which keep standing in shallow water for hours waiting for prey to come to them." *Plava* is a generic term for waterfowl: coot, cormorant, duck: see Dave 2005: 299, 371–375. The *cakra* is the ruddy sheldrake called the Brahmani duck. The fidelity of a mated pair to each other and their grief when separated is celebrated in Indian poetry and folklore. See Dave 2005: 450–453. *Balāka* is the flamingo; the term is sometimes applied to other waterfowl, such as the egret. Dave 2005: 409–421. *Kṛsara* is a kind of porridge made with rice, sesame seeds, and milk, or with rice and peas boiled together. *Saṃyāva* is a fried cake made with wheat flour, ghee, milk, sugar, and spices. *Śaṣkulī* is a large round cake made with rice flour, sugar, and sesame seeds and fried in oil.

78 *Kalaviṅka* is a species of sparrow, identified as the "village sparrow" by Vijna on *YDh* 1.174. According to Dave (2005: 487), the word is used for blackbirds, magpies, and finches. The term *kurara* applies to ospreys and eagles that eat fish. See Dave 2005: 185–187, 489. *Rajjudālaka* is often called a species of wild fowl. Dave (2005: 54) identifies it as the paradise flycatcher. *Khañjarīta* is the yellow wagtail: see Dave 2005: 105.

79 The Vulg reads "intentionally" in place of "unintentionally." The latter reading is supported by the parallel passage in *MDh* 5.20. *Cāṣa* is a genre of birds, both jays and rollers (bee-eaters): see Dave 2005: 146–154.

80 For the lunar fast, see *YDh* 3.324–325.

81 The *siṃhatuṇḍa,* literally "lion-faced," is a kind of fish. The *rohita* is a kind of red fish said to feed on moss. The *pāṭhīna* is a kind of sheat-fish: *Silurus pelorius* or *boalis. Saśalka,* literally "with scales," is a kind of fish.

82 Aquatic articles are items such as pearl, coral, and conch. A *camasa* is a square ladle made of banyan wood and used for a variety of purposes in a sacrifice, including serving as a container or a drinking vessel for *soma. Caru* is a porridge prepared from rice or barley and cooked in water with butter or milk. *Sruc* is the common name for ladles (including *juhū, upabhṛt,* and *dhruvā*) used for pouring ghee into the sacred fire.

83 The Vulg reads "large quantities of grain and clothes" in place of "large quantities of clothes." Note that most of the articles

mentioned in these verses are ritual implements. The cart, for example, refers to the small cart used ritually and not to normal carts used for transportation. A *sphya* is a wooden sword made of *khadira* wood and used within the Vedic ritual for a variety of ritual purposes. A *śūrpa* is a winnowing basket made of bamboo or reed and used to winnow grain for a Vedic ritual.

84 The Vulg reads "cloth of sheep wool and silk" in place of "cloth of sheep wool and woven textiles." *Ariṣṭa* is the soapberry tree: *Sapindus detergens.*

85 Smearing here refers especially to smearing the land or the floor of the house with cow's dung.

86 The Vulg reads "impurities issuing from men" instead of "impurities issuing from the bodily orifices of men."

87 The Vulg reads "the best knowers of the highest self" in place of "those who contemplate the highest self."

88 See ch. 1, n. 29.

89 "A cow facing both ways" refers to a cow in the act of delivering her calf. The mother faces one way and the calf the other. After this verse, the Vulg adds a verse intended to define the above expression: "As long as the two feet and face of the calf are seen in the vagina, for that long the cow should be recognized as the earth, so long as she does not deliver the fetus."

90 The Vulg reads "lamp" in place of "farm animal."

91 The Vulg reads "tree and what is cherished" in place of "water for trees."

92 See ch. 1, n. 64.

93 The "special new-moon day" (*vyatīpāta*) is when the new moon falls on a Sunday and it is in a specific constellation. The "elephant's shadow" is also called *kuñjarasya prākchāyā* (see *MDh* 3.274). As Kane (1965–1975, IV: 371 n.) has shown, medieval authors interpret this word differently, some even taking it literally. Most, however, interpret it astronomically: it is the thirteenth day of Bhadrapada (August–September) when the moon is in the *māgha* constellation and the sun in the *hasta* constellation.

94 *Jyeṣṭhasāman,* "the most senior or best *sāman* chants," refers to *Tāṇḍya Brāhmaṇa* 21.2.3. *Trimadhu* refers to the three verses beginning with Madhu: *ṚV* 1.90.6–8. *Trisuparṇa* refers to the three verses *ṚV* 10.114.3–5.

95 *Triṇāciketa:* Bodewitz (1985, 8–10, 25) has shown that this term

refers not to particular fires but to the building of a special fire-altar bearing the name of Naciketas, the central figure in the *Kaṭha Upaniṣad.*

96 The five sacred fires are the three Vedic fires: offertorial fire (*āhavanīya*), householder's fire (*gārhapatya*), and southern fire (*dakṣiṇāgni*), along with the two other fires: hearth fire (*āvasathya*) and hall fire (*sabhya*).

97 The Vulg reads "impotent man" in place of "cruel man."

98 The Vulg reads "teacher" (or "elder"; *guru*) in place of "son." "Someone whose son is a Shudra" (*vṛṣlātmaja*): I follow the interpretation of Vishvarupa, taking the compound as a *bahuvrīhi,* which is also mentioned by Apararka. Vijnaneshvara takes the compound as a *tatpuruṣa* to mean: "son of a Shudra," which is unlikely, because then he would be a Shudra himself, while this list pertains to Brahmans who are disqualified.

99 "Purifying rings" are made with the sacred *kuśa* grass and worn around the fingers.

100 *Ṛg Veda* 2.41.13.

101 *Ṛg Veda* 10.9.4.

102 *Vājasaneyi Saṃhitā* 5.26; *TS* 1.3.1.1.

103 *Taittirīya Brāhmaṇa* 2.7.15.4.

104 "Welcome water" (*arghya*) consists of perfumed water with flowers and forms an integral part of the welcoming ceremony for important guests. After this verse many Vulg sources, including Vijna, add a half-verse: "likewise, the offering of clothes, as also water to clean the hands."

105 *Ṛg Veda* 10.16.12.

106 *Vājasaneyi Saṃhitā* 19.58.

107 After the citation from the *VS,* many Vulg sources, including Vijna, add another half-verse: "after spreading sesame seeds all around, saying: 'The demons have been driven away'" (*VS* 2.29).

108 The formula "The earth is your vessel" is found in *Āpastambamantrapāṭha,* 2.20.1; *HirGṛ* 2.3.4. "Vishnu strode out..." is *ṚV* 1.22.17.

109 *Ṛg Veda* 1.90.6–8.

110 "Inexhaustible water" (*akṣayyodaka*) refers to the rite of offering water mixed with sesame seeds to the Brahmans, asking them to pronounce "May it be inexaustible!," from which formula is derived the name of this water offering.

111 According to the Vulg reading the translation would be: "... water on the ground, and when the Brahmans have said: 'May the All-Gods be pleased,' he should softly recite this."

112 See *MDh* 3.259, *ViDh* 73.28.

113 *Ṛg Veda* 7.38.8.

114 Although the Vulg reading differs, the meaning remains the same.

115 *Vājasaneyi Saṃhitā* 19.25–26.

116 The Vulg reads "He should perform the rest as before" in place of "The rest, however, beginning with the welcome-water is performed as before." The rite of "making rice-ball-sharers" (*sapiṇḍīkaraṇa*) is performed one year after death or the eleventh day after death. This rite makes the newly deceased person take his place among the forefathers and a sharer in the balls of rice offered monthly to the forefathers.

117 The *eṇa* is the blackbuck (also called *kṛṣṇasāra: MDh* 2.23), an antelope with black hair on the back and sides and white under the belly: *Antilope cervicapra.* The *ruru* is a species of spotted antelope.

118 The *mahāśalka* is a kind of large prawn. The *kālaśāka* is the plant *Ocimum sanctum,* commonly referred to as holy basil or the Tulasi plant. The term *vārdhrāṇasa,* literally "leather-snouted," sometimes refers to the rhinoceros, but in dharma texts it refers to a type of bird, probably a hornbill. At *BDh* 1.12.6, however, it is classified as a bird that scratches with its feet in searching for food, which would argue against a waterbird.

119 The meaning is that a person offers an ancestral offering every day during the fourteen days from the first day of the dark fortnight (*kṛṣṇapakṣa*) until the new-moon day, excluding the fourteenth, that is, the day before the new moon. When he does so, each day he obtain a specific reward beginning with a daughter on the first day and ending with all desires—that is, the thirteen given before—on the new-moon day.

120 The Vulg reads "prosperity, primacy, good fortune" in place of "offspring, primacy, sons." There appears to be some confusion regarding the repetition of various items. Scribes and commentators attempt to eliminate repetitions. However, each item corresponds to the reward obtained from an ancestral offering offered on a particular day, and thus some items are repeated. *Kṛttikā* is the third constellation, Pleiades; *bharaṇī* is the name of a constellation (*nakṣatra*) containing three stars:

35, 39, and 41 Arietis.

121 The Vulg reads "offspring" in place of "intelligence."

122 This section appears to be a synopsis of *MānGṛ* 2.14. The term *gaṇa* is applied to large groups or hosts of divine beings. Their chief is Ganapati, the son of Shiva.

123 The Vulg variant reading does not materially affect the meaning. Vishvarupa explains that a woman who is pregnant fails to obtain offspring (i.e., she has miscarriages) and a woman who has regular periods fails to conceive.

124 The Vulg reads "after his body has been rubbed with a paste of white mustard along with ghee" in place of "after his body has been rubbed with a newly prepared paste of white mustard." Here the rare term *sādya* means newly prepared. Clearly the reference is to the bathing of the individual possessed by Vinayaka or Ganapati.

125 The four ritual formulas are: *mitāya svāhā, saṃmitāya svāhā, sālakaṭaṅkaṭāya svāhā,* and *kūśmāṇḍarājaputrāya svāhā.* Vijnaneshvara, however, takes these as six formulas, dividing the compounded words: *sālāya svāhā, kaṭaṅkaṭāya svāhā, kūśmāṇḍāya svāhā, rājaputrāya svāhā.*

126 *Pūrikā,* often paired with *apūpa,* appears to be a cake or bread. Vijna (on *YDh* 1.288) appears to say that *apūpa* is cooked without oil, while *pūrikā* is cooked with oil, perhaps fried. This could be the same as modern puri. After this verse, the Vulg adds an extra verse: "Curd, boiled rice, milk rice, balls of molasses and flour, and sweetmeat—bringing all these and placing the head on the ground." The added verse forms a syntactic unit with verse 286.

127 See ch. 1, n. 104.

128 Ambika, literally "mother," is another name of Parvati, the wife of Shiva.

129 The Vulg reads "Grant me wealth" in place of "prosperity and merit."

130 According to the Vulg reading, as interpreted by Vijna, the reading would be: "By always performing the worship of the sun and making the forehead-mark of Skanda and Great Ganapati, he obtains success." It is unclear why Skanda is referred to as *tilakasvāmin* ("Lord of *tilaka*"): see n. 43 to the edition.

131 Rahu is the name of one of the nine Indian planets, considered the descending node and the head of the demon Saihikeya, identified with the Vedic *svarbhānu* (Jamison 1991: 282), whose body is *ketu.*

Ketu is the name of one of the nine Indian planets, considered the descending node and the body of the demon Saihikeya, identified with the Vedic *svarbhānu* (Jamison 1991: 282), whose head is Rahu.

132 Each planet has a color represented by the substance out of which it is manufactured. Mercury and Jupiter are both made of gold. That still leaves an extra planet. Vishvarupa says that the images of both Rahu and Ketu are made of lead, while Apararka says that Ketu is made of *kāṃsya* (bell metal or brass), which, however, is listed only in the Vulg reading. The *Matsya Purāṇa* (93.17) says that both Saturn and Rahu are black and are made of iron.

133 *Ṛg Veda* 1.35.2.

134 *Vājasaneyi Saṃhitā* 9.40.

135 *Ṛg Veda* 8.44.16.

136 *Vājasaneyi Saṃhitā* 15.54.

137 The nine mantras are given in vv. 296 and 297, and each of them is used in making the offerings to the nine planets, respectively.

138 *Ṛg Veda* 2.23.15.

139 *Vājasaneyi Saṃhitā* 19.75.

140 *Ṛg Veda* 10.9.4.

141 *Vājasaneyi Saṃhitā* 13.20.

142 *Ṛg Veda* 1.6.3.

143 *Arka* is the madder tree: *Calotropis procera* or *gigantea*. *Palāśa* is a variety of fig tree called Dhak with a beautiful trunk and abundant leaves; *Butea frondosa*. *Khadira* is the Black catechu, cutch tree; *Acacia catechu*. *Apāmārga* is a plant commonly called prickly chaff flower or devil's horsewhip: *Achyranthes aspera*. The *pippala* is the peepal or bo tree, *Ficus religiosa*. The name *śamī* covers two plants. First, *Mimosa suma* (Hindi: *chikkur*), a thorny shrub. Second, *Prosopis spicigera*.

144 The Vulg reads "dipped in honey, ghee, curd, and milk" in place of "dipped in honey, ghee, and curd."

145 Sixty-day rice is said to be a kind of rice that matures in sixty days.

146 The Vulg reads "not petty, not harsh" in place of "possessing a council that is not petty"; and "not given to vice" in place of "firmly loyal." For an analysis of the section on the dharma of kings, see Tokunaga 1993.

147 The Vulg reads "he should confer about the kingdom" in place of "he should confer about what has to be done." See the parallel at *KAŚ* 1.15.1. The referent of "Brahman" here is unclear, but possibly

refers to the chaplain, even though his appointment is mentioned only in the next verse.

148 The reading of the edition, *alabdhaṃ labdhum īheta,* is conjectural. But the various readings do not create differences in meaning. The Vulg reads "increase through right policy what has been protected" in place of "increase constantly what has been protected."

149 The Vulg reads "good" in place of "avaricious."

150 The Vulg reads "with the mind" (or intelligently: *buddhyā*) in place of "after waking up" (*buddhvā*).

151 The Vulg reads "providing protection to his subjects" in place of "providing protection justly."

152 In Indian jurisprudence, the justification for kings taking taxes from people is based on his providing them protection especially from thieves. When the king fails to provide such protection he loses the right to taxes. See *YDh* 2.38.

153 The Vulg reads "the king should honor" in place of "he should always honor."

154 This advice to the king about how to administer a conquered territory is dependent on *KAŚ* 13.5.4, 24.

155 The theory of the circle of kingdoms (*maṇḍala*) is spelled out in detail in *KAŚ* 6.2.13–22. The idea is that each kingdom is surrounded by other kingdoms vying for power. The immediate neighbors are considered natural enemies, while circles beyond those are natural allies.

156 These six tactics are called *ṣāḍguṇya* and discussed extensively in *KAŚ* 7.1.

157 The Vulg reads "When the enemy's kingdom is endowed with the quality consisting of good crops" in place of "When the enemy's kingdom lacks the proper strategic advantages," which is both the more difficult reading and agrees with the other conditions for attacking an enemy when he is weak.

158 The Vulg has a very different reading of this verse: "Some people with excellent minds take the fruit (of actions) to proceed from fate, some from inherent nature, some from human effort, and some through the combination of them." See n. 53 to the edition.

159 For the image of a cart with one wheel, see *ChU* 4.16.3.

160 This verse is based on *KAŚ* 6.1.1. Here the word *jana* clearly stands for *janapada* ("the countryside") as opposed to the *durga* ("fort"). For the technical use of the term *prakṛti* as constituent part of a

kingdom, see *KAŚ* 6.1–2 (Olivelle 2013: 658).

161 The Vulg reads "It cannot be justly wielded by someone" in place of "It cannot be wielded, therefore, by someone."

162 The Vulg reads "provided with choice sacrificial fees" in place of "provided with one hundred thousand in sacrificial fees."

163 For "assessors," see ch. 2, n. 1. After this verse, the Vulg places the verse given as 2.34 in my edition.

164 The *trasareṇu* is the smallest quantity in the list of weights. The *likṣā*, literally, "egg of a louse," is a minute measurement of weight equal to eight *trasareṇus*. A *rājasarṣapa* is a kind of mustard seed (*Sinapis ramosa*) used as a unit of measurement.

165 A *gaurasarṣapa* is a white mustard seed (*Sinapis glauca*) used as a unit of measurement. A *yava*, literally a barley corn, is a measurement of weight, approximately 0.039 gm.

166 A *niṣka* is a measurement of weight said to be four *suvarṇas*, i.e., 37.76 grams.

167 See ch. 1, n. 32.

## *2 Legal Procedure*

1 The Vulg reads "knowers of dharma" in place of "belong to distinguished families." The term *sabhāsad* ("court officer") is probably synonymous with the more common *sabhya* ("assessor") used in v. 3. Generally, three such assessors are appointed to each court (*MDh* 8.10). They are versed in law and assist the king or principal judge (*prāḍvivāka;* Olivelle 2016b), who may not be a jurist, and are responsible for the proper conduct of court proceedings and for reaching a verdict. For the Sanskrit legal vocabulary, see Olivelle 2015.

2 The Vulg reads: "out of greed" in place of "out of hatred."

3 The four feet or parts of the legal procedure outlined above are: plaint, plea, evidence or proof that includes the litigation proper (evidence offered by the plaintiff and the defendant), and verdict. For a detailed analysis, see Olivelle and McClish 2015.

4 The surety should be capable of paying the amount under dispute and any fine that may be assessed in case a litigant is unable or unwilling to do so.

5 The meaning of the first provision appears to be that the plaintiff attempts to settle his doubtful claim (e.g., a claim that the defendant

has denied) not by proper legal means of proof, such as witnesses or documents, but by extra-judicial means such as arresting or threatening the defendant.

6 The issue here relates to who has the burden of proving his case. The person on whom this burden falls is called by the technical term *pūrvavādin,* lit. "prior litigant." Most commonly this person is the appellant or plaintiff. Thus, his witnesses are called to testify first. There are conditions, however, under which the "prior litigant" status falls on the defendant. The commentator Vijnaneshvara gives the example of a suit concerning a piece of land that the plaintiff claims he received as a gift but is now occupied by the defendant. The defendant admits that the plaintiff received the land as a gift, but claims that it was subsequently purchased by the king and given to the defendant. In this case, the claim of the plaintiff being superseded by the plea of the defendant, the onus of proof falls on the latter, and he becomes the "prior litigant." In this case, his witnesses are deposed first (see *YDh* 2.23). The explanation relates to the two kinds of plea: "special plea" (*kāraṇokti* or *pratyavaskanda*) and "prior judgment" (*prāṅnyāya*). In the first case, the defendant admits the charges but pleads innocent for a specific reason: e.g., admits that he borrowed the money as stated in the plaint, but says that he returned it. In the second case, the defendant claims that the same charges against him have been already dismissed by the judgment of another court. In each of these cases, the burden of proof falls on the defendant, and he becomes the "prior litigant."

7 The wager appears to have been a curious custom where either the plaintiff or the defendant—or both—publicly boasts that he will bet a certain amount that he will win the suit. This was probably done in public and as part of the court proceedings, because it was enforced by the court. See Lariviere 1981b.

8 "Discarding subterfuge" means that the judge must detect and dismiss all kinds of deceits and tricks that the litigants may use to win the case.

9 According to the Vulg reading, the translation would be: "When two traditional texts are in conflict, principles of interpretation have greater force than legal procedure."

10 The technical term "enjoyment" (*bhukti* or *bhoga*) refers to legal possession and usufraction of the thing under litigation.

If someone, for example, has tilled a particular field or milked a particular cow for an extended period of time without objection, then the presumption is that he has ownership of it. See, however, *YDh* 2.27, where title to a property is given greater force than possession.

11 The Vulg reads "in all monetary litigations" in place of "in all litigations."

12 "Property" here is probably either the purloined pledge that is the subject of the legal dispute or its value. The statement "and the like" (*ādi*) refers to a boundary, an open deposit, the property of the mentally handicapped, children, and the king, and a sealed deposit.

13 This verse is omitted in the Vulg.

14 The Vulg reads "officials appointed by the king" in place of "king, officials authorized to adjudicate lawsuits." These are the five traditional forums for trying lawsuits. Vijnaneshvara defines an association as one based on residence, for example, a village, that includes people belonging to different castes. A guild, on the other hand, is based on occupation and may include people of the same or different castes and living in the same or different localities, for example, a guild of weavers or goldsmiths. A family probably refers to an extended family or lineage, where disputes may be resolved by the paterfamilias.

15 The Sanskrit term *vyavahāra* refers both to a legal transaction (such as taking out a loan) and to a lawsuit, so is here translated as "legal action" to maintain the ambiguity of the term as used by Yajnavalkya. The two verses 32–33 are dependent on the parallel in the *KAŚ* 3.1.2, 12, 13, where the reference is clearly to legal transactions. Yajnavalkya, however, uses the term within his discussion of lawsuits, but some of the disabilities mentioned here apply rather to transactions. "Outside" probably refers to outside a village or town, paralleling the *KAŚ* term wilderness (*araṇya*). The mention of enemy clearly refers to a lawsuit brought by an enemy of the accused; it is difficult to see how someone would make a business transaction with an enemy, unless it was done under threat of force.

16 The Vulg gives this verse as 1.361 in its enumeration (after 1.356 in the enumeration of my edition).

17 A secured loan is one guaranteed by a pledge or collateral. Such

pledges are dealt with below, *YDh* 2.58–64. One-eightieth translates into 1.25% interest per month. For a general treatment of debt in classical Indian law, see Chatterjee 1971.

18 The text of Vijnaneshvara transposes the verses 40 and 41. "Women" here refers to slaves. Another interpretation of this compound takes the term to mean "female farm animals." But see *YDh* 2.59 where the same expression occurs. In general, Indian law stipulated that interest accrued on a loan can only equal the amount of the loan itself. Thus, when the interest plus the principal becomes double the loan taken out, then the interest ceases to accrue and the loan becomes payable. Here we have different upper limits for accrued interest on non-monetary loans.

19 The Vulg places this verse after verse 52. This list of persons responsible for the debts of a dead man is somewhat confusing. That heirs inherit both the assets and the debts of a deceased person is a general rule of ancient Indian jurisprudence. Vijnaneshvara specifies that the list contains a hierarchy of those obliged to pay the debt; those listed later are so obliged only when those listed earlier are unavailable. The person who marries the widow of the dead man also becomes liable for his debts if there is no son who has inherited the property. The reasons for incurring this liability are left unstated. A son is liable for his father's debts even if he has not inherited any property, so long as the property has not been inherited by someone else (the first provision).

20 Undivided coparceners are father and sons or, in the absence of the father, the group of brothers who live in a joint family where the ancestral property has not been divided among the heirs.

21 A surety for appearance only undertakes the obligation to produce the person for whom he is acting as surety when he is needed, e.g., in court at the appointed time. He becomes liable for the payment of the debt in question only if he fails to produce the debtor. A surety for trustworthiness presents the debtor to the creditor as a trustworthy person with the means to repay the debt. In the case of default, he is liable for the debt. The obligations undertaken by these two types of sureties are personal and do not devolve to their sons or heirs. The third type of surety, on the other hand, guarantees the payment of the debt in the case of default, and this obligation falls on his sons and heirs at his death.

22 There are two ways in which several sureties can guarantee a

single loan. Each could guarantee a portion of the loan, or all could guarantee the entire loan individually. In the first case, each is liable only for that part of the loan guaranteed by him. In the second case, each is liable for the entire loan, and the creditor could press any one of them to pay the entire loan.

23 These amounts are the same as the rates of interest specified in vv. 39–40. Verse 59 records the amounts to be returned to the surety who has settled the debt over and above the amount (twice the loan) fixed in verse 58.

24 The third kind of pledge is one used in some way by the creditor (*bhogyādhi*), for example, milk from a cow or grain from a field. When such a pledge is given, there is no interest on the loan, the use of the pledge acting as the interest. Given that the interest is not added on to the loan and, thus, the loan never becomes double, the pledge is never forfeited. This is distinguished from a pledge that is to be safeguarded (*gopyādhi*), dealt with in the next verse.

25 The issue concerns a pledge given as collateral that the creditor is not allowed to use. In case he either uses the yield, such as the milk of a pledged cow, or otherwise uses the pledge, such as a bullock for transportation, then he has to repay any interest that may have been paid on the loan.

26 Here also the issue concerns a pledge that is to be utilized by the creditor in lieu of interest. It comes into force as such a pledge the moment the creditor appropriates (*svīkaraṇa*), that is, begins to make use of it. If it loses its value—for example, if the pledged cow ceases to give milk—then another similar pledge should be given or the loan returned.

27 Generally, loans are secured through pledges. When a loan is given purely on the basis of the good character of the debtor, interest has to be paid on the loan. The exact meaning of the technical expression *satyaṃkāra* is not altogether clear, but it probably refers to the earnest money paid to secure a loan (see *KātSm* 541). The meaning appears to be that the borrower loses the earnest and in addition has to pay twice the loan (principal plus interest: see ch. 2, n. 18).

28 According to the Vulg reading, the translation would be: "otherwise, he becomes a thief." This and the next verse have been subject to much misunderstanding by the commentators of the *YDh*. They correspond to *KAŚ* 3.12.11–14, where the meaning and

the readings are transparent. I have followed it in the edition and the translation.

29 The Vulg reads "placed within a cloth" in place of "placed within a box."

30 According to the reading of Vishva and M, the translation would be: "If the fault happened after."

31 The Vulg reads "who are devoted to rites given in the Vedas and texts of recollection" in place of "who delight in rites associated with the five sacrifices." See 1.101 for the five (great) sacrifices.

32 Vishvarupa and M read "physical assault" in place of "theft, assault."

33 Verses 75 and 76 are placed after verse 79 in the Vulg.

34 See *YDh* 3.228.

35 The issue here is whether there is an *avagraha* (elision of initial *a*) before *samāḥ*. Vishva and Apar assume it and read *asamāḥ* ("uneven number"), while Vijna takes it as a positive: *samāḥ* ("even number").

36 This verse is omitted in the Vulg.

37 According to Vijna, "marks" refers to unique symbols that may be on the document. "Connection" refers to the previous dealings that the creditor and debtor may have had.

38 The Vulg reads "every time a payment is made by the debtor" in place of "any payment received from the debtor."

39 The Vulg places this verse after verse 103. The ordeal of the plowshare is somewhat obscure (Lariviere 1981a: 48), and often it is identical to the fire ordeal. Separately, however, it may refer to the touching of a plowshare that is red-hot.

40 The Vulg reads "the blind" in place of "the afflicted." In *pāda*-c, there is a difference in interpretation as to whether the reading is *aśūdrasya* (*vā* + *aśūdrasya* = *vāśūdrasya*) or *śūdrasya* (*vā śūdrasya*). In the manuscripts there is no orthographic difference between the two readings, given that they do not put spaces between words. Vishva glosses: *aśūdrasyāgnir jalaṃ vā syāt* ("Fire or water is for a non-Shudra"). Vijna, on the other hand, takes fire as intended for a Kshatriya, water for Vaishya, and poison for a Shudra. Apar is silent on this point. I follow Vishva's interpretation. It appears that in a *sūtra*-like manner, Yajnavalkya takes *vāśūdrasya* twice, once with the sandhi and once without, making the prescription in *pāda*-d apply to a Shudra.

41 The person administering the ordeal inspects both hands after they have been rubbed with unhusked rice to reveal any hidden injuries on the hand. These are then marked so that after the ordeal they are not viewed as burn marks.

42 Fifty *palas* equal 1.89 kilograms.

43 Sixteen *aṅgulas* equal 32 centimeters.

44 This a very abbreviated description. According to Vishva's explanation, while the man undergoing the ordeal is standing in water, someone shoots three arrows. A fast runner is placed near the middle arrow. Another fast runner runs from the place where the arrows were shot to the place where the arrow fell, and the man undergoing the ordeal immerses his entire body under water. At the same time, the other runner runs to the place from where the arrow was shot. If he does not see any part of the man under water, then the latter is considered innocent. Otherwise he is deemed guilty.

45 The *śārṅga* poison is extracted from the *śṛṅga* plant, which is a species of *Aconitum*. The name is derived from the fact that the flower has the appearance of a horn: see *KātSm* 446–450; Lariviere 1981a: 40.

46 According to Vishva, fierce deities are Aditya and so forth, while Vijna identifies them as Durga, Aditya, and the like. "Handfuls" here may also have a more technical sense of a particular measurement of volume (*prasṛti*). In that case, it would be either 165 cc or 275 cc (Srinivasan 1979: 71).

47 "Women's property" (*strīdhana*) is a technical term referring to wealth that a married woman owns and is under her control. For the different kinds of such property, see *YDh* 2.147. For a detailed study of inheritance in Indian law, see Rocher 2002b.

48 This provision gives the father authority to make the partition in a manner he thinks best. The procedure followed in partition is normally called *dāyadharma* (*MDh* 9.103) and *vibhāgadharma* (*NSm* 13.36). Here Yajnavalkya says that this dharma is determined by the father.

49 The Vulg places this verse after verse 122.

50 The Vulg reads "should receive an equal share" in place of "should receive a share." See *YDh* 1.119.

51 A Brahman can marry women from all four social classes, while, according to the rule of hypergamy, a Kshatriya can marry women

from three, and a Vaishya from two (see *YDh* 1.57). Thus sons of a Brahman father from Brahman, Kshatriya, Vaishya, and Shudra mothers take four, three, two, and one shares, respectively. Sons of a Kshatriya father from Kshatriya, Vaishya, and Shudra mothers take three, two, or one shares, respectively. Sons of a Vaishya father from Vaishya and Shudra mothers take two and one shares, respectively. Given that Shudras can only marry Shudras, such a distribution of shares does not obtain. This view contradicts what is stated in 1.56, where twice-born men are forbidden to take Shudra wives.

52 See *YDh* 1.68–69.

53 The female son (*putrikā*) is actually one's daughter who has been appointed to be the father's legal son, so that the son she begets is ritually and legally the son of his maternal grandfather. The second kind of son is the one born through the leviratic process (1.68–69).

54 With reference to the term *dāsī* ("slave woman") in *MDh* 9.179, Rocher (2002a) has argued that it refers to a Shudra woman rather than to a slave as such. In this context, however, given the statement in the very next verse, the reference is probably to a slave or "kept woman" (*avarodhaka* according to Vishvarupa) of a Shudra man.

55 There are four kinds of heirs for three kinds of people. This problem is solved by Apar by saying that each subsequent heir inherits only in the absence of each preceding irrespective of the three kinds of ascetics. Vijna says that "due order" (*krameṇa*) actually means "in the inverted order" (*pratilomakrameṇa*). And he takes spiritual brother and someone belonging to one's own order to be a single category. I think Apar's solution is simpler and more credible. Vishva does not comment on this.

56 The Vulg reading has caused a lot of confusion and a variety of forced interpretations of this verse (see Rocher 2002b: 215–223). Rocher translates the Vulg version literally as follows: "A half brother gets the property if he was reunited, not any half brother; he who was not reunited gets it as well, not the half brother who was reunited." Rocher (personal communication) has indicated that the reading adopted in this edition resolves the textual issues underlying the confusion and controversy.

57 Vishvarupa and M read "son" in place of "husband."

58 See *YDh* 1.58–61.

59 See ch. 1, n. 32.

60 For *āyatana* as shrine in this context, see *NSm* 11.4 and Lariviere's (1989) translation. Apar glosses the term with *devālaya,* temple.

61 The distinction between *maryādā* ("border) and *sīmā* ("boundary") is not altogether clear (see KAŚ 3.9.3). I think Kangle (1972, notes to KAŚ 3.9.21 and 5.1.43) is correct in taking the first as referring to the property lines between fields, houses, and the like (private property), and the second as referring to the boundaries between villages and other public property. The reading of the Vulg changes the sequence: "for encroaching on a boundary and for seizing a field" thus inverting the seriousness of the two offenses and the respective fines. For the three levels of seizure-fines, see 1.361.

62 The Vulg reads "the fine is twice what was given above" in place of "but do not abide there, the fine is doubled."

63 According to the Vulg, the translation would be: "Stud bulls and ritually released cattle; a cow that has just delivered, a stray cow, and the like; ones without a herdsman; and those hounded by fate or the king, should be set free."

64 Many Vulg sources including Vijna read: "from anywhere always" in place of "from anywhere as if they were his own."

65 A "bow" (*dhanuḥ*) is a measurement of length, approximately 6 feet or 1.82 meters.

66 The payment is made to the king by the man who lost his property as compensation for recovering and keeping it safe. "Human being" refers to a slave.

67 The Vulg reads: "what has been promised to someone else" in place of "what is jointly held with someone else."

68 The process of weaving (mentioned in the next verse) is expected to increase the weight of the raw material (cotton, silk, etc.) used, while the process of manufacturing finished products reduces the weight of metals. For an extended discussion of this issue, see KAŚ 4.1.8–9, 36–43.

69 The Vulg reads "more than that" in place of "less than that." Either reading produces the same result: a middling textile loses five *palas.*

70 *Kauśeya* is a kind of Indian silk that in the KAŚ (2.11.107–114) is distinguished from imported Chinese silk and the less valued *parṇorṇā* probably made from uncultivated silk worms growing naturally in a variety of trees.

71 See 1.361.

72 According to the Vulg reading, the translation would be "he should be made to give an equal amount." Most interpreters take *kāryam* as referring to *samam,* thus giving a meaning similar to that of the Vulg. I follow the better interpretation of Vishva, who takes *samam* as connected to *āvahet* of *pāda*-b, and takes *kāryam* (with the sense of *kārayitavyam*) as connected with *karma* of *pāda*-a. This is a good example of Yajnavalkya's *sūtra*-like verses. See the parallel in *NSm* 6.5.

73 According to the Vulg, the translation would be: "A man's wages, however, are in direct proportion to the amount of work he does; if it cannot be accomplished by both, the wages should be paid for the work done according to the agreement." The difference in the two readings appears to rest on the meaning of *ubhayoḥ* ("of both"). Vishva, whose reading I follow, takes it to mean the worker and the employer, while Vijna, who follows the Vulg reading, takes the term to refer to two workers who carry out the work, envisaging a scenario when the first worker is unable to carry out the task and entrusts the work to another.

74 According to the Vulg, the master takes 5 percent from a gambler whose winnings amount to one hundred or more. I have followed the reading and interpretation of Vishva, according to which the master takes 5 and 10 percent from the winner and the loser, respectively, for providing the place and dice for gambling.

75 The master of the gambling hall seizes the winnings from the loser and gives them to the winning gambler.

76 According to the Vulg, the translation would be: "I will fuck your mother *or* sister." One factor to prefer the reading of the edition is that vv. 208–209 deal with insults about the other person's disabilities or character, while the section on harming the other person begins at v. 212.

77 People of the lowest social class are Shudras. When they abuse a person of a higher class, the fines are increased: for a Brahman four times, for a Kshatriya three times, and for a Vaishya two times. In the opposite case, a Brahman reviling a Kshatriya is assessed half of four times, i.e., two times; a Vaishya, one and a half times; and a Shudra, one time, that is, simply the original fine. The Vulg reading, however, differs and the translation would then be: "When reviling is done in the inverse order of social class, the

fines are increased by two and three times, respectively. When it is done in the direct order of social class, those same fines are reduced progressively by one half." These increases affect Kshatriyas and Vaishyas, respectively, when they revile a Brahman. Vijnaneshvara explains the omission of the Shudra by saying that he is not fined but beaten.

78 See *YDh* 1.361.

79 The marks refer to wounds, fractures, and the like suffered by the person bringing the accusation. But, given that a man may injure himself and falsely accuse someone else of assault, the king is instructed to conduct a proper trial using both the marks of assault and other evidence such as legal reasoning and reports of witnesses.
After this verse, Vishva and M add a verse: "In a case where due to negligence none of the noble ones [i.e., authors of dharma treatises] has prescribed a fine, one should thoroughly investigate the case and impose a punishment."

80 See *YDh* 1.361.

81 See *YDh* 1.361.

82 In place of my conjectural reading, "twisting, squashing," Vishva and the Vulg read "binding with a cloth."

83 The Vulg reads "middle seizure-fine" (see *YDh* 1.361) in place of "highest seizure-fine."

84 For tolls at ferries and on land transportation, see *MDh* 8.404–405. The failure to invite a neighbor refers to a ritual, such as an ancestral offering. For more details, see *MDh* 8.392. The Vulg places this verse after v. 267.

85 Here, according to the commentators, we have three fines for four offenses of increasing gravity. Vishva takes the fine of twenty as referring to both the last two offenses, while Vijna thinks that when the wall is knocked down the three fines are combined (= 35 *paṇas*) and Apar connects the payment of the expenses for repair only with the last offense. I have taken the final *kuḍyāvapātane* as a *bahuvrīhi* compound qualifying *chede,* thus giving rise only to three offenses.

86 "Part" of an animal refers to a horn, ear, or tail, while a limb is a foot or eye. This succinct statement of the fines means that for causing pain the fine is two *paṇas;* for drawing blood, four; for cutting a part, six; and for cutting a limb, eight. Small animals are goats and sheep, and large animals are cattle, buffaloes, horses, and camels.

87 According to the Vulg reading, the translation would be: "For hacking branches, the trunk, and the entirety of tree with sprouting branches." This makes little sense. The reading of the edition is supported also by the parallel passage in *KAŚ* 3.19.28, where, however, the trees in question are those of city parks and not those belonging to private individuals, and the fines begin with six *paṇas* and are progressively doubled.

88 The Vulg reads "temple" in place of "royal palace."

89 In the original Sanskrit, the title of this Topic 32 is simply *sāhasa.* But this term has two meanings in its legal usage: violent acts and forcible seizure (or mugging). I have given both the meanings in the title. Both kinds of offenses are given under this topic.

90 In place of my conjectural reading, "seizing a property by force in the presence of the victim," Vishva, M, and the Vulg (even though they have somewhat different readings) have "seizing common property by force."

91 The Vulg reads "strikes his brother's wife" in place of "strokes his brother's wife." See the note to the edition for further comment.

92 Both Vijna and Apar interpret *svacchandavidhavāgāmī* to mean a man who, of his own choice, has sex with a widow. However, the *KAŚ* passage (3.20.16), on which this verse is based, reads: *vidhavāṃ chandavāsinīm,* clearly referring to a widow who lives on her own.

93 This verse is based on *KAŚ* 3.20.16–17. It is clear that Shudra recluses here refer to heretical ascetics such as Buddhists and Ajivakas listed in the *KAŚ*. Further, there the reference is not to a person who administers an oath without authorization but to a person who carries out a judicial interrogation under oath without being authorized to do so.

94 The meaning of "who comes between them" (*sāntara* or in the Vulg *antare*) is far from clear. It probably refers to a person who has in some way facilitated or encouraged the rift between father and son. This is the interpretation of Vishva, while Vijna and Apar take him to be someone who provided surety in a dispute with a wager.

95 The Vulg reads "the highest seizure-fine" in place of "lowest seizure-fine" (see *YDh* 1.361).

96 This verse appears to be a condensation of the *KAŚ* passage (4.2.20–21), which reads "For a weigher or a measurer who by sleight of hand causes a diminution that amounts to one-eighth

of an article valued at one *paṇa*, the fine is 200 *paṇas*. That also explains successive 200-*paṇa* increases in fines." The last phrase of the *YDh* verse, "adjusted according to the increase or decrease," is somewhat unclear. The meaning appears to be that when the value of the article in question is higher or lower, the fines are proportionately adjusted. This is stated in the last sentence of the *KAŚ* passage: when the value of the article is two *paṇas*, the fine would be increased to 400 *panas*. See below vv. 252–253.

97 The Vulg reads "the fine is the highest when deliberately carried out" in place of "the fine is said to be 1,000 *paṇas*."

98 The last clause appears to envisage a scenario where the seller is a merchant who sells a product, fails to deliver it, and then goes abroad to sell the same product for a larger profit. In this case, he is made to give that profit to the original buyer.

99 This verse is omitted by Vishva and M.

100 According to the Vulg reading, translation would be: "A trader who does not know the decrease...." This does not make much sense, unless we take it to mean that even if the trader does not know. As Vishva points out, a merchant is supposed to know how the value of a commodity may fluctuate and is thus not allowed to rescind a sale because the article may have increased in price between the time of purchase and delivery.

101 In *pāda*-d of v. 271, *mukha* refers to the face rather than mouth and *śuṣka* should go with *svara*. This is clear from the parallel passage in *KAŚ* 4.6.2: *śuṣkabhinnasvaramukhavarṇam*.

102 The phrase "unless it has gone outside" refers to an animal or human who was killed or stolen after leaving the village. Commentators take *anirgate* as referring to the thief, but the accusative *anirgatam* in the parallel passage at *KAŚ* 4.13.8 clearly refers to what has been killed or stolen: *muṣitam pravāsitam*.

103 According to the Vulg reading, the translation would be: "outside one *krośa* (about 3.6 km)" in place of "outside the plowed area." It is unclear what exactly they give. Stenzler and the commentators think it is compensation for the loss. But the *KAŚ* 4.13.11–12 speaks about permitting a search: *vicaya*.

104 The parallel passage in *ViDh* 5.136–137 makes it clear that the cloth thief has his hand cut off and the cutpurse his thumb and forefinger, which he used to pick someone's pocket. The punishment appears not to be distributive for the second offense, because the cutting

of the hand was already stated. So, for the second offense both the hand and foot are cut. Given that the cloth thief has already lost his hand during the first offense, it is unclear how he is to lose it again, unless it is the other hand used for the second offense.

105 Vijnaneshvara cites verses from Narada giving examples of the three kinds of articles. Small ones are earthenware, grain, and the like. The middling are clothes other than silk, non-precious metal, animals except cows and the like. And the great are gold, silk, and the like.

106 According to the reading of Vishva and the Vulg, the translation would be: "He should tie a rock and dump in water a woman who administers poison [Vulg: "who is depraved"] or who kills a man [probably, husband]—unless she is pregnant—and a woman who breaks a dike." For my conjectural reading, see note 48 of the edition.

107 Verses 284–285 condense the passage on the criminal investigation into a sudden death in *KAŚ* 4.7.14–22.

108 The source of this provision is *KAŚ* 4.11.20 where the reading is *dravyahastivana* ("produce and elephant forest") in place of *grāmavana* ("village, forest"). I think there was a lack of understanding of what a *dravyavana* (a produce forest in Kautilya's vocabulary) meant, and *dravya* was changed to *grāma*, thus adding a new category to the list. It is unclear whether this mistake was made by the author of the *YDh* or by a subsequent scribe or commentator. It is also unclear whether *grāmavana* should be taken as a *tatpuruṣa* compound ("a forest/woods of a village") or a *dvandva* ("village and forest"). Clearly, because of the transposition of *grāma* and *vana* (*vanagrāma*) in the Vulg, at least that tradition took the compound to be *dvandva*.

109 See *YDh* 1.361.

110 The Vulg reads "for the woman, the cutting of the ear and so forth" in place of "while the woman's nose and so forth are cut off." In this and the following verses, "direct order" means that the woman belongs to a lower class/caste than the man, and in the "inverse order" the woman belongs to a higher class/caste than the man.

111 The Vulg reads "thigh" in place of "navel," and "staying together in one place" in place of "lingering together." According to the Vulg reading of verse 290, the translation would be: "When prohibited, the woman should pay a fine of one hundred and a man

two hundred. When both have been prohibited, the punishment is the same as for a sexual offense." The changes to the text were probably carried out because of the failure to fully comprehend the meaning of the original. The Vulg seems to assume that the first line refers to a situation when the woman and the man have been admonished individually and separately, while the second line refers to a situation when both have been admonished together. This is somewhat farfetched. I think Vishva's interpretation is correct. The first line refers to a situation when the woman has been admonished against this conduct by the man with whom she is about to engage in this behavior, and when the man has been similarly admonished by the woman. The second line refers to a situation when such prohibitions were not made, but both willingly participated in the activity.

112 A virgin who is adorned refers to a context when she is being prepared for her imminent wedding. The man thus abducts the woman on her wedding day.

113 In all likelihood, the female slave (*dāsī*) here is actually a prostitute in exclusive keeping of a man (see the added verse after the next verse). Thus, she is not available for sex with other men. See *KAŚ* 4.12.7.

114 After this verse, many sources of the Vulg add a verse: "A prostitute who, after receiving payment, is unwilling to have sex should present twice that amount. The man who does so when she has not received payment should pay an equal amount." See *NSm* 6.20.

115 The expression "lowest-born" (*antya*) refers to an outcaste lower than even a Shudra, and Arya refers to the three twice-born social classes. For this provision, see *KAŚ* 4.13.34–35.

116 See *YDh* 1.361.

117 The *KAŚ* in the parallel passage at 4.10.14 identifies the three limbs as the left hand and both feet. Regarding unfit meat, see *YDh* 1.171–177.

118 According to the Vulg reading, the translation would be: "an injury is caused with a piece of wood, a clod, an arrow, a stone, hands, or vehicle."

119 The verse refers to someone who shouts "Thief!" and lets the woman off the hook for an illicit affair. The reading of Vishva and M is: "calls out a thief as 'Thief!' This makes little sense, and Vishva's explanation that the man tries to shield the real thief by calling

someone else a thief is rather lame. See *KAŚ* 4.12.34.

120 The term for sending into exile is *pravāsayet.* This term in the *Arthaśāstra* vocabulary has also the meaning of executing a man, which may well be the meaning here.

121 The Vulg reads "the highest seizure-fine" in place of "middle seizure-fine." "Anything attached" to a corpse refers to clothes, garlands, and the like.

### *3 Expiation*

1 The Yama-hymn is *ṚV* 10.14 consisting of sixteen verses. Apar identifies the Yama-verses as the three verses beginning *yo 'sya kauṣṭhya jagataḥ* (*KS* 28.12; *TĀ* 6.5.2).

2 The hymn to be recited on this occasion is *ṚV* 1.97, whose first verse is cited here in abbreviation. Vishva takes seventh and tenth as referring to generations. That is, relatives as distant as seven or ten generations from the deceased are expected to perform this rite, the former being *sagotras* and the latter *samānodakas.* Vijna and Apar, on the other hand, take the numbers as referring to the number of days the relatives must perform this rite.

3 The Vulg reads "for deceased maternal grandfathers and teachers," while the reading of the edition following Vishva and M read "for maternal grandfathers, teachers, and married daughters." I think the correct reading should be *aprattānāṃ* ("unmarried daughters"), rather than *prattānām* ("married daughters"), because the former belong to the same *gotra* as the father and because the married daughter is again listed in the second line. The translation follows this emendation.

4 The Vulg reads *pāṣaṇḍy anāśritāḥ.* The first is a member of a heretical sect and the second is interpreted by Vijna as referring to people who do not belong to an order of life (*āśrama*). The issue here is whether there is one category of person here (those who have joined a heretical sect) or, as Vijna thinks, two. I think Vishva and Apar are correct in taking this as a single category of persons who have joined a heretical sect.

5 The individuals who should console the mourners are not identified. Vijna says that they are the elders of the family (*kulavṛddha*), while Apar identifies them simply as "elders" (*vṛddha*).

6 According to the Vulg reading, the translation would be "rites with

the use of Vedic and domestic fires should be carried out."

7 The Vulg places vv. 16–17 before verse 14. The syntax of verse 16 is rather convoluted. I have followed the interpretation of Vishva, who joins syntactically *icchatām* with *pretasaṃsparśinām*. Vijna gives a different explanation: "The rites beginning with entering the house may be carried out also by those who have come into contact with the newly deceased. Others, if they desire immediate purification, become pure after taking a bath and maintaining self-control."

8 Votary (*vratin*) probably refers to a Vedic student (*brahmacārin*).

9 Impurity resulting from a death lasts ten days and nights for those belonging to the same lineage (*gotra*), and for three days and nights for the more distant relatives called *samānodakas*, a relationship based on offering libations to a common ancestor (see *MDh* 5.60). For the impurity resulting from a birth, see below, note 18.

10 The first half of this verse is omitted in the Vulg. From this verse the sequence of verses in the critical edition and the Vulg diverge. For the sequence, see Concordance of Verses.

11 The Vulg reads "For a Shudra thirty days, and half that much for one whose conduct is righteous" in place of "For a Shudra . . . thirty days."

12 The issue here is the death of a relative while he was in a distant region. When the relatives back home hear about his death, they are purified after the number of days still remaining for the period of impurity. Thus if a Brahman's relatives gets the news of the death after five days, then they are purified after the lapse of the remaining five days. If the news comes after the lapse of the statutory period of impurity, then they are purified by simply making a water offering to the departed person.

13 See *YDh* 2.132.

14 The great journey consists of walking toward the north or northeast without food or water until one drops dead. See *YDh* 3.55.

15 I take *saṃgrāme* ("in a war") as a separate category, following *MDh* 5.95. Vijna and Apar connect it with *gobrāhmaṇārthe:* "in a battle for the sake of cows and Brahmans."

16 The Vulg reads "A Brahman should never follow a deceased Shudra or twice-born person" in place of "A Brahman . . . deceased Shudra."

17 See ch. 3, n. 8. Here, however, since the Vedic student is mentioned immediately afterward, the term *vratin* probably refers to a person

engaged in performing a vow or penance.

18 The verse is very cryptic. The meaning is that, unlike the period of impurity following a death, which affects all close relatives, impurity following a birth affects only the parents of the child. Even there, the full period of generally ten days affects only the mother; the father becomes pure by bathing, while other close relatives are not affected at all.

19 See ch. 1, n. 12.

20 This verse contains two technical terms: knower of the field (*kṣetrajña*), which refers to the spirit that observes the body and its activities as if they were a field (*kṣetra*), and elemental self (*bhūtātman*), a term that is less clear but probably referring to a self made of material elements but acting as a center of consciousness (see v. 179). These terms are defined in *MDh* 12.12: "The one who makes this body act is called *kṣetrajña,* the knower of the field; the one who does the actions, on the other hand, the wise call *bhūtātman,* the elemental self."

21 The Vulg reads "poison, land" in place of "poison, fish."

22 The Vulg reads "lead" in place of "lethal substances" (*hetavaḥ*). The meaning of the latter term is unclear. Vishva says that they are substances such as poison that are means of killing people (*hetavo vadhasādhanāni viṣādīni*). It is also possible that *hetavaḥ* is an error and the original should be *hetayaḥ* ("weapons"; see *heti* in *YDh* 1.322).

23 The Vulg reads "Selling lac, salt, or meat" in place of "Selling salt, a daughter, or lac."

24 The Vulg reads "grain" (*dhānya*) in place of "provisions" (*dhanam,* which is a generic term for money or other valuables). These two terms occur together in a compound frequently: see v. 219.

25 According to the Vulg reading, the translation would be: "After finding out his conduct, family, character, learning, education, austerity, and household, the king should provide for him a righteous livelihood."

26 The Vulg reads "go to the forest" in place of "live in the forest," and omits "and remaining patient."

27 According to the Vulg reading, the translation would be: "he should satisfy the fires, ancestors, gods, guests, and dependents, keeping his beard, matted hair, and bodily hair uncut, and remaining self-possessed."

28 September-October.

29 See ch. 3, n. 151.

30 For the definitions of lunar fast and the set of fasts called "arduous penances" (*kṛcchra*), see *YDh* 3.315–325.

31 He sits in the middle with four fires burning at each cardinal point, with the sun overhead as the fifth fire. Note also that there are five ritual fires associated with Vedic and domestic rituals.

32 The Sanskrit term *mokṣa* literally means freedom or liberation. Already in Manu, however, a technical meaning is attached to the term; it is used as a synonym of renunciation and the fourth order of life (*āśrama*) dedicated exclusively to the search after personal liberation. The term *mokṣa* has this meaning when used in the common compound *mokṣadharma,* which is a section of the *MBh* and a distinct topic in medieval legal digests (*nibandha*). Yajnavalkya is following Manu in using this term for the life of a wandering mendicant.

33 The Vulg adds: "distress" after "bodily diseases."

34 The image of sparks bursting out of a fire is from the *Muṇḍaka Upaniṣad,* 1.2.1.

35 Vishvarupa gives two possible interpretations of *bhava* (process of coming into being). According to the first, the reference is to actions that are performed simply by being in existence, such as an infant sucking its mother's breast. According to the second, the reference is to actions that cause future births. The Vulg, however, here reads "actions that are in keeping with dharma, contrary dharma, or part of both."

36 Vishvarupa reads *ādatte 'bhavann api* (with an *avagraha*). The translation would then be: "so he also gathers them as he reverses the process of coming into being." The reference is to the coming into being of *ātman* as multiple *ātmans* (see v. 67). See also v. 27 where too the term *ādatte* is used with reference to taking on the five elements. Each succeeding element has one more attribute than the preceding: ether has sound; wind has sound and touch; light has sound, touch, and form; water has sound, touch, form, and taste; and earth has sound, touch, form, taste, and smell.

37 The source of this and the following verse is the doctrine of five fires given in both the *BāU* (6.2) and the *ChU* (5.3–10).

38 For the developmental stages of a fetus, see *Caraka Saṃhitā, śarīrasthāna,* 4.9–12. For the meaning of *arbuda,* see Yaska's

*Nirukta* 14.6. On the relationship of the doctrine of self (*atman*), embryology, and anatomy to the dharma of an ascetic, and the close connection of this section to the *Caraka Saṃhitā*, see Yamashita 2001–2002.

39 The Vulg reads "touching" in place of "propelling" (or "impelling").

40 The Vulg reads "from bile" in place of "from fire." The chief quality of bile is heat.

41 The Vulg reads "it comes to possess skin, flesh, and memory" in place of "it comes to possess skin, as also memory."

42 For this enumeration of body parts, especially the 360 bones, see *Caraka Saṃhitā, śarīrasthāna*, 7.4–6. But *Suśruta* (*śarīrasthāna*, 5.17) lists only 300 bones. The commentators give varying explanations of the six parts, skins, and limbs. Six parts—Vishva: the five elements and the "unseen," probably the self; Vijna: essence of food, blood, fat, bone, marrow, and "last element" (*caramadhātu*), probably semen; Apar: the six kinds of living beings—those born of placenta, egg, and sweat, sprouts, fleeting (*ātivāhika*), and body destined to suffer torments (*yātanārthīya*). Six skins—Vishva: feces, blood, etc.; Vijna: blood, flesh, fat, bone, marrow, and semen; Apar does not specify. Six limbs are enumerated the same way by all: head, torso, two arms, and two legs.

43 The Vulg reads "forehead, eyes, and cheeks, and the solid bone of the nostrils" in place of "bone of the forehead; the solid bone of the cheeks and nostrils." The number of bones listed in this half-verse is calculated differently by the three commentators. Vishva takes the number as four (two at base of chin, one bone of the forehead, and one of cheeks and nostrils). Vijna sees nine bones here (two at the base of the chin, two bones each in the forehead, eyes, and cheeks, and one in the nostril), and Apar eight (agreeing with Vijna in all except that he takes the forehead as a single bone). So, along with the seventy-two listed in the second half of the verse, the three commentators count seventy-six, eighty-one, and eighty, respectively.

44 In the *Caraka Saṃhitā* (*śarīrasthāna*, 7.6) the number of chest bones is given as fourteen.

45 A different set of ten seats of vita breaths (*prāṇāyatana*) are listed in *Caraka Saṃhitā, śarīrasthāna*, 7.9. Our list appears to be drawn from another section of the *Caraka* (*sūtrasthāna*, 29.3), which lists

ten taking the two temporal bones as two items.

46 The Vulg reads *vasāvahananam* in place of *vapāvahananam*, and both Vijna and Apar take this as two terms and not a compound: *vasā* is fat attached to flesh, and *avahanana* is lungs. The meaning and reading of the first two items, *vapā vapāvahananam*, are unclear. The parallel passage in the *Caraka Saṃhitā* (*śarīrasthāna*, 7.10) has simply *vapāvahananam* meaning the omentum. The meaning of *udaraṃ ca gudaḥ* is unclear; the parallel in the *Caraka* reads *adharagudaṃ*, "lower rectum," i.e., anus. Given that the number of inner organs (*koṣṭha*) are given as fifteen in the *Caraka*, here *udara* cannot be a separate item.

47 The four pathways of the eyes have been interpreted by the translators of the *Caraka Saṃhitā* (*śarīrasthāna*, 7.11) as the four eyelids. Apar, however, takes them to be the two white and the two black areas of the eyeball. The nine openings are two eyes, two ears, two nostrils, mouth, anus, and generative organ.

48 According to the readings of the Vulg, the translation would be: "There are three hundred thousand hairs of the head and beard of embodied beings, 107 vital points,..."

49 This is a very succinct verse, and the meaning is less than clear. Scribes and commentators have tried to modify the reading, and they give varying interpretations. From the parallel in the *Caraka Saṃhitā*, *śarīrasthāna*, 7.17, it appears that the most minute segments of the human body cannot be counted because they are too numerous, too subtle, and beyond sensory perception. The causes of their juncture and disjuncture are wind (*vāyu*) and the effects of past karma.

50 The text turns here to liquid components of the body that can be measured by volume. The basic unit here is *añjali*, the amount contained when the two hands are brought together to form a cup. The exact modern equivalent is uncertain, but if we take it to be equal to a *kuḍuba*, which is 150 gm, then the volume would be 0.15 liters. Srinivasan (1979: 71) gives two possible equivalents that are larger: 330 cc and 550 cc (0.33 or 0.55 liters). Sap (*rasa*) here probably refers to the first stage of digestion creating a fluid mixture, which gives rise to blood.

51 The *Āraṇyaka* here probably refers to the *Bṛhadāraṇyaka Upaniṣad*, which is part of the *Yajur Veda* that Yajnavalkya is supposed to have received from the sun. Given that the very

opening verse of the text refers to Yajnavalkya as the "lord of yogis," it may well have been that a text on yoga was ascribed to him. I have not been able to identify any such text.

52 According to the Vulg reading, the translation would be: "Reciting the *sāman* song according to the proper procedure without stumbling, so a man, being quite attentive, attains the highest Brahma through constant practice."

53 For a detailed description of these seven *gītikās* (or *gītakās*), collectively called *saptarūpa,* see Bharata's *Nāṭyaśāstra,* ch. 31; *Dattilam* 171–221 and Nijenhuis's (1970) commentary on them; Rowell 1988, especially pp. 158–183, and notes 28 and 29; and Nijenhuis 1977: 7.

54 The Vulg reads "having the name 'liberation'" in place of "having the stated names," and "the path of liberation" in place of "the path of yoga." On *pāṇikā* and the like, see *Dattilam* 232–233 and Nijenhuis's (1970) commentary on it. The vina (*vīṇā*) is a string instrument similar to a sitar and harp.

55 According to the Vulg reading, the translation would be: "In the form of food of Viraj, he takes on the nature of the sacrifice." Verses 119–120 are referring back to the Purusha hymn of *ṚV* 10.90. Viraj, literally "the wide-ruling one," is presented as the first creature in the Ṛgvedic creation story of the Purusha hymn (*ṚV* 10.90).

56 These verses deal with the cosmic cycle centered around the offerings made to the sacrificial fire. This theory is derived from the doctrine of the five fires found in both the *BāU* (6.2) and the *ChU* (5.3–10).

57 This and the following verses are, once again, based on the Purusha hymn of *ṚV* 10.90.

58 The Vulg reads "from his touch" in place of "from his skin."

59 According to the Vulg reading, the translation would be: "A person who tells lies, commits slander, and is cruel, as also. . . ."

60 Unsanctioned killing refers to killing that is not for a ritual purpose (see *YDh* 1.178–180). For the view that ritual killing is not really killing, see *MDh* 5.27–56.

61 This verse responds to one of the questions posed in verse 130. The syntax is complex and there are diverse readings. But the intent appears to be to assert that a yogi in his yogic concentration can, indeed, know the thoughts of all, but he does not appropriate them or make those thoughts his own.

62 This is again a laconic verse. For the elements and the Lord as the sixth, as well as the process of creation, see *YDh* 3.72–73. I have separated *brahma* from *khānilatejāṃsi,* while most editions present all as a single compound. Vijna also takes only the five as elements, with Brahma as the source of the elements. It appears that the verse presents the basic ingredients that give rise to the world as we know it, somewhat in the manner of the twenty-five categories of Samkhya philosophy.

63 Following Vishva, I connect this verse with the following verse. Vijna and Apar take this also as part of the previous questions.

64 For *amātya* as a member of the household, see *YDh* 1.157 and note 18 to the edition.

65 Various versions of the Vulg read "the knower of what is to be known" and "what is to be known" in place of "the knower and the non-knower."

66 The reading of the first word of the verse is unclear and my *-tamastā* is conjectural. However, the different readings have the same meaning.

67 According to the Vulg reading, the translation would be: "Deformity of the fetus, such as the lack of an organ, seen at birth, arises from. . . ." According to Vishva's explanation, defects of time refers to intercourse at a forbidden time, defects of action refers to the defective performance or non-performance of rites such as the impregnation ceremony, defects of self refers to the progenitor thinking of another woman during intercourse, and defects of semen refers to the weakness or the small quantity of semen.

68 This verse is omitted in most Vulg sources.

69 According to the Vulg reading, the translation would be: "With that he attains the bodies of gods along with their abodes."

70 The issue in *pāda*-b is whether the word is *āmaraṇena* (through sandhi) or simply *maraṇena.* I have opted for the latter as it corresponds to the other positives and negatives in this verse. Vishva, however, opts for the former and explains it as directives that must be observed until death.

71 The Vulg reads "those relating to the waking state" in place of "results from water." I take the two terms *jalajaiḥ* and *svapnajaiḥ* as connected to *phalaiḥ,* which is the last word of the previous sentence. They refer to results or fruits obtained through "water"

or dreams. According to Vishva, water here refers to pilgrimages to *tīrthas,* or sacred fords.

72 In the Indian cosmological tradition, each world age (*kalpa*), which is the largest time span and is considered a day of Brahma, contains fourteen units called *manvantara* ("Manu intervals or epochs"), each presided over by a different Manu. See Kane 1962–1975, V: 686–693.

73 This list parallels the one at *YDh* 3.73. "Life" (*jīvita*) here appears to parallel *preraṇa* in that verse, given as the opposite of *dhāraṇā.*

74 The Vulg reads "heaven and dream" in place of "creation of entities in dream."

75 The Vulg reads *avyaktam,* and takes it as the unmanifest material principle (*prakṛti*) and part of the list of Samkhya cosmic categories given in the previous verse. The edition takes the reading to be *avyakte* (locative), that is, the self (*atman*) abiding within *prakṛti,* which then is the knower of the field consisting of the manifest evolutes of *prakṛti.* In the second sentence, the Vulg reads "He is the lord residing in all beings" in place of "He is the lord of all beings."

76 For the increasing number of attributes in each successive element, see ch. 3, n. 36.

77 The Vulg reads "the one among these elements from which each of them arises" in place of "the one among these elements on which each of them is based."

78 This verse refers back to verses 129–130 in which the sages pose a question to Yajnavalkya, who answers the question in the intervening verses.

79 The meaning of *liṅgendriya* is unclear. With all three commentators, I take it as a *dvandva* compound, but unlike them, who take *liṅga* as referring to the inner senses of ego, intellect, and mind, I take the term in the sense *cihnāni* (where the Vulg reads *liṅgāni*), a term that was used previously in verse 177, namely, the signs or clues that are present revealing the highest self given in verses 175–176.

80 The Vulg reads "desire heaven" in place of "desire offspring." *Ajavīthi* is one of the three divisions of the southern path by which the moon, sun, and planets move, while *agastya* is the name of the star Canopus of the southern sky.

81 The eight qualities of the self are enumerated in *GDh* 8.23: compassion toward all creatures, patience, lack of envy,

purification, tranquility, having an auspicious disposition, not being niggardly, and lack of greed (*dayā sarvabhuteṣu kṣāntir anasūyā śaucam anāyāso maṅgalam akārpaṇyam aspṛhā*).

82 For a longer passage on the eighty-eight thousand sages, see *ĀpDh* 2.23.4–5. For the promulgators of dharma, see *YDh* 1.4–5.

83 The seven seers are the seven stars of Ursa Major. The serpent's way is the passage of the moon through the asterisms *svāti* (or *aśvinī*), *bharaṇī*, and *kṛttikā*.

84 "From them," that is, from the two kinds of sages mentioned above.

85 The Vulg reads "faith, fasting, and independence" in place of "the constant engagement in faith and fasting." This verse is based on *BāU* 4.4.22.

86 According to the Vulg reading, the translation would be: "For it is he whom all the orders of life should understand." This verse is based on *BāU* 4.5.6.

87 The verses from here until v. 198 are derived from *BāU* 6.2.15–16 dealing with the doctrine of the five fires and the passage of a person from the cremation fire to the heavenly regions, either to return back to earth as rain or to enter the orb of the sun and attain immortality. The term *āraṇyaka* ("wilderness") may have a double entendre, referring also to the *Bṛhadāraṇyaka Upaniṣad* in which Yajnavalkya is a prominent teacher. See *YDh* 3.110 where the term is a clear reference to the *BāU*.

88 According to the Vulg reading, the translation would be: "The person who, self-possessed, does not know these two paths."

89 This passage is reproduced with variants in *ViDh* 97.1.

90 The meaning of *śrotrajñatā* is unclear. Vijnaneshvara takes it to mean the ability to hear sounds from places far away. I think here the original reading was *śrotraṃ jñatā* and have translated it accordingly. The term *jñatā* is found also in v. 142. The extraordinary powers called *vibhūti* acquired by a person performing Yoga are described in the third chapter of Patanjali's *Yogasūtras*.

91 The Vulg reads "while living in the forest" in place of "while living with his son." Verses 205–206 parallel the section on *saṃnyāsa* in *MDh* 6.87–96.

92 The Vulg reads "dreadful" in place of "contemptible." For grievous sins causing loss of caste, see ch. 1, n. 36 and 3.228.

93 A Pulkasa is an outcaste individual considered to be particularly impure. He is said to be the son of a Nisada man (born to a Brahman

father and a Vaishya mother) and a Shudra woman: *MDh* 10.38. A Vena also is an outcaste born of a Vaidehaka man (born to a Vaishya man and Brahman woman) and an Ambashta woman (when the mother is two classes lower than the father): *MDh* 10.19.

94 The Vulg reads "dwells together" in place of "drinks water with." See note 46 to the edition.

95 The Vulg reads "by stealing water, a water bird" in place of "by stealing a farm animal, a goat."

96 The Vulg reads "endowed with knowledge" in place of "endowed with auspicious marks."

97 The issue here is whether an expiation can wipe out a sin intentionally and deliberately committed. The controversy is briefly alluded to in *MDh* 11.44–47. Yajnavalkya comes down on the side of those who think that such a sin cannot be erased in this life, even though after the performance of the appropriate penance people should associate with him as before.

98 The Vulg reads *mahāpatha* in place of *nadīpatha*. For the enumerations of various kinds of hells and their descriptions, see Kane 1962–1975, IV: 261–264.

99 The Vulg reads "dwells together" in place of "drinks water with." See note 46 to the edition.

100 On the *vrātya*, see *YDh* 1.38.

101 The Vulg reads "base metal" (or "forest produce") in place of "silver," and "son" (or "child") in place of "friend."

102 The Vulg reads "breaking a vow" in place of "neglecting the Veda."

103 Both Vijna and Apar, following the Vulg reading of *pāda*-b *strīhiṃsauṣadhi*, take the compound to contain three items: women, harmful things (such as hunting), and medicine. But in the very next compound *hiṃsra* is used adjectivally to qualify *yantra* ("harmful equipment"). After this verse, the Vulg adds the following verse: "being a servant of a Shudra; friendship with a lowly person; having sex with a woman of low birth; living in a state that is outside the orders of life; being nourished with other people's food."

104 For the penitent carrying a bowl consisting of a human skull and carrying a human head as a banner, see *GDh* 22.4; *BDh* 2.1.3. For the head banner, see *MDh* 11.73.

105 Eight parts of the body are offered: hair, skin, blood, flesh, sinew, fat, bone, and marrow. Each mantra contains the name of the

respective body part. See *VaDh* 20.26 for this rite. The mantras are found in the *VS* 39.10.

106 For the Vulg readings here, see the note to the edition. The Vulg variants, however, do not affect the meaning.

107 The meaning is that when a person kills a fetus, he should observe the penance prescribed for killing a man of the same class of society as the fetus. A woman soon after her menstruation is called by the technical term *ātreyī,* which is given an interesting etymological spin in *VaDh* 20.35–36. The woman is then in her fertile period and killing her is tantamount to killing a future Brahman. There is the added possibility that the woman is pregnant. For a detailed study of this provision, see Jamison 1991: 213–223; Wezler 1994.

108 Some Vulg sources read "he should eat ... at night for three years" in place of "he should eat ... at night for one year."

109 The Vulg reads "the three twice-born social classes" in place of "the three social classes."

110 The *prājāpatya,* lunar penance, and others listed in the following verses are defined below in verses 315–325.

111 The Vulg reads "dwells together" in place of "drinks water with." See note 46 to the edition.

112 This is a rather elliptical verse. Vishva interprets inferior persons as referring to those belonging to social classes below oneself; in the case of Shudras the reference is to those born through *pratiloma* (woman of higher class than man) marriages. Vijna, however, takes them to refer solely to the latter kind of socially excluded individuals. Shudras are not entitled to recite mantras and other ritual acts connected with the lunar fast. Yet, they are purified by observing the fast for a full month.

113 "Double the guilt" means double the guilt of actually committing that crime.

114 The meaning is that the sinner should live in a cowshed, following the cows as they go out to pasture, returning home with them, and sleeping in the cowshed. See the description of this penance in Kalidasa's *Raghuvaṃśa,* Canto 2.

115 For the arduous penance (*kṛcchra*) and extreme arduous penance (*atkṛcchra*), see *YDh* 3.315–325.

116 See *YDh* 3.321.

117 *Krauñca* is a species of large water bird, probably the common crane: see Dave 2005: 312.

118 The Vulg adds "ruddy goose" before vulture. *Bhāsa* is a species of vulture, identified by Dave (2005: 188) as the bearded vulture.

119 The Vulg reads "tin and lead" in place of "a *māṣaka* of tin." The meaning of *guñjā* is unclear. Apar takes it to be a piece of gold weighing a *guñja* (taken by Vishva to be a *kṛṣṇala*), about 0.118 gm.

120 The term *tittira* is used for a variety of partridges: see Dave 2005: 269. *Droṇa* is a measurement of capacity, approximately five liters.

121 Many Vulg sources, including Vijna, place 278ab before 276ab.

122 The Vulg reads "a dog, camel, etc., and a bird," while Apar reads "a camel, etc., and a bird" in place of "by dogs or birds." The Vulg places 278cd before 277ab.

123 The *BāU* 6.4.5.

124 The *BāU* 6.4.6.

125 Nirriti (*nirṛti*) is a goddess personifying death, destruction, and adversity.

126 The *TĀ* 2.18.1.

127 The *TĀ* 2.18.1.

128 The Vulg transposes the first and second sentences of the verse.

129 The Vulg omits "through such means as administering medicine and food, and by remedies such as medical procedures."

130 An appointment to have sex with a brother's wife refers to levirate: see *YDh* 1.68, n. 33. After sex during a woman's menstrual period, a man should fast for three days at the end of which he should consume some ghee.

131 The Vulg transposes verses 289 and 290.

132 The meaning of "ruins the Veda" is unclear. Commentators take it to mean that the man has engaged in Vedic recitation either when it is forbidden (see *YDh* 1.143–150) or while he is impure.

133 The Vulg reads "eats" in place of "sleeps."

134 The Vulg reads "or ties him up with a cloth" in place of "or strikes or ties him up." "You" here refers to the familiar address using *tvam* rather than a formal form of address, similar to the French distinction between *tu* and *vous*. "*Huṃ*" is an expletive directed at someone in anger.

135 The Vulg reads "outside the village" in place of "filled with water."

136 The Vulg reads "dwell together with" in place of "drink water with." See note 46 to the edition.

137 The Vulg reads "dwell together with" in place of "drink water with." See note 46 to the edition.

138 The Vulg reads "one should treat him with respect" in place of "one may associate with him."
139 See *YDh* 1.9.
140 *Aghamarṣaṇa* means literally "effacing sins"; this is the hymn *ṚV* 10.190.
141 The Vulg reads "having stood in water" in place of "having remained lying down in water."
142 The *sahasraśīrṣa* hymn is the same as the Purusha hymn: *ṚV* 10.90. "These people" are the three sinners identified in these two verses: one who has drunk liquor, stolen gold, and had sex with an elder's wife.
143 The three junctures are sunrise, noon, and sunset.
144 The Vulg reads "especially of the *gāyatrī* verse" in place of "of the *gāyatrī* verse a thousand times." Vijna identifies *śukriya* as the verse "All difficulties impel away, god Savitar. What is beneficial, that impel here to us" (*ṚV* 5.82.5; *VS* 30.3), and *āraṇyaka* as *VS* 36.1–22. The eleven *rudra* verses consist of *TS* 5.1–11; *VS* 16.1–66.
145 For the five great sacrifices, see *YDh* 1.101.
146 The Vulg reads "gift giving" in place of "meditation," and "non-injury, not stealing, tenderness, and self-control" in place of "non-injury, not stealing, not hating, and self-control."
147 The Vulg reads "refraining from anger and from carelessness" in place of "refraining from anger, and giving gifts."
148 The Vulg reads "cow's urine, dung, milk, curd, ghee, and a decoction of *kuśa* grass" in place of "the five products of the cow—cow's milk, curd, urine, dung, and ghee."
149 *Parṇa* is the same as *palāśa,* which is a variety of fig tree: *Butea frondosa. Bilva* is the bel tree, *Aegle marmelos.*
150 The lunar fast described here begins on the new moon day. On the first day of the bright half, the penitent eats one ball of rice and increases the number by one ball each day until on the full-moon day he eats fourteen balls. The number is decreased in the same manner during the dark half of the month. The other method is to start with fourteen mouthfuls on the full-moon day and decrease the number of balls each day, and then increase them again during the bright half. See *MDh* 11.217–218.
151 The meaning of "purificatory verses" (*pavitrāṇi*) is unclear. Commentators of *MDh* 11.226 identify these verses variously as the *aghamarṣaṇa* (*ṚV* 10.190), *pāvamānī* verses (*ṚV* 9.67.21–27 or

*ṚV* 9.1–114), and the like. The three appointed times for bathing are morning, noon, and evening.

152 The Vulg reads "with a collected mind" in place of "without a doubt."

153 The Vulg reads "the seers said this to that most noble king of yogis" in place of "the most noble seers said this to the king of yogis."

154 According to the Vulg reading, the translation would be: "When a learned man, self-restrained, makes people listen to this at the days of the moon's change." For the days of the moon's change, see ch. 1, n. 42.

# GLOSSARY

ADITYAS literally the son(s) of Aditi, the term in the plural refers to a group of gods, including some prominent ones such as Varuna, Mitra, and Indra. Early texts give their number as eight, but the Brāhmaṇas already show their number as twelve, which has remained the norm ever since. Together with the Vasus and the Rudras, they constitute the three major classes of gods. In the singular, the term Aditya refers to the sun

ALL-GODS the name of a class of gods. In the later Dharma texts they are listed as ten in five pairs: Kratu and Daksha, Vasu and Satya, Dhuri and Locana, Kala and Kama, and Pururavas and Ardrava. See Kane 1962–1975, IV: 457

*apūpa* small round cake made with wheat flour, sugar, and spices and cooked without oil

*atharva-aṅgirasa* the reference likely is to the verses found in the *Atharva Veda,* and more generally to incantations that can produce desired results

*baka* this term is applied to a wide variety of waterfowl, including heron, ibis, stork and the common flamingo. Dave 2005: 383–387, 408–409

BALI a ritual offering of food given to various beings and spirits

BRAHMA depending on context, the Sanskrit term *brahman* has several meanings: the ultimate being, the god Brahma, and the Veda

BRIHASPATI a god, viewed as the preceptor of the gods. Several works of political science and *dharmaśāstra* are ascribed to him

CALLS these are the names of the seven worlds in ascending order: *bhur* (earth), *bhuva* (mid-space), *svar* (sky), *mahar* (great), *janas* (people), *tapas* (austerity), *satya* (truth). These names are considered sacred and powerful. The first three are generally referred to as simply calls (*vyāhṛti*), whereas all seven are referred to as great calls (*mahāvyāhṛti*). See *MDh* 2.76–81

*dhamanī* a kind of tube within the human body, artery; distinguished from *sirā*

*dharaṇa* a measure of weight; approximately 377.6 grams; a silver *dharaṇa,* however, is said to weight only 3.776 grams

*dūrvā* panic grass; *Panicum dactylon*

GANDHARVA in the early Vedic literature Gandharvas appear as a class of divine beings alongside the gods and the forefathers. They are associated with the *soma* drink and are said to be fond of females. They are often associated with the celestial nymphs, Apsarases. In later literature, especially the epics, the Gandharvas are depicted as celestial singers and are associated with music

*gāyatrī* same as *sāvitrī*

*hitā* along with *sirā*, a kind of tube emerging from the heart

INDRA a major Vedic god noted for his victory in battle over demons

*kākola* a species of raven, although the term is used to refer to a wide variety of ravens and crows. Dave 2005: 1–9

*kārṣika* a copper coin, the same as *kārṣāpaṇa* or *paṇa*

*kṛṣṇala* a measure of weight approximately 0.118 grams

*kuśa* the most common of the sacred grasses (see *darbha*) used for ritual purposes. *Poa cynosuroides*

*kūṣmāṇḍī* these verses are *TĀ* 2.3, sometimes identified also as *TĀ* 2.6

*magha, maghā* the tenth lunar constellation, Regulus

*māṣa/māṣaka* literally a bean, it is a measure of weight; approximately 0.59 grams. As a coin, the value depended whether it was silver or gold. In the *KAŚ* a *māṣaka* was 1/16 of a *paṇa*, both being silver coins. The rates in later literature are unclear

*pala* a measure of weight, approximately 37.76 grams

*paṇa* this is the standard currency in ancient Indian texts. It was probably a silver coin in the early texts such as the *KAŚ* but became a copper coin later

PRAJAPATI the name of a Vedic god viewed as the creator and later identified with the creator god Brahma

PURIFICATOR VERSES commentators provide different identifications of the purificatory verses (*pāvamānī*): Purusha hymn (*ṚV* 10.90); *ṚV* 9.67.21–27; *ṚV* 9.1–114 (that is the entire ninth Maṇḍala; so Medhatithi on *MDh* 11.258); and *ṚV* 9.14–67 (so Bharuci on the same *MDh* verse)

PURUSHA the term mean "man," but often it has a cosmological meaning. In the Purusha hymn (*ṚV* 10.90) it is a primeval male human whose sacrifice created the world, often identified with Prajapati. In later philosophical traditions, it is the spiritual principle

RAHU (*rāhu*) the name of one of the nine Indian planets. Considered the descending node and the head of the demon Saihikeya, identified with the Vedic *svarbhānu* (Jamison 1991: 282), whose body is *ketu*

*rājīva* the term has two meanings:

(1) A kind of lotus-colored fish, or one with stripes. (2) The same as *aravinda,* a kind of lotus

*ṛc* the verses found in the *Ṛg Veda*

*rohiṇī* the red constellation, Aldebaran

RUDRA in the singular, the name refers to a prominent Vedic god later identified with Shiva

RUDRAS in the plural, the term refers to a group of eleven gods; one of the three class of gods, the others being Vasus and Adityas

*rudra* VERSES the eleven *rudra* verses consist of *TS* 5.1–11; *VS* 16.1–66

*sāman* chants found in the *Sāma Veda*

*śatamāna* a silver coin weighing approximately 11.66 gm

SAVITAR a name for the sun as the impeller to action. The name is used in the famous *sāvitrī/gāyatrī* verse

*sāvitrī* also called *gāyatrī,* this is the most sacred of ritual formulas: *ṚV* 3.62.10. Sometimes the term is used with reference to Vedic initiation, because teaching this verse to the initiated boy forms a central part of that rite

*sirā* along with *hitā,* a kind of tube coming from the heart

SKANDA the name of a god, one of the sons of Shiva

*soma* a plant from which the central libation of the Vedic sacrifice was made; the term is applied also to that libation

*sruva* the *sruva* is a kind of ladle used in Vedic sacrifices and is smaller than the other ladle called *sruc.* The *sruva* has a long handle at the end of which there is a small globular spoon without a spout

*surā* a kind of liquor, which was in a special way prohibited to Brahmans

*suvarṇa* a measure of weight; approximately 9.44 grams

*svadhā* the exclamation accompanying the offering of an oblation to ancestors

*yajus* the ritual formulas found in the *Yajur Veda*

*udumbara* a type of fig tree whose wood is used for ritual purposes: *Ficus glomerata* or *Ficus racemosa*

VARUNA a prominent Vedic god who later is associated with the western direction and water

VASUS one of the three classes of gods, the others being Adityas and Rudras

VINAYAKA another name for the god Ganapati

*vrātya* this term is used in ancient literature to refer to groups of people, at least some of whom appear to have led a wandering or nomadic life. In later times the term is used to refer to either mixed-caste people or to Brahmans who have not undergone Vedic initiation at the proper time

# BIBLIOGRAPHY

*Editions and Translations*

Stenzler, Adof Friedrich, ed. and trans. 1849. *Yājñavalkya's Gesetzbuch: Sanskrit und Deutsch*. Berlin: Ferd. Dümmler's Buchhandlung.

Mandlik, Vishvanath Narayan, ed. 1880. *The Vyavahāramayūkha and the Yājñavalkya Smṛti*. Part I. Bombay: Education Society's Press, Byculla.

*Yājñavalkyasmṛti*. 1903–1904. Edited with Aparārka's commentary. 2 vols. Ānandāśrama Sanskrit Series 46. Pune: Ānandāśrama.

Gharpure, J. R., ed. 1914. *Yājñavalkyasmṛiti or the Institutes of Yājñavalkya, together with the Commentary Called Mitāksharā by Śrī Vijñāneśvara*. Collections of Hindu Law Texts, Vol. 1. Bombay: n.p.

Ganapati Sastri, T., ed. 1922–1924. *The Yājñavalkyasmṛti with the Commentary Bālakrīda of Visvarūpāchārya*. 2 parts. Trivandrum: Government Press. Reprint, New Delhi: Munshiram Manoharlal, 1982.

Panśīkar, Wāsudev Laxmaṇ Śāstrī, ed. 1936. *Yādnyavalkyasmṛiti of Yogīshvara Yādnyavalkya with the Commentary Mitākṣarā of Vidnyāneshvara*. Bombay: Nirṇaya Sāgar Press.

Pandey, Umesh Chandra, ed. 1967. *Yājñavalkyasmṛti of Yogīshwara Yājñavalkya with the Mitākṣarā Commentary of Vijñāneshwar*. Kashi Sanskrit Series 178. Varanasi: Chowkhamba Sanskrit Series.

Rai, Ganga Sagar, ed. 1998. *Yājñavalkyasmṛti of Yogīśvara Maharṣi Yājñavalkya with the Mitākṣarā Commentary of Vijñāneśvara*. Vrajajivan Prachyabharati Granthamala 90. Delhi: Chowkhambha Sanskrit Pratishthan.

Röer, Edward, and W. A. Montriou, trans. 1859. *Hindu Law and Judicature from the Dharma-Śāstra of Yājnavalkya in English with Explanatory Notes and Introduction*. Calcutta/London: R. C. Lepage.

Mandlik, Vishvanath Narayan, trans. 1880. *The Vyavahāramayūkha and the Yājñavalkya Smṛti: An English Translation and Notes*. Part II. Bombay: Education Society's Press, Byculla.

Vasu, Srisa Chandra, trans. 1909. *Yajnavalkya's Smriti with the Commentary of Vijnaneśvara called the Mitakṣara and the Gloss of Bālambhaṭṭa*. Sacred Books of the Hindus. Allahabad: Panini Office.

Vidyārṇava, Srisa Chandra, trans. 1918. *Yajnavalkya Smriti with the*

*Commentary of Vijnaveśvara called the Mitaksara, Book I: The Āchāra Adhyāya*. Allahabad: Panini Office.

Gharpure, J. R., trans. 1936–1942. *Yājñavalkyasmṛiti with the Mitākshara by Vijñanesvara Bhikshu and the Vīramitrodaya by Mitramiśra*. Collections of Hindu Law Texts, Vol. 2 in 7 Parts. Bombay: n.p.

*Other Sources*

*Agnipurāṇa*. 1984–1987. Edited by N. Gangadharan. 4 vols. Ānandāśrama Sanskrit Series 41. Delhi: Motilal Banarsidass. First published, Poona, 1900.

*Aitareyabrāhmaṇa*. 1896. Edited with Sāyaṇa's commentary by Bābā Śāstrī Phaḍke. 2 vols. Ānandāśrama Sanskrit Series 32. Poona. Translated in Keith 1920.

Aiyangar, K. V. Rangaswami. 1941. "Additional Verses of Kātyāyana on Vyavahāra." In *A Volume of Studies in Indology Presented to Prof. P. V. Kane*, ed. S. M. Kartre and P. K. Goode, pp. 2–17. Poona: Oriental Book Agency.

———. 1942. *Bṛhaspatismṛti (Reconstructed)*. Gaekwad's Oriental Series 85. Baroda: Oriental Institute.

*Āpastambadharmasūtra*. Edited and translated in Olivelle 2000.

*Āpastambamantrapāṭha*. 1897. Edited by Maurice Winternitz. Oxford: Clarendon Press. Reprint, Delhi: Sri Satguru Publications, 1985.

*Arthaśāstra* of Kauṭilya. Edited in Kangle 1969. Translated in Olivelle 2013.

*Atharva Veda*. 1960–1964. Edited with Sāyaṇa's commentary by Vishva Bandhu. Vishveshvaranand Indological Series 13–17. Hoshiarpur: Vishveshvaranand Vedic Research Institute. Translated by W. D. Whitney. Harvard Oriental Series 7–8. Cambridge, Mass.: Harvard University Press, 1905.

Balogh, Dániel. 2015. *A Textual and Intertextual Study of the Mudrārākṣasa*. Doctoral dissertation. Budapest: Eötvös Loránd University.

*Baudhāyanadharmasūtra*. Edited and translated in Olivelle 2000.

Bodewitz, H. W. 1985. "Yama's Second Boon in the Kaṭha Upaniṣad." *Wiener Zeitschrift für die Kunde Südasiens* 29: 5–26.

*Bṛhadāraṇkaya Upaniṣad*. Edited and translated in Olivelle 1998.

*Bṛhaspatismṛti*. Edited in Aiyangar 1942. Translated in Jolly 1889.

Bronkhorst, Johannes. 2007. *Greater Magadha: Studies in the Culture of Early India*. Leiden: Brill.
Bryant, Edwin F., ed. and trans. 2009. *The Yoga Sūtras of Patañjali*. New York: North Point Press.
Bühler, Georg, trans. 1879–1882. *Sacred Laws of the Āryas* (containing the Dharmasūtras of Āpastamba, Gautama, Baudhāyana, and Vasiṣṭha). 2 vols. Sacred Books of the East 2, 14. Reprint, Delhi: Motilal Banarsidass, 1965.
Buitenen, J.A.B. van, trans. 1973–1978. *Mahābhārata*. 3 vols. (Books 1–5). Chicago: University of Chicago Press.
*Carakasaṃhitā* of Caraka. 1997–1998. Edited and translated by Ram Karan Sharma and Vaidya Bhagwan Dash. 5th ed. Varanasi: Chowkhamba Sanskrit Series Office.
*Chāndogya Upaniṣad*. Edited and translated in Olivelle 1998.
Chatterjee, Heramba Nath. 1971. *The Law of Debt in Ancient India*. Calcutta: Sanskrit College.
Courtright, Paul. 1985. *Gaṇeśa: Lord of Obstacles, Lord of Beginning*. New York: Oxford University Press.
*Dattilam*. Translated in Nijenhuis 1970.
Dave, K. N. 2005. *Birds in Sanskrit Literature*. Rev. ed. of 1985. Delhi: Motilal Banarsidass.
Davis, Donald R., Jr. 2007. "On *Ātmatuṣṭi* as a Source of *Dharma*." *Journal of the American Oriental Society* 127: 279–296.
Derrett, J. Duncan M. 1973a. *Dharmaśāstra and Juridical Literature*. Wiesbaden: Harrassowitz.
———. 1973b. *History of Indian Law (Dharmaśāstra)*. Leiden: Brill.
*Dharmakośa*. 1937. Edited by Laxmanshastri Joshi. Vol. 1. Wai: Prājñapāṭhaśālā Maṇḍala.
Dresden, Mark J. 1941. *Mānavagṛhyasūtra: A Vedic Manual of Domestic Rites*. Groningen: J. B. Wolters.
Fitzgerald, James L., trans. 2004. *Mahābhārata*. Books 11–12. Chicago: University of Chicago Press.
*Garuḍapurāṇa*. 1964. Edited by R. Bhaṭṭacharya. Kashi Sanskrit Series 165. Varanasi: n.p.
*Gautamadharmasūtra*. Edited and translated in Olivelle 2000.
Goldman, Robert P., et al. 1984–2009. *The Rāmāyaṇa of Vālmiki*. 6 vols. Princeton: Princeton University Press.
Heesterman, J. C. 1962. "Vrātya and Sacrifice." *Indo-Iranian Journal* 6: 1–37.

*Hiraṇyakeśigṛhyasūtra.* Translated in Oldenberg 1886–1892.

Jamison, Stephanie. 1991. *The Ravenous Hyenas and the Wounded Sun: Myth and Ritual in Ancient India.* Ithaca, N.Y.: Cornell University Press.

———, and Joel Brereton, trans. 2014. *The Rigveda: The Earliest Religious Poetry of India.* 3 vols. New York: Oxford University Press. Translations of the *ṚV* are taken from this.

Jayaswal, K. P. 1930. *Manu and Yājñavalkya: A Comparison and a Contrast: A Treatise on the Basic Hindu Law.* Calcutta: Butterworth.

Jha, G. 1920–1939. *Manusmṛti with the 'Manubhāṣya' of Medhātithi.* 10 volumes. Reprint, Delhi: Motilal Banarsidass, 1999.

Jolly, Julius, trans. 1880. *The Institutes of Vishnu.* Sacred Books of the East 7. Oxford: Clarendon Press.

———, trans. 1889. *The Minor Law-Books,* Part I: *Nārada. Bṛhaspati.* Sacred Books of the East 33. Oxford: Clarendon Press.

Kalidasa, 1984. *Raghuvaṃśa,* in *Works of Kālidāsa,* Vol. II: *Poetry.* Edited by C. R. Devadhar. Delhi: Motilal Banarsidass.

Kane, P. V. 1933. *Kātyāyanasmṛti on Vyavahāra (Law and Procedure).* Poona: Oriental Book Agency.

———. 1962–1975. *History of Dharmaśāstra.* 5 vols. Poona: Bhandarkar Oriental Research Institute.

Kangle, R. P. 1964. "Manu and Kauṭilya." *Indian Antiquary* (3rd series) 1: 48–54.

———. 1969. *The Kauṭilīya Arthaśāstra,* Part I: *A Critical Edition and Glossary.* 2nd ed. Bombay: University of Bombay. Original edition, 1960.

———. 1972. *The Kauṭilīya Arthaśāstra,* Part II: *An English Translation with Critical and Explanatory Notes.* 2nd ed. Bombay: University of Bombay. Original edition, 1963.

*Kāṭhakasaṃhitā.* 1900–1910. Edited by Leopold von Schroeder. 3 vols. Leipzig: F. A. Brockhaus.

*Kātyāyanasmṛti.* Edited and translated in Kane 1933; further verses edited in Aiyangar 1941.

Keith, Arthur Berriedale, trans. 1914. *The Veda of the Black Yajus School entitled Taittiriya Sanhita.* 2 vols. Harvard Oriental Series 18–19. Cambridge, Mass.: Harvard University Press. Reprint, Delhi: Motilal Banarsidass, 1967.

———, trans. 1920. *Rigveda Brhamanas: The Aitareya and Kauṣītaki Brāhmaṇas of the Rigveda.* Harvard Oriental Series, 25. Cambridge,

Mass.: Harvard University Press. Reprint. Delhi: Motilal Banarsidass, 1981.

Kobayashi, Masato. 2001–2002. "Nominal Compounds in the Yājñavalkyasmṛti." *Zinbun: Annals of the Institute for Research in Humanities* (Kyoto University) 36.2: 131–151.

Lariviere, Richard W. 1981a. *The Divyatattva of Raghunandana Bhaṭṭācārya: Ordeals in Classical Hindu Law.* New Delhi: Manohar.

———. 1981b. "The Judicial Wager in Hindu Law." *Annals of the Bhandarkar Oriental Research Institute* 62: 135–145.

———, ed. and trans. 1989. *The Nāradasmṛti.* 2 vols. Philadelphia: Department of South Asia Regional Studies, University of Pennsylvania. Reprinted in one volume, Delhi: Motilal Banarsidass, 2003.

Lindquist, Steven. 2018. *Creating a Sage: The Literary Life of Yājñavalkya.* Albany: State University of New York Press.

Lingat, Robert. 1973. *The Classical Law of India.* Translated by J. D. M. Derrett. Berkeley: University of California Press.

*Mahābhārata.* 1933–1959. Critically edited in 19 volumes. General editor, Vishnu Sitaram Sukthankar. Poona: Bhandarkar Oriental Research Institute. Translated in van Buitenen 1973–1978; Fitzgerald 2004.

*Mahānārāyaṇopaniṣad.* Edited and translated by Jean Varenne. 2 vols. Paris: de Boccard, 1960.

Majumdar, Susmit Basu and S. Bajpai. 2015. *Select Early Historic Inscriptions: Epigraphic Perspectives in the Ancient Past of Chhattisgarh.* Raipur: Shatakshi Prakashan.

*Mānavadharmaśāstra.* Edited and translated in Olivelle 2005.

*Mānavagṛhyasūtra.* Edited by F. Knauer. St. Petersburg: J. Glassounof, 1897. Translated in Dresden 1941.

*Matsyapurāṇa.* 1907. Ānandāśrama Sanskrit Series 54. Pune: n.p. Reprint, 1981. Translation originally published by Panini Office, Allahabad, 1916–1917. Reprint, Delhi: Oriental Publishers, 1972.

McClish, Mark. 2009. *Political Brahmanism and the State: A Compositional History of the Arthaśāstra.* Ph.D. dissertation, University of Texas at Austin.

Medhātithi. *Manubhāṣya,* commentary on the *MDh.* Edited and translated in Jha 1920–1939.

*Nāradasmṛti.* Edited and translated in Lariviere 1989. Translated in Jolly 1889.

*Nāṭyaśāstra of Bharatamuni with the Commentary Abhinavabhāratī by Abhinavaguptācārya.* 1926–1964. Edited by Manavalli Ramakrishna

Kavi. Gaekwad's Oriental Series 36, 68, 124, 145. Baroda: Oriental Institute.

Nijenhuis, Emmie te, trans. 1970. *Dattilam: A Compendium of Indian Music.* Leiden: Brill.

———. 1977. *Musicological Literature.* Wiesbaden: Harrassowitz.

*Nirukta* of Yaska. 1940. Edited by V. K. Rajavade. Poona: Bhandarkar Oriental Research Institute. Translated by Lakshman Sarup. Reprint of 1920–1927. Delhi: Motilal Banarsidass, 1967.

Oldenberg, Hermann, trans. 1886–1892. *The Gṛhya-Sūtras.* 2 vols. Oxford: Oxford University Press. Reprint, Delhi: Motilal Banarsidass, 1964.

Olivelle, Patrick. 1991. "From Feast to Fast: Food and the Indian Ascetic." In *Rules and Remedies in Classical Indian Law,* ed. Julia Leslie, pp. 17–36. Panels of the VIIth World Sanskrit Conference, vol. 9. Leiden: Brill.

———, ed. and trans. 1998. *The Early Upaniṣads: Annotated Text and Translation.* New York: Oxford University Press.

———. ed. and trans. 2000. *Dharmasūtras: The Law Codes of Āpastamba, Gautama, Baudhāyana, and Vasiṣṭha.* Delhi: Motilal Banarsidass.

———. 2002a. "*Abhakṣya* and *abhojya:* An Exploration in Dietary Language." *Journal of the American Oriental Society* 122: 345–354.

———. 2002b. *"Food for Thought: Dietary Regulations and Social Organization in Ancient India."* 2001 Gonda Lecture. Amsterdam: Royal Netherlands Academy of Arts and Sciences.

———. 2004. "Manu and the *Arthaśāstra*: A Study in *Śāstric* Intertextuality." *Journal of Indian Philosophy* 32: 281–291.

———, ed. and trans. 2005. *Manu's Code of Law: A Critical Edition and Translation of the Mānava-Dharmaśāstra.* New York: Oxford University Press.

———. 2006. "When Texts Conceal: Why Vedic Recitation Is Forbidden at Certain Times and Places." *Journal of the American Oriental Society* 126: 305–322.

———, ed. and trans. 2009. *The Law Code of Viṣṇu: A Critical Edition and Translation of the Vaiṣṇava-Dharmaśāstra.* Harvard Oriental Series 73. Cambridge, Mass.: Harvard University Press.

———. 2010. "Dharmaśāstra: A Textual History." In *Hinduism and Law: An Introduction,* ed. Timothy Lubin, Donald R. Davis, Jr., and Jayanth K. Krishnan, pp. 28–57. Cambridge: Cambridge University Press.

———. 2013. *King, Governance, and Law in Ancient India: Kauṭilya's* Arthaśāstra. New York: Oxford University Press.
———. 2015. *A Sanskrit Dictionary of Law and Statecraft.* Delhi: Primus Books.
———. 2016a. *Dharma Reader: Classical Indian Law.* Historical Sourcebooks in Classical Indian Thought, ed. Sheldon I. Pollock. New York: Columbia University Press.
———. 2016b. "Judges and Courts in Ancient India: On *dharmastha* and *prāḍvivāka.*" In *Festschrift Stephanie Jamison,* ed. Dieter Gunkel et al., pp. 305–313. Ann Arbor, Mich.: Beech Stave Press.
———. Forthcoming. *Yājñavalkya Smṛti: A Textual History and Critical Edition of a Hindu Legal Code.* Delhi: Primus Books.
Olivelle, Patrick and Mark McClish. 2015. "The Four Feet of Legal Procedure and the Origin of Jurisprudence in Ancient India." *Journal of the American Oriental Society* 135: 33–47.
*Pāraskaragṛhyasūtra.* Edited with five commentaries by M. G. Bakre. Bombay: Gujarati Printing Press, 1917. Translated in Oldenberg 1886–1892.
Pollock, Sheldon. 1989. "The Idea of *Śāstra* in Traditional India." In *The Sastric Tradition in the Indian Arts,* ed. A. L. Dallapiccola and S. Zingel-Avé Lallemant, pp. 17–26. Wiesbaden: Steiner.
*Rāmāyaṇa.* 1960–1975. *The Vālmīki-Rāmāyaṇa.* Critically edited in 7 volumes. General editors, Govindlal Hargovind Bhatt and Umakant Premanand Shah. Baroda: Oriental Institute. Translated in Goldman et al. 1984–2009.
*Ṛgveda.* 1849–1874. Edited with Sāyaṇa's commentary by F. Max Müller. 6 vols. London: Wm. H. Allen & Co. Translated in Jamison and Brereton 2014, from which all the translations are taken.
Rocher, Ludo. 1986. *The Purāṇas.* Wiesbaden: Harrassowitz.
———. 2002a. "*Dāsadāsī.*" *Journal of the American Oriental Society* 122: 374–380.
———. 2002b. *Jīmūtavāhana's Dāyabhāga: The Hindu Law of Inheritance in Bengal.* New York: Oxford University Press.
Rowell, Lewis. 1988. "Form in the Ritual Theatre Music of Ancient India." *Musica Asiatica* 5: 140–190.
*Śatapathabrāhmaṇa.* 1855. Edited by Albrecht Weber. Berlin: Ferd. Dümmler's Verlagsbuchhandlung. Reprint, Cowkhamba Sanskrit Series 96. Varanasi, 1964. Translated by J. Eggeling in Sacred Books of the East 12, 26, 41, 43, 44. Oxford: Clarendon Press, 1882–1900.

Srinivasan, Saradha. 1979. *Mensuration in Ancient India.* Delhi: Ajanta Publications.

Stietencron, Heinrich von. 1985–1986. "Political Aspects of Indian Religious Art." *Visible Religion* 4–5: 16–36.

*Suśrutasaṃhitā.* 1992. Edited by Jādavji Trikamji Ācārya. 5th ed. Vārāṇasī: Caukhmbha Orientālīyā.

*Taittirīyāraṇyaka.* 1898. Edited with Sāyaṇa's commentary by Bābā Śāstrī Phaḍka. 2 vols. Ānandāśrama Sanskrit Series 36. Poona: Ānandāśrama.

*Taittirīyabrāhmaṇa.* 1898. Edited with Sāyaṇa's commentary by Nārāyaṇa Śāstrī Goḍabole. 3 vols. Ānandāśrama Sanskrit Series 37. Poona: Ānandāśrama.

*Taittirīyasaṃhitā.* 1900–1908. Ed. with Sāyaṇa's commentary by Kāśīnātha Śāstrī Āgāśe. 9 vols. Ānandāśrama Sanskrit Series 42. Poona: Ānandāśrama. Translated in Keith 1914.

Tokunaga, Muneo. 1993. "Structure of the *Rājadharma* Section in the Yājñavalkyasmṛti." *Memoirs of the Faculty of Letters,* Kyoto University, 32: 1–42.

*Vājesaneyisaṃhitā.* 1852. Edited by Albrecht Weber. Berlin: Ferd. Dümmler's Verlagsbuchhandlung.

*Vasiṣṭhadharmasūtra.* Edited and translated in Olivelle 2000.

*Viṣṇudharmasūtra.* Edited and translated in Olivelle 2009. Translated in Jolly 1880.

Wezler, Albrecht. 1994. "A Note on Sanskrit *brūṇa* and *bhrūṇahatyā.*" In *Festschrift Klaus Bruhn,* ed. N. Balbir and J. Bautze, pp. 623–646. Reibek: Verlag für Orientalistische Fachpublikationen.

Willis, Michael. 2009. *The Archaeology of Hindu Ritual: Temples and the Establishment of the Gods.* Cambridge: Cambridge University Press.

Yamashita, Tsutomu. 2001–2002. "On the Nature of the Medical Passages in the *Yājñavalkyasmṛti.*" *Zinbun: Annals of the Institute for Research in Humanities* (Kyoto University) 36.2: 87–129.

*Yogasūtra* of Patañjali. Edited and translated in Bryant 2009.

# CONCORDANCE OF VERSES

## CRITICAL EDITION AND COMMENTARIES

### *Chapter One*

| Critical Edition | Vishvarupa | Vijnaneshvara | Aparark a |
|---|---|---|---|
| 1–30 | 1–30 | 1–30 | 1–30 |
| 31–34 | 31–34 | 32–35 | 32–35 |
| 35 | 35 | 31 | 31 |
| 36–75 | 36–75 | 36–75 | 36–75 |
| 0 | 0 | 76 | 76 |
| 76 | 76 | 77 | 77 |
| 77–85 | 77–85 | 78–86 | 78–86 |
| 86 | 86 | 88 | 88 |
| 87 | 87 | 89 | 89 |
| 88 | 88 | 87 | 87 |
| 89–163 | 89–163 | 90–164 | 90–164 |
| 164 | 164 | 165 | 165ab, 166ab |
| 165 | 165 | 167 | 166cd–167ab |
| 166 | 166 | 168 | 167cd, 165cd |
| 167 | 167 | 166 | 168 |
| 168 | 168 | 169 | 169 |
| 169–194 | 169–194 | 170–195 | 170–195 |
| 195 | 0 | 197 | 197 |
| 196 | 195 | 196 | 196 |
| 197–205 | 196–204 | 198–206 | 198–206 |
| 0 | 0 | 207 | 207 |
| 206 | 205 | 208 | 208 |
| 207–229 | 206–228 | 209–231 | 209–231 |
| 0 | 0 | 232ab | 0 |
| 230 | 229 | 232cd–233ab | 232 |
| 231–285 | 230–284 | 233cd–288 | 233–287 |
| 0 | 0 | 289 | 288ab |
| 286 | 285 | 290 | 288cd–289ab |
| 287–356 | 286–355 | 291–360 | 289cd–359ab |
| (=2.34) | (=2.34) | 361 | 359cd–360ab |
| 357–363 | 356–362 | 362–368 | 360cd–366 |

*Chapter Two*

| | | | |
|---|---|---|---|
| 1–28 | 1–28 | 1–28 | 1–28 |
| 29 | 29 | 0 | 0 |
| 30–33 | 30–33 | 29–32 | 29–32 |
| 34 | 34 | (=1.361) | (=1.359-60) |
| 35–39 | 35–39 | 33–37 | 33–37 |
| 40 | 40 | 39 | 39 |
| 41 | 41 | 38 | 38 |
| 42–46 | 42–46 | 40–44 | 40–44 |
| 47 | 47 | 51 | 51 |
| 48–49 | 48–49 | 45–46 | 45–46 |
| 50 | 50 | 48 | 48 |
| 51–52 | 51–52 | 49–50 | 49–50 |
| 53 | 53 | 47 | 47 |
| 54–74 | 54–74 | 52–72 | 52–72 |
| 75 | 75 | 76 | 76 |
| 76 | 76 | 77 | 77 |
| 77–79 | 77–79 | 73–75 | 73–75 |
| 80–89 | 80–89 | 78–87 | 78–87 |
| 90 | 90 | 0 | 0 |
| 91–99 | 91–99 | 88–96 | 88–96 |
| 100 | 100 | 99 | 99 |
| 101 | 101 | 0 | 0 |
| 102–103 | 102–103 | 97–98 | 97–98 |
| 104–122 | 104–122 | 100–118 | 100–118 |
| 123–125 | 123–125 | 120–122 | 120–122 |
| 126 | 126 | 119 | 119 |
| 127–216 | 127–216 | 123–212 | 123–212 |
| 0 | 217 | 0 | 0 |
| 217–226 | 218–227 | 213–222 | 213–222 |
| 228–259 | 229–260 | 223–254 | 223–254 |
| 260 | 0 | 255 | 255 |
| 261–267 | 261–267 | 256–262 | 256–262 |
| 227 | 228 | 263 | 263 |
| 268–287 | 268–287 | 264–283 | 264–283 |
| 288 | 288 | 286 | 286 |
| 289–290 | 289–290 | 284–285 | 284–285 |
| 291–295 | 291–295 | 287–291 | 287–291 |
| 0 | 0 | 292 | 0 |

| | | | |
|---|---|---|---|
| 296–310 | 296–310 | 293–307 | 292–306 |

## *Chapter Three*

| | | | |
|---|---|---|---|
| 1–13 | 1–13 | 1–13 | 1–13 |
| 14–15 | 14–15 | 16–17 | 16–17 |
| 16–17 | 16–17 | 14–15 | 14–15 |
| 18 | 18 | 18 | 18 |
| 19ab | 19ab | 0 | 0 |
| 19cd | 19cd | 22ab | 22cd |
| 20 | 20 | 22cd, 20ab | 23ab, 20ab |
| 21 | 21 | 20cd, 21cd | 20cd, 21cd |
| 0 | 0 | 0 | 22ab |
| 0 | 0 | 23 | 0 |
| 22 | 22 | 24 | 23cd, 24ab |
| 23 | 23 | 25 | 24cd, 25ab |
| 24ab | 24ab | 0 | 0 |
| 24cd | 24cd | 21ab | 21ab |
| 25 | 25 | 27 | 25cd, 26ab |
| 26 | 26 | 26 | 26cd, 27ab |
| 27 | 27 | 28 | 27cd, 28ab |
| 28 | 28 | 29 | 28cd, 29ab |
| 29 | 29 | 19 | 19 |
| 30 | 30 | 30 | 29cd, 30ab |
| 31 | 31 | 31 | 30cd, 31ab |
| 32 | 32 | 32 | 31cd, 32ab |
| 33 | 33 | 33 | 32cd, 33ab |
| 34 | 34 | 34 | 33c–f |
| 35–164 | 35–164 | 35–164 | 34–163 |
| 165 | 165 | 0 | 164 |
| 166–221 | 166–221 | 165–220 | 165–220 |
| 222 | 222 | 226 | 221 |
| 223–227 | 223–227 | 221–225 | 222–226 |
| 228–241 | 228–241 | 227–240 | 227–240 |
| 0 | 0 | 241 | 241 |
| 242–243 | 242–243 | 242–243 | 242–243 |
| 244 | 244 | 247 | 247 |
| 245–247 | 245–247 | 244–246 | 244–246 |

| | | | |
|---|---|---|---|
| 248 | 248 | 249 | 249 |
| 249 | 249 | 248 | 248 |
| 250–260 | 250–260 | 250–260 | 250–260 |
| 0 | 261–262 | 0 | 0 |
| 261–262 | 263–264 | 261–262 | 261–262 |
| 263 | 265 | 284cd–285ab | 263 |
| 264–275 | 266–277 | 263–274 | 264–275 |
| 276 | 278 | 275cd, 276ab | 276 |
| 277 | 279 | 277 | 277 |
| 278 | 280 | 275ab, 276cd | 278 |
| 279–284 | 281–286 | 278–283 | 279–284 |
| 285ab | 287ab | 0 | 0 |
| 285cd | 287cd | 284ab | 285ab |
| 285ef | 288ab | 0 | 0 |
| 286–288 | 288cd–290 | 285cd–287 | 285cd–288ab |
| 289 | 291 | 289 | 288cd–289ab |
| 290 | 292 | 288 | 289cd–290ab |
| 291–335 | 293–337 | 290–334 | 290cd–334 |

# INDEX

# ABOUT THE BOOK

Murty Classical Library of India volumes are designed by Rathna Ramanathan and Guglielmo Rossi. Informed by the history of the Indic book and drawing inspiration from polyphonic classical music, the series design is based on the idea of "unity in diversity," celebrating the individuality of each language while bringing them together within a cohesive visual identity.

The Sanskrit text of this book is set in the Murty Sanskrit typeface, commissioned by Harvard University Press and designed by John Hudson and Fiona Ross. The proportions and styling of the characters are in keeping with the typographic tradition established by the renowned Nirnaya Sagar Press, with a deliberate reduction of the typically high degree of stroke modulation. The result is a robust, modern typeface that includes Sanskrit-specific type forms and conjuncts.

The English text is set in Antwerp, designed by Henrik Kubel from A2-type and chosen for its versatility and balance with the Indic typography. The design is a free-spirited amalgamation and interpretation of the archives of type at the Museum Plantin-Moretus in Antwerp.

All the fonts commissioned for the Murty Classical Library of India will be made available, free of charge, for non-commercial use. For more information about the typography and design of the series, please visit *http://www.hup.harvard.edu/mcli.*

Printed on acid-free paper by Maple Press, York, Pennsylvania.